THE FALL OF A PRESIDENT

THE FALL OF A
PRESIDENT

BY THE STAFF OF
The Washington Post

DELACORTE PRESS / NEW YORK

Published in cooperation with
The Washington Post Writers Group

Manufactured in the United States of America
First printing

ISBN: 0-440-04550-9

Contents

INTRODUCTION

By Howard Simons and Benjamin C. Bradlee

Howard Simons and Benjamin C. Bradlee are, respectively, the managing editor and the executive editor of The Washington Post.

Few men have dominated American politics as did Richard Milhous Nixon for almost a generation. Yet, strangely, few people really knew him—least of all the American Press, and even fewer really understood this controversial, contradictory, insulated man.

To Mr. Nixon, the press was a cross to bear, an institution to be used and manipulated to serve his version of the national purpose. To the press, Mr. Nixon was also a cross to bear, a man committed more to image than to truth.

But in one of those ironies that marked his public life, Nixon did more for the press than any President in recent history. He made folk heroes out of reporters. He made some newspapers household words. And he provided more copy, more headlines, more magazine covers, and more TV footage than any man since World War II.

In short, the man who disliked and distrusted the press came to dominate the press. He was never off Page One, whether it was achieving detente with Russia and China, ending the war that had seared the psyche of America, bringing home the prisoners of war—or becoming ensnarled in the madness that was Watergate.

Watergate. As history it began June 17, 1972, as a simple "B & E" (breaking and entering), one of roughly 50 committed in an average day in the District of Columbia. As a story in The Washington Post it began with a simple headline "5 Held in Plot to Bug Democrats' Office Here" the next day. It was on Page One only because this is a political town, that was a political year, and it was the most political of offices, the Democratic National Committee.

Watergate. For days the story remained a bizarre burglary. Then slowly, painfully, it changed through laundered money, White House connections, red wigs, forged cables, dirty tricks, grand jury investigations, perjured testimony, Senate hearings, indictments, guilty pleas, convictions, and impeachment inquiry—and finally the resignation of a President, for the first time in the history of the Republic.

Watergate. For The Washington Post, at first it was routine. Then it was lonely, as the rest of the press hesitated. Then it was seige, as the newspaper came under the strongest attack ever launched by one administration against one newspaper.

There was one memorable week in October of 1972 that none of us will ever forget:

• October 18, Clark MacGregor, director of the Committee for the Re-Election of the President: "The Washington Post's credibility has today sunk lower than that of George McGovern . . . Using innuendo, third-person hearsay, unsubstantiated charges, anonymous sources and huge scare headlines, The Post has maliciously sought to give the appearance of a direct connection between the White House and the Watergate . . . a charge which The Post knows, and half a dozen investigations have found . . . to be false."

• October 24, Senator Robert Dole, chairman of the Republican National Committee: "The Post's reputation for objectivity and credibility has sunk so low that they have almost disappeared from the Big Board altogether. The Post's hand in this disreputable enterprise, is visible for all to see."

• October 25, Ronald Ziegler the President's spokesman: "The Washington Post ran a story based on hearsay and to my view it is based upon the shabbiest journalistic techniques . . . This matter has reached the level of unbelievable absurdity . . . I respect the free press. I don't respect the shabby journalism that is being practiced by The Washington Post."

Watergate joined the issue of credibility as it had never been joined before. White House attacks on newspapers and television quite literally forced the reader and the listener to choose between the White House and the press. Only one could be credible, and in midsummer 1974, it became tragically clear: the press was to be believed.

Significantly, the best journalists took no satisfaction in vindication. The best journalists are all too aware that they practice their trade in a crisis atmosphere with a crisis mentality; that they, at best, catch history on the run; that truth is hard to come by under the disciplines of deadlines and emerges only in time, and sometimes never.

The best journalists know they are as strong and frail as other human beings. Other Presidents liked them more than Richard Nixon did, and perhaps they responded by liking other Presidents more than they liked Richard Nixon. But during the 2,027 days of the Nixon presidency some of the men closest to the President decided they had a better notion of how to govern than anyone else in the historic past of this country. They substituted contempt for communication, hubris for humility, and lèse-majesté for law and order. And so with the judiciary and the legislature, the fourth branch of government—the press—responded instinctively and inevitably to the threat to the fragile experiment that is democracy.

But Watergate was only the latest chapter in the crises-filled life of one of the truly remarkable men produced in this century. From a modest beginning in Whittier, Calif., to the most powerful office in the world, Richard Nixon's determined life intruded upon most of the stormy moments of the last 30 years: Communism and Alger Hiss, anti-Communism and Joe McCarthy, the Cold War and Dwight Eisenhower, the New Frontier and John F. Kennedy . . . until he finally had America in the palm of his hand, elected by the greatest majority ever achieved by any President, to lead it to the greatness of which he dreamed.

This book chronicles that extraordinary voyage— its controversies, its successes, its crises, and its ultimate demise. Edited by Washington Post staff writer Haynes Johnson, *The Fall of a President* is the story of the Nixon years on the American scene, the many Nixons that torment our memories.

PROLOGUE I

TO THE PEOPLE, FOR THE LAST TIME

Following is the official text of President Nixon's resignation address, Aug. 8, 1974.

Good evening.

This is the 37th time I have spoken to you from this office, where so many decisions have been made that shaped the history of this nation. Each time I have done so to discuss with you some matter that I believe affected the national interest.

In all the decisions I have made in my public life, I have always tried to do what was best for the Nation. Throughout the long and difficult period of Watergate, I have felt it was my duty to preserve, to make every possible effort to complete the term of office to which you elected me.

In the past few days, however, it has become evident to me that I no longer have a strong enough political base in the Congress to justify continuing that effort. As long as there was a base, I felt strongly that it was necessary to see the constitutional process through to its conclusion, that to do otherwise would be unfaithful to the spirit of that deliberately difficult process, and a dangerously destabilizing precedent for the future.

But with the disappearance of that base, I now believe that the constitutional purpose has been served, and there is no longer a need for the process to be prolonged.

I would have preferred to carry through to the finish whatever the personal agony it would have involved, and my family unanimously urged me to do so. But the interest of the nation must always come before any personal considerations.

From the discussions I have had with Congressional and other leaders, I have concluded that because of the Watergate matter I might not have the support of the Congress that I would consider necessary to back the very difficult decisions and carry out the duties of this office in the way the interests of the nation would require.

I have never been a quitter. To leave officer before my term is completed is abhorrent to every instinct in my body. But as President, I must put the interest of America first. America needs a full-time President and a full-time Congress, particularly at this time with the problems we face at home and abroad.

To continue to fight through the months ahead for my personal vindication would almost totally absorb the time and attention of both the President and the Congress in a period when our entire focus should be on the great issues of peace abroad and prosperity without inflation at home.

Therefore, I shall resign the Presidency effective at noon tomorrow. Vice President Ford will be sworn in as President at that hour in this office.

As I recall the high hopes for America with which we began this second term, I feel a great sadness that I will not be here in this office working on your behalf to achieve those hopes in the next 2½ years. But in turning over direction of the government to Vice President Ford, I know, as I told the nation when I nominated him for that office ten months ago, that the leadership of America will be in good hands.

In passing this office to the Vice President, I also do so with the profound sense of the weight of responsibility that will fall on his shoulders tomorrow and, therefore, of the understanding, the patience, the cooperation he will need from all Americans.

As he assumes that responsibility, he will deserve the help and the support of all of us. As we look to the future, the first essential is to begin healing the wounds of this nation: to put the bitterness and the divisions of the recent past behind us and to rediscover those shared ideals that lie at the heart of our strength and unity as a great and as a free people.

By taking this action, I hope that I will have hastened the start of that process of healing which is so desperately needed in America.

I regret deeply any injuries that may have been done in the course of the events that led to this decision. I would say only that if some of my judgments were wrong, and some were wrong, they were made in what I believed at the time to be the best interest of the nation.

To those who have stood with me during these past difficult months, to my family, my friends, to many others who joined in supporting my cause because they believed it was right, I will be eternally grateful for your support.

And to those who have not felt able to give me your support, let me say I leave with no bitterness toward those who have opposed me, because all of us, in the final analysis, have been concerned with the good of the country however our judgments might differ.

So, let us all now join together in affirming that common commitment and in helping our new President succeed for the benefit of all Americans.

I shall leave this office with regret at not completing my term, but with gratitude for the privilege of serving as your President for the past 5½ years. These years have been a momentous time in the history of our nation and the world. They have been a time of achievement in which we can all be proud, achievements that represent the shared efforts of the administration, the Congress and the people.

But the challenges ahead are equally great and they, too, will require the support and the efforts of the Congress and the people working in cooperation with the new administration.

We have ended America's longest war, but in the work of securing a lasting peace in the world, the goals ahead are even more far-reaching and more difficult.

We must complete a structure of peace so that it will be said of this generation, our generation, of Americans, by the people of all nations, not only that we ended one war, but that we prevented future wars.

We have unlocked the doors that for a quarter of a century stood between the United States and the People's Republic of China.

We must now ensure that the one quarter of the world's people who live in the People's Republic of China will be and remain not our enemies but our friends.

In the Middle East, 100 million people in the Arab countries, many of whom have considered us their enemy for nearly 20 years, now look on us as their friends. We must continue to build that friendship so that peace can settle at last over the Middle East and so that the cradle of civilization will not become its grave.

Together with the Soviet Union we have made the crucial breakthroughs that have begun the process of limiting nuclear arms. But we must set as our goal not just limiting, but reducing and finally destroying these terrible weapons so that they cannot destroy civilization and so that the threat of nuclear war will no longer hang over the world and the people.

We have opened the new relation with the Soviet Union. We must continue to develop and expand that new relationship so that the two strongest nations in the world will have together in cooperation rather than confrontation.

Around the world, in Asia, in Africa, in Latin America, in the Middle East, there are millions of people who live in terrible poverty, even starvation. We must keep as our goal turning away from production for war and expanding production for peace so that people everywhere on this earth can at least look forward in their children's time, if not in our own time, to having the necessities for a decent life.

Here in America, we are fortunate that most of our people have not only the blessings of liberty, but also the means to live full and good and, by the world's standards, even abundant lives. We must press on, however, to a goal of not only more and better jobs, but of full opportunity for every American, and of what we are striving so hard right now to achieve, prosperity without inflation.

For more than a quarter of a century in public life I have shared in the turbulent history of our era. I have fought for what I believe in. I have tried to the best of my ability to discharge those duties and meet those responsibilities that were entrusted to me.

Sometimes I have succeeded and sometimes I have failed, but always I have taken heart from what Theodore Roosevelt once said about the man in the arena, "whose face is marred by dust and sweat and blood, who strives valiantly, who errs and comes short again and again because there is not effort without error and shortcoming, but who does actually strive to do the deeds, who knows the great enthusiasms, the great devotions, who spends himself in a worthy cause, who at the best knows in the end the triumphs of high achievements and who at the worst, if he fails, at least fails while daring greatly."

I pledge to you tonight that as long as I have a breath of life in my body, I shall continue in that spirit. I shall continue to work for the great causes to which I have been dedicated throughout my years as a congressman, a senator, a Vice President and President; the cause of peace not just for America but among all nations, prosperity, justice and opportunity for all of our people.

There is one cause above all to which I have been devoted as long as I live.

When I first took the oath of office as President 5½ years ago, I made this sacred commitment: "To consecrate my office, my energies and all the wisdom I can summon to the cause of peace among nations."

I have done my very best in all the days since to be true to that pledge. As a result of these efforts, I am confident that the world is a safer place today, not only for the people of America, but for the people of all nations, and that all of our children have a better chance than before of living in peace rather than dying in war.

This, more than anything, is what I hoped to achieve when I sought the presidency.

To have served in this office is to have felt a very personal sense of kinship with each and every American. In leaving it, I do so with this prayer: May God's grace be with you in all the days ahead.

THE EAST ROOM FAREWELL

*Following is the text of Richard Milhous Nixon's fare-
well address as President to members of his administration in the East Room of the White House, Aug. 9,
1974.*

Well, members of the Cabinet, members of the White
House staff, all of our friends here. I think the record
should show this is one of those spontaneous things
we always arrange whenever the President comes in to
speak. And it will be so recorded in the press, and we
don't mind, because they've got to call it as they see it.
But on our part believe me it is spontaneous. You are
here to say goodby to us. And we don't have a good
word for it in English; the best is *au revoir*. We'll see
you again.

I just met with the members of the White House
staff, you know, those that served here in the White
House, day in and day out, and I asked them to do
what I ask all of you to do to the extent that you can
and of course are requested to do so, to serve our next
President as you have served me and previous Presidents, because many of you have been here many
years, with devotion and dedication. Because this office,
great as it is, can only be as great as the men and
women who work for and with the President. This
house, for example, I was thinking of it as we walked
down this hall, and I was comparing it to some of the
great houses of the world I've been in. This isn't the
biggest house; many and most, in even smaller countries, are much bigger. This isn't the finest house. Many

in Europe particularly, in China, Asia, have paintings of great, great value, things that we just don't have here. But this is the best house. And it's the best house because it has something far more important than numbers of people who serve, far more important than numbers of rooms or how big it is, far more important than numbers of magnificent pieces of art. This house has a great heart and that heart comes from those who serve it. I was rather sorry they didn't come down; we said goodby to them upstairs. But they're really great. And I recall after so many times I've made speeches, some of them pretty tough, you always come back, or after a hard day, my days usually have run rather long, I'd always get a lift from them, because I might be a little down, but they always smiled.

And so it is with you. I look around here and I see so many on this staff that, you know, I should have been by your offices and shaken hands and I'd loved to have talked to you and found out how to run the world. Everybody wants to tell the President what to do and, boy, he needs to be told many times. But I just haven't had the time. But I want to know, I want you to know that each and every one of you, I know, is indispensable to this government. I'm proud of this Cabinet. I'm proud of our . . . all the members who have served in our Cabinet. I'm proud of our sub-Cabinet. I'm proud of our White House staff. As I pointed out last night: sure, we've done some things wrong in this administration, and the top man always takes the responsibility and I've never ducked it. But I want to say one thing: no man or no woman came into this administration and left it with more of this world's goods than when he came in. No man or woman ever profited at the public expense or the public till. That tells something about you, mistakes, yes, but for personal gain, never. You did what you believed in, sometimes right, sometimes wrong, and I only wish that I were a wealthy man—at the present time I've got to find a way to pay my taxes. And if I were I'd like to recompense you for the sacrifices that all of you have made to serve in government. But you are getting something in government and I want you to tell this to your children, and I hope the nation's children will hear it too, something in government service that is far more important than money. It's a cause bigger than yourself, it's the cause of making this the greatest nation in the world, the leader of the world, because without our leadership the world would know nothing but war, possibly starvation or worse in the years ahead. With our leadership it will know peace, it will know plenty. We have been generous, and we will be more generous in the future if we are able to. But most important we must be strong here, strong in our hearts, strong in our souls, strong in our beliefs, and strong in our willingness to sacrifice as you have been willing to sacrifice in a pecuniary way to serve in government.

There's something else I'd like for you to tell your young people. You know, people often come in and say "What'll I tell my kids." You know, they look at government and consider the rugged life and they see the mistakes that are made, they get the impression that everyone is here for the purpose of feathering his nest. That's why I made this earlier point, not in this administration, not one single man or woman. And I say to them, there are many fine careers. This country needs good farmers, good businessmen, good plumbers, good carpenters. I remember my old man, I think that they would have called him sort of a little man, a common man. He didn't consider himself that way. You know what he was, he was a streetcar motorman first, and then he was a farmer, and then he had a lemon ranch—it was the poorest lemon ranch in California I can assure you. He sold it before they found oil on it. And then he was a grocer, but he was a great man. Because he did his job, and every job counts up to the hilt regardless of what happens.

Nobody'll ever write a book, probably, about my mother. Well, I guess all of you would say this about your mother. My mother was a saint. And I think of her, two boys dying of tuberculosis, nursing four others in order that she could take care of my older brother for three years in Arizona and seeing each of them die.

And when they died it was like one of her own. Yes, she will have no books written about her, but she's a saint. Now, however, we look to the future. I had a little quote in a speech last night from TR [Teddy Roosevelt's]. As you know, I kind of like to read books. I'm not educated but I do read books. And, uh, the TR quote was a pretty good one. Here's another one I found as I was reading my last night in the White House. And this quote is about a young man, he was a young lawyer in New York. He'd married a beautiful girl. And they had a lovely daughter. And then suddenly, she died.

This is what he wrote. This is in his diary. He said: "She was beautiful in face and form. And lovelier still in spirit. As a flower she grew. And as a fair young flower, she died. Her life had been always in the sunshine.

"There had never come to her a single great sorrow. None ever knew her who did not love and revere her for her bright and sunny temper, and her saintly unselfishness.

"Fair, pure and joyous as a maiden; loving, tender, happy as a young wife. When she had just become a mother and her life seemed to be just begun. And then the years seemed so bright before her. And by a strange terrible fate, death came to her. And when my heart's dearest died, the life went from my life forever." That was TR in his 20's. He thought the life had gone from his life forever. But he went on. And he not only became President, but as an ex-President, he served his country. Always in the arena, tempestuous, strong, sometimes wrong, sometimes right, but he was a man, and as I leave let me say, that's an example I think all of us should remember. We think sometimes when things happen, things don't go the right way, we think that when you don't pass the bar exam the first time. I happened to, but I was just lucky. I mean my writing was so poor the bar examiner said, "We just got to let the guy through." (Laughter.)

We think that when someone dear to us dies, we think that when we lose an election, we think that when we suffer a defeat, that all is ended. We think as TR said that the life has left his life forever. Not true. The old must know it. They must always sustain it because the greatness comes not when things go always good for you, but the greatness comes when you're really touchy, when you take your knocks, some disappointment, when sadness comes, because only if you've been in the deepest valley can you ever know how magnificent it is to be on the highest mountain.

And so I say to you on this occasion, we leave, we leave proud of the people who have stood by us and worked for us and served this country.

We want you to be proud of what you've done. We want you to continue to serve in government if that is your wish. Always give your best. Never get discouraged. Never be petty. Always remember: others may hate you. Those who hate you don't win unless you hate them. And then you destroy yourself.

And so we leave with high hopes, in good spirits, and with deep humility. And with very much gratefulness in our hearts. I can only say to each and every one of you we come from many faiths. We pray perhaps to different Gods, but really the same God in a sense.

But I want to say for each and every one of you, not only will we always remember you, not only will we always be grateful to you, but always you will be in our hearts and you will be in our prayers. Thank you very much. (Applause.)

CHAPTER ONE

THE FALL OF A PRESIDENT

By Richard Harwood and Haynes Johnson

When the day finally came, the anger and tensions and recriminations that had so enveloped this capital for weeks had been subdued in the solemnity of change. A sense of calm and a tenuous spirit of conciliation began to emerge.

There was no chorus of jubilation in Washington and no cries for vengeance or retribution. There was an absence of turmoil, mobs, violence, massive protests.

The crowds that had begun to gather at the White House two days earlier had remained quiet, solemn and patient. They were witnesses to history, yes, and some-day they would tell their grandchildren about it. But on this Thursday, Aug. 8, 1974, they seemed more pre-occupied by personal feelings of sorrow and sadness.

"Think of it," said a tourist from Wheaton, Ill. "The most beautiful building in the country, right across the street, and the man that lives there, that has worked all his life to get there, has to give it up. . . . It's a sad ter-rible thing, but he brought it all on himself. But it makes me sad that he has to be humiliated like this."

Another visitor who had driven up from Myrtle Beach, S.C., was philosophical: "Our country will sur-vive. In a way, this is like the Kennedy assassination. It is a sad time for everyone but we'll pull through."

By nightfall, the crowd had swelled to large propor-tions, blocking traffic on historic Pennsylvania Avenue, filling up beautiful Lafayette Park with its flower beds, benches and statues.

With darkness, the atmosphere changed. Cars moved slowly down the avenue past the White House, frequently honking as they rolled by. Some bore Nixon-Agnew stickers and American flags.

In the park, some people milled about aimlessly and some sat on blankets, watching portable TV sets. Others stared silently and thoughtfully at a White House bathed in lights. The stirring crowds, the sense of the moment, the night, the realization of what was happening inside the mansion behind the iron fence—all combined to create a scene of somberness tinged with festivity.

On Capitol Hill, where the Congress had been engaged in bitter debate for months and engaged, too, in a great constitutional struggle with the executive, there was talk—although no substantial action—about granting immunity for the 37th man ever to serve as President of the United States.

Inside the White House, there were no last-minute theatrics, no public relations gimmicks, no coyness about what was to happen and no rancorous remarks about enemies. Ronald L. Ziegler and Gerald L. Warren, who, as presidential spokesmen, had spent the last months in acrimonious confrontations with reporters, were now emotionally spent. They struggled to keep from crying as they performed their last tasks for the President.

It was an orderly thing, this passing of power. The decision was made known early, the time and place announced, the necessary meetings held. Vice President Ford met with Richard Nixon at midday and then canceled a political trip to the West. There were routine announcements of changes among federal judges, the Atomic Energy Commission, the National Science Foundation, the Combined Federal Campaign for the National Capital Area, the International Pacific Salmon Fisheries Commission.

And in what may have been his last executive act, the President vetoed the appropriations bill for the Agriculture Department and the Environmental Protection Agency.

Richard Nixon, in his 37th and final report to the American people went out with grace and strength and dignity—but with no confession of high crimes.

2

The night before, Saul Pett of the Associated Press reported, there had been an emotional scene in the White House living quarters. The President had made his decision to resign and his family took it hard. Tears welled up in the eyes of Pat Nixon and Julie Nixon Eisenhower and when the President embraced his other daughter, Tricia Nixon Cox, she broke down and wept without control.

Later there were other farewells. The leaders of Congress were called in for a last meeting. A time was set aside for a chance to gather privately with old friends and supporters. It was civil and done with dignity.

In response, themes of hope for a kind of national reconciliation and healing were heard, even the hope that in leaving office after such a stormy passage, the President might at last achieve the goal that had been a campaign slogan in 1968—bringing the country together.

Democratic Gov. Milton Shapp of Pennsylvania composed an instant poem:

In the aftermath,
No wrath.
Just sorrow
And hope for tomorrow.

Another Democrat, Terry Sanford, the president of Duke University, expressed sympathy for Mr. Nixon and concluded: "It's time to gird up our loins and get going again."

House Minority Leader John J. Rhodes, who had called for the President's impeachment some days earlier, confessed to feelings of "sadness and deep regret. At the same time, I'm glad for the country in two ways.

"The matter is going to be over with and we have a completely capable man to take over. I'm optimistic about the future . . . I look for a healing time. There are those who would continue to harass President Nixon. I don't believe this group will be large in numbers. He will be allowed to go in peace. The country should then turn itself to constructive tasks."

Nevertheless, the trauma remained. Never in the

3

history of the Republic has a President been driven from office.

Only eight times had a President failed to complete his term. Four were assassinated—Lincoln, Garfield, McKinley, Kennedy. Four died of disease—Harrison, Taylor, Harding, Franklin Roosevelt. But only Richard Nixon had resigned in the face of inevitable House impeachment and almost certain conviction by the Senate.

The day before his announcement, he had been warned by Republican congressional leaders that only 10 of the 435 House members were likely to oppose impeachment and that only 15 of 100 senators would vote to acquit him of "high crimes and misdemeanors" —obstruction of justice, the abuse of power and contempt of Congress.

He could have chosen to "tough it out," to "stonewall it" and to take himself and the nation through the long ordeal of impeachment and trial. He could have raised the specter of crisis in a last effort to rally support.

In the end, he chose the other course. After the final blow had fallen on Monday, Aug. 5, with the release of the most damaging of his secretly-recorded conversations, he moved swiftly.

Rhodes said on Wednesday that the decision probably was sealed Sunday, Aug. 4, at Camp David. By Wednesday, when Rhodes met with Mr. Nixon at the White House, it was apparent that this presidency was at an end:

The President knew that the situation was hopeless. He really behaved like a champion and made it easy on all of us. It was the President who said there were only 10 votes for him in the House. I didn't disagree with that although I actually thought there were more. Just before we left . . . the President said, 'Just make it plain that whatever decision I make will be completely in the national interest.' "

Until the end, his daughter, Julie, had urged him to stay on and make a fight in the Senate. So had a tiny band of congressmen, and one of them, Rep. Earl

4

Landgrebe (R-Ind.), got one of the last of the presidential letters on Wednesday, Aug. 7.

Landgrebe had said that the "liberals are lynching our President" and Mr. Nixon replied to him:

"I cannot predict whether your comments will go down in history but I want to assure you, they will remain forever in my heart and in the hearts of all the Nixons."

The manner of his departure was regarded everywhere as an affirmation of the stability of the American system. The constitutional processes, it was said, had proved adequate. The Congress had risen to its mission. The country had reacted with understanding and maturity and Nixon himself had seemed serene and composed.

At the Wednesday, Aug. 7, meeting with Rhodes and Sens. Barry Goldwater and Hugh Scott, the President put his feet on the desk in the Oval Office and listened quietly to their grim assessment. All three, Scott said, told him the situation was "gloomy."

"He asked me," Scott said. "I said, 'Gloomy.' He said, 'Damn gloomy?' I said, 'Yes, sir.' "

That set the stage for the final act.

By Thursday morning, the government was taking it it all in stride. Agriculture Secretary Earl Butz was able to joke in a speech to the American School Food Association.

Referring to the retiring president of the organization, he observed, "You are going to discover shortly that there is nothing paster than a past president."

At the Treasury Department, Mary Brooks was sworn in for a second five-year term as director of the Mint. "This is a very unhappy day for many of us," she said. "But the past is prologue. The government hasn't stopped. It's going on . . ." Foreign governments were notified that a transfer of power was imminent.

In the Senate, Edward W. Brooke of Massachusetts, the first Republican to call for the President's resignation, introduced a "sense-of-the-Congress" resolution. It would have the effect of urging Watergate Special Prosecutor Leon Jaworski, who aggressively pressed

5

the investigation against the President anad his men, not to prosecute the President after he became a private citizen. It also would urge the same course for prosecutors at state and local levels.

Hubert H. Humphrey and George McGovern, both defeated for the Presidency by Mr. Nixon, said they were considering joining Brooke as co-sponsors.

On television early in the morning, before an audience estimated at 60 million Americans, Rep. Peter W. Rodino Jr. of New Jersey spoke with emotion of his own feelings. Rodino, who had chaired the congressional hearing that led to the fateful committee votes for articles of impreachment and had himself cast three "Aye" votes, told of his "reverence for the presidency." He wept, he said, after those first articles were adopted.

As always in a crisis, Americans were rallying around the presidency. It happened to Dwight D. Eisenhower at the time of the U-2 crisis, to John F. Kennedy at Bay of Pigs, to Lyndon B. Johnson at the Kennedy assassination. It seems certain to happen to the man who will become the 38th President of the United States, Gerald R. Ford of Michigan.

With Ford as President and a new Vice President to be chosen, for the first time in American history the two most important national offices will be filled by persons who have not been elected to their positions. In other places, such a situation could create tensions, but that prospect has scarcely raised a ripple in the nation.

The same sense of calm acceptance was not as apparent elsewhere when the dramatic news instantly sped around the world. In Moscow, Tass tersely announced the resignation without comment. In Paris, the foreign minister, Jean-Pierre Fourcade, said the resignation might unleash speculative upheavel in the world money markets. In London, there were reports of a wave of international concerns and fears of unknown repercussions.

In this, alone, were expressed the ancient fears about the fall of kings being accompanied by cataclysmic actions.

The problems that will confront the new President were also evident throughout the day.

In the Midwest, where Richard Nixon always looked for the heart of his constituency, a searing drought continued. It held a warning that foreign countries may receive less American grain during the coming year, further fueling an already dangerous worldwide inflation.

In Washington, the government announced that wholesale prices had spurted to their highest point, led by increases in food and industrial costs and "continuing adjustments to energy problems."

On Wall Street, the stock market began the day with another round of heavy trading that has marked the uncertainty of the week. When the first rumors about the President's possible resignation sped through the nation, Wall Street rallied dramatically. In three days, the Dow Jones industrial average rose 45 points. But Wednesday, after initial move upward, the market reacted more warily and then the average dropped six points as investors took their profits and awaited further developments.

The first reports of historic change came in midmorning with bulletins from the White House quoting unnamed White House aides. Shortly after noon, Ronald Ziegler, his voice quavering, issued a one-minute statement to the press.

"I am aware of the interest of the American people and you in this room concerning developments today and over the last few days. This, of course, has been a difficult time.

"The President of the United States will meet various members of the bi-partisan membership of Congress at the White House early this evening.

"Tonight, at 9 o'clock Eastern Daylight Time, the President of the United States will address the nation on radio and television from his Oval Office."

He had not mentioned the President's name.

There was an ironic note in the names of three television programs that had been scheduled—and immediately canceled—for that hour in Washington.

The programs were: "The Taste of Ashes," on NBC; "The Nature of Evil," on ABC; and "The Lost Man," on CBS.

Unintentionally those names evoked the turmoil and passions that have surrounded Richard Nixon and the American people for the past two years. For month after month, year after year, the Watergate scandal spread like a poison through the body politic. For month after month, year after year, the President stubbornly fought off a host of investigators, public and private. Slowly, reluctantly, the nation began to conceive that the once-unthinkable ultimate act of impeachment might be employed—drawing the sword from the temple, as the young congressman, William S. Cohen of Maine, described it.

The sword was finally unsheathed. Less than two weeks before the resignation, a committee of the Congress took its first roll call on impeachment in more than a century. It was only the second time such an action had been taken against a President.

A coalition of Democrats and Republicans, liberals and conservatives, men and women from all corners of the country voted nearly 3 to 1 against the President. That, coupled with the unanimous Supreme Court ruling compelling him to turn over still more of those destructive tape recordings, was a near-fatal blow.

But still the President continued his struggle, still he maintained he would not resign, still he said he would carry the case until the constitutional process had run its course.

Monday, Aug. 5, saw the final blow. He released three more transcripts. They contained the final seeds of his destruction. He conceded he had withheld critical evidence from his lawyer, his aides and stanchest supporters—and that he had personally approved plans for the Watergate cover-up only six days after the break-in on June 17, 1972.

All his previous public statements about his role were demolished by his own words.

The last week of Richard Nixon's presidency brought

8

evidence of a President wrestling alone with his fates. The White House logs told of his isolation and search for a solution:

Aug. 1 (Thursday) White House: Canceled meeting with economic advisers.

Aug. 2 (Friday) White House: No meetings.

Aug. 3 (Saturday): Left in afternoon for Camp David with Mrs. Nixon, daughters and sons-in-law, and Bebe Rebozo.

Aug. 4 (Sunday) Camp David: Called meeting with Alexander Haig, his chief of staff; Ziegler; Patrick Buchanan and Ray Price, speech writers and advisers; James St. Clair, his lawyer.

Aug. 5 (Monday) White House: Released statement on tapes. No meetings.

Aug. 6 (Tuesday) White House: Cabinet meeting 11 a.m., private meeting following with Henry Kissinger.

Aug. 7 (Wednesday) White House: Morning meetings with Haig, Ziegler, William Timmons; meeting with Rabbi Baruch Korff early afternoon; meeting with Rhodes, Goldwater and Scott, 5 p.m.

Out of those private sessions came the decision that will live in history.

The denouement of Thursday evening, Aug. 8, came on a day of paramount significance to Richard Nixon. It was exactly six years ago to the day that he stood before the cheering Republican National Convention and accepted his party's call as its presidential nominee.

"America is in trouble today not because her people have failed," he said then to great applause, "but because her leaders have failed."

Richard Nixon already had come a long way by that August night in Miami Beach. For more than a generation he had been a central figure on the American scene: congressman, senator, Vice President, defeated presidential candidate and then triumphant President.

But for all his battles, his defeats and victories, Richard Nixon always had wrestled with crises and had somehow survived. In those last tape recordings that finally brought him down, he was speaking of those

9

crises again, drawing lessons from the past, seeking a way out of his troubles.

But this time, still the existential loner, he had met a crisis he could not overcome.

CHAPTER TWO

RICHARD MILHOUS NIXON, THE 37th PRESIDENT, WHOSE TRUST WAS IN HIMSELF

By Haynes Johnson

Haynes Johnson is a Pulitzer prize winning reporter for The Washington Post and author or co-author of seven books about contemporary American life.

Pathos is not ordinarily associated with the American presidency. Tragedy, majesty, loneliness, nobility, yes, but a pathetic quality of the Presidency now seems uniquely Richard Milhous Nixon's own.

In those April days of 1973 when the President and his men were desperately wrestling with Watergate and finally, reluctantly, realizing that some form of public accounting had to be made, Mr. Nixon unburdened himself in the privacy of his office. He was speaking to his old friend and counselor, William P. (Bill) Rogers, then the Secretary of State but long before that a trusted companion in Nixon crises from other days. Although they were alone, the secret tape recorders that were to prove so destructive to the President captured an intimate glimpse of Richard Nixon in the throes of his final crisis and Richard Nixon still wanting to believe in his old dreams.

He had just spoken to Henry Petersen, the chief government prosecutor in the Watergate case, the President was saying. Then he said:

"Well, I'm not going to talk to him any more about that. After all, I'm the President of the country—and I'm going to get on with it and meet Italians and Germans and all these others. You know, really—"

"Oh, you do that," Rogers said consolingly. "I think you. I think that—"

The President interrupted. He had been living with Watergate for a long time now, spending at least half of his time on it, knew the immediate impact would be "terrible," knew it was a "mess," but he was confident that within a year it would all be seen in a better perspective.

"When it's finished—" Rogers began.

And the 37th President of the United States again interrupted to say: "I'll be here all along, Bill. The jury indicts, moves. We're going to get on with this country."

Richard Nixon never really was able to get on with the business of the country and the world. In the narrowest sense, he became a casualty of a third-rate, bungled burglary, but in a larger perspective he was a victim of himself. His ambitions, his insecurities, his aloofness, his resentments, his humorlessness, his inability to inspire popular confidence, his misplaced trust in others, his taste for the second-rate, his penchant for secrecy, for maneuver, for deviousness—these were the attributes that ultimately destroyed him.

In the end, they brought ruin to Richard Nixon, left a vast wreckage of shattered reputations, did incalculable damage to political, presidential and legislative institutions, and dealt a psychic blow to America's self-esteem.

And it was all so unnecessary.

When he was campaigning for President in 1968, Richard Nixon set out basic themes that he promised would characterize his administration. "The next President must unite America," he said. "He must calm its angers, ease its terrible frictions and bring its people together once again, in peace and mutual respect. He has to take *hold* of America before he can move it forward."

He spoke of articulating the nation's values, defining its goals, marshaling its will; of an administration of "open doors, open eyes and open minds"; of bringing dissenters into policy discussions, not freezing them out; of a government of scholars and thinkers drawn from the broadest possible base, not an administration of "yes men." But most important of all, he talked of a

President who listens to the quiet, inner voices—voices that "speak from the heart and the conscience." These, he said, are the voices that "carry the real meaning and the real message of America."

He came to office in a time of chaos and promised calm. He offered himself for leadership after a period of irrationality, of war and riots and assassinations, and pledged peace and reason and stability. Whatever Americans thought of Richard Nixon in the past—he knew he was not beloved as a Roosevelt or Kennedy had been, and apparently never expected to be—they believed his promise and supported his aspirations.

Instead, the Nixon years proved to be at least as traumatic as the decade that had foreshadowed them. Crisis became the keynote of those years—the energy crisis, the economic crisis, the pollution crisis, the Mideast crisis, the Agnew crisis, the Watergate crisis.

Calm never came for very long to America, confidence never was restored, unity never was achieved. Instead, America lived through the Manson murders and the Mylai atrocities, skyjackings and terroristic attacks, bombings and the Berrigans' trial, political kidnapings and conspiracy trials, Kent State and Jackson State, hardhats and campus "bums," Chappaquiddick and men on the moon, positive political polarization and the effete corps of rotten apples, Middle Americans and the Silent Majority, Carswell and Haynsworth, Woodstock and the counterculture, law-and-order and the Wallace shooting, "hooked" Vietnam veterans and moratorium demonstrations, the Pentagon Papers and the Calley trial, Women's Lib and Gay Lib, hard-core pornography and X-rated films, radiclibs and the media, inflation and devaluation of the dollar, the stock market slide and wage-price controls, political corruption and "laundered" money—and, toward the end, a President who was forced to proclaim, "I am not a crook."

There is irony—and tragedy—in all of this.

Despite the tensions that remained in the country and the new problems that arose, the President's public prescription for leadership was correct. Americans desperately did want to put aside the searing divisions of the 60s. They did want to "lower their voices." And, disturbing as the existing problems were, the President did offer hope for future tranquility. The cities were not scarred by race riots, the war was, in the cliche of the times, "winding down." Most hopeful yet was the prospect of real peace, genuine detente, true rapprochement. His initiatives toward China and the Soviet Union were universally acclaimed. Richard Nixon had in his grasp all he ever had dreamed.

The tragedy lies in Nixon himself. When America finally began to trust Richard Nixon, Richard Nixon found himself incapable of trusting America and its institutions.

With peace in his grasp and history waiting to vindicate him, the President saw a different country. The America he and his aides viewed from inside the White House was still in turmoil, still dangerous, still filled with enemies. They saw themselves as beleaguered and besieged. They took steps, secretly and in the name of "national security," to counter these perceived threats.

"In the spring and summer of 1970, another security problem reached critical proportions," the President told the public in May of 1973, in trying to explain why certain operations had been set in motion, among them Watergate. "In March a wave of bombings and explosions struck college campuses and cities. There were 400 bomb threats in one 24-hour period in New York City alone. Rioting and violence on college campuses reached a new peak after the Cambodian operation and the tragedies at Kent State and Jackson State. The 1969-70 school year brought nearly 1,800 campus demonstrations and nearly 250 cases of arson on campus. Many colleges closed. Gun battles between guerrilla-style groups and police were taking place. Some of the disruptive activities were receiving foreign support.

"Complicating the task of maintaining security was the fact that, in 1966, certain types of undercover FBI operations that had been conducted for many years had been suspended. This also had substantially impaired our ability to collect foreign intelligence information. At the same time, the relationships between the FBI and other intelligence agencies had been deteriorating. By May 1970, FBI Director Hoover shut off his agency's liaison with the CIA altogether."

Out of this fearsome, conspiratorial portrait grew the darker side of the Nixon years. The President and his men put in motion the activities that led to their own disintegration:

Surveillance operations, bugging teams, surreptitious entries, "deep-sixing" of evidence, obstruction of justice, perjury, hush money, blackmail, enemies' lists, the secret bombing of Cambodia, the Pentagon spying on the White House, the White House spying on itself, $100,000 in cash and Bebe Rebozo, San Clemente and tax write-offs, using the FBI, the CIA, the Justice Department for political purposes, ITT and the milk fund, fabricated polls, doctored documents, missing tapes, falsification of past presidential records, a cancer in the presidency, the transcripts, impeachment.

When he finally fell from power, Richard Nixon had failed to keep those promises of '68. His name will not be associated with political realignment, with taking the lead in building an emerging new Republican majority for the rest of the century, with setting a new—and higher—standard of government service. The legacy he has bequeathed is one of public cynicism and disbelief.

Those Nixon years are examined here, and a preliminary assessment is attempted of Mr. Nixon's impact on foreign affairs and domestic life, on politics and the presidency, on the moral and ethical climate of America and on hopes for reform and the restoring of confidence.

When it has all been said, though, two key questions intrude. They are about Richard Nixon, the man, and Richard Nixon, the politician, as perceived by the American people. Among his intimates, who *really* knew him or was able to unravel the enigmatic character of the private Nixon? And why, after so long an exposure to him publicly, were the American people surprised at how his presidency turned out?

The psycho-historians, now so much in vogue, are going to have a field day with the private personality of Richard Milhous Nixon, the boy from Whittier who became President. Some already have. They have examined his obsessive preoccupation with crisis and his need to prove himself. Already they have proclaimed him a paranoid.

With Mr. Nixon, however, there is no need to indulge in amateur analysis or idle speculation. He has long been trying to tell us about himself. Our most introspective President figuratively scattered pieces of himself, his values and basic attitudes, over the American landscape for decades.

The self-portrait that emerges is of a driving, calculating, tense, grimly assured man who approached every task and obstacle with fiercely single-minded determination. If there is any evidence of humor or sheer joy and exuberance, it has not come to the surface.

"It's important to live like a Spartan," he told an interviewer on the eve of his second inauguration. "That's not to say I don't enjoy a good time. But the worst thing you can do in this job is to relax, to let up. One must have physical and mental discipline here. . . ."

Richard Nixon, quite obviously, always had an extraordinary amount of self-discipline and tenacity. It is, he has said again and again, the hallmark of his success, the reason why he was able to face and succeed in self-proclaimed personal crisis after personal crisis. His words themselves ring with a martial sound: It is the contest, the battle, the struggle that sustained him. "I believe in the battle, whether it's the battle of a campaign or the battle of this office, which is a continuing battle," he said in that same pre-inaugural interview. "It's always there wherever I go. I perhaps, carry it more than others because that's my way."

In Caracas, in 1958, during one of those crises that helped shape his career, Richard Nixon displayed another telling aspect of his personal "battle" psychology.

16

"As we got into the car," he has written, "the rocks were flying around us, but I could not resist the temptation to get in one other good lick. I stood up on the rear seat at the car moved slowly away and asked [Secret Service Agent Jack] Sherwood to brace my legs so that I would not fall. I shouted, with [Vernon] Walters [later to be deputy CIA director during the Watergate episode] translating in rapid-fire Spanish, 'You are cowards, you are afraid of the truth! You are the worst kind of cowards.' I felt the excitement of battle as I spoke but I had full control of my temper as I lashed out at the mob. Those nearby who heard me quieted down, but the rocks from the rear continued to fly."

In that most revealing book, "Six Crises," written after his defeat in the 1960 presidential election Richard Nixon gave a general description of how crisis affected him—and how he had learned to handle it. "When a man has been through even a minor crisis, he learns not to worry when his muscles tense up, his breathing comes faster, his nerves tingle, his stomach churns, his temper becomes short, his nights are sleepless. He recognizes such symptoms as the natural and healthy signs that his system is keyed up for battle. Far from worrying when this happens, he should worry when it does not."

Years later, as he faced the denouement of his most serious crisis shortly after releasing his secret presidential transcripts, he again referred to those earlier struggles. Having profited from all those previous crises, he told columnist James J. Kilpatrick, he had been able to survive Watergate without "tingling nerves and a churning stomach." And, he remarked to Kilpatrick in a familiar Nixon personal reference, "I am a disciplined man."

As Washington Post staff writer Lou Cannon recounted, his intimates over the years saw another Nixon —a man of shyness, gentleness, generosity. His own edited transcripts of his Watergate conversations offer an even more contradictory picture.

The Nixon who emerges from those critical discus-

17

sions is neither the strong, decisive, commanding figure that he himself has described so often nor the magnanimous, compassionate figure known to his friends. In fact, if one didn't know what the letters identifying the speakers in those transcripts meant, one would have difficulty determining which man was the President of the United States. "H" (Haldeman) comes over as stronger and far more decisive, "E" (Ehrlichman) as the shrewdest and craftiest, while "P" (President) is the vaguest, most confused and disorganized. Richard Nixon, in these moments, was hardly even master in his own house.

But however history finally judges the private Nixon —and that record is far from being written—the country has had to deal with a series of changing public perceptions of the man. To the end, even after all his years at the center stage of American public life, Richard Nixon still retained the capacity to surprise and bewilder friends and foes alike. Those who have proclaimed or denounced him have seen Nixon the conservative, Nixon the liberal, Nixon the centrist, Nixon the pragmatist, Nixon the peacemaker, Nixon the Cold Warrior, Nixon the old and Nixon the new.

Somewhere early in his career (the generally accepted time is during his 1950 race for the Senate), Richard Nixon acquired the derisive description of "Tricky Dick." He never was able entirely to live it down, but as he climbed from senator to Vice President and finally to the presidency, he did gain a new measure of respect.

Part of this was inevitable: Richard Nixon simply had been around longer than any major political figure in American history. The people came to believe they knew him, strengths, weaknesses and all. For a generation he stood at the center of political life. No other Republican basked so long in the national spotlight. In all of our history only Franklin Roosevelt had been on a national political ticket as many times, five. In time, he outlived his major political contemporaries— two Kennedys, Johnson, Stevenson, Eisenhower.

But part of his eventual presidential success sprung from a more complicated public view of him. It is too much to suggest that Mr. Nixon's old foes believed he had been transformed by the passage of years. Yet the people at large did see a different Nixon—a man who had changed, who had risen from defeat, who had tempered his harsher positions, who had become less strident, less accusatory, more accessible.

Thus his promise, thus his success.

Even so, his victory in 1968 was extraordinarily narrow. He had been defeated by one-tenth of a percentage point in his first try for the presidency in 1960. Eight years later he was elected by seven-tenths of a percentage point. And not since 1846 had a President been elected without having a majority of his party in control of either house of Congress.

Americans have always been indulgent toward their Presidents. Once elected, they are seldom subsequently defeated. Only seven times has an incumbent President trying for reelection been rejected: the two Adamses, Van Buren, Cleveland, Harrison, Taft and, the last time in this century, Hoover. Over the decades the power of the presidency continued to increase. Whatever else may have been troubling the country, the President stood alone. He held the one symbolic office above petty partisanship and ignobility. A President, until recently, had been taken at face value. He was believed, trusted.

Richard Nixon built on that reservoir of public goodwill with more than words. In foreign affairs, with his trips to China and Russia he helped ease the tensions of the Cold War era. He presided over the final withdrawal of American ground forces from Vietnam, bringing to an end, for Americans at least, the longest, most divisive war in their history. In domestic affairs, he appealed to the mythical "Middle Americans" who have felt most acutely the frustrations of rapid change and who believe they have been overlooked.

To many citizens, the President personified the problems of the ordinary American. Throughout his career he had evoked his own background of hardship, meager means, family tragedies and a determination to succeed against all odds. He also touched a responsive chord when he promised to bring into line the vast governmental bureaucracy and to return decision-making power to states and local communities. Like a majority of citizens, he stood strongly for law and order, for an end to permissiveness, for morality and decency.

There will always be a debate, of course, about whether a Democrat other than George McGovern would have fared better against Mr. Nixon in 1972. The strong probability is that no one could have beaten him. Certainly, the President and his men did not need Watergate and its related activities to help them.

As it was, Watergate and corruption did figure largely in the '72 campaign. It never took hold, however, as a major issue. Never, it seems clear, because of two facts about most citizens: They tend to think of politics as vaguely corrupt anyway—and they refuse to believe their President could have anything to do with such a sordid business.

They refused to believe that Richard Nixon,· whatever his stormy past, had not been redeemed by the majesty of the presidency. They refused to believe that a President who had struggled so long, had triumphed over adversity and defeat, had espoused such noble goals in such moral terms, could be party to such deceit and manipulation. They certainly refused to believe that he would view them privately with such cynicism and contempt.

"Nobody is a friend of ours," he said at one point in his taped conversations. "Let's face it! Don't worry about that sort of thing." And at another point, when he was wondering out loud just how serious a crisis Watergate was, he said: "The point is, everything is a crisis. (Expletive deleted) it is a terrible, lousy thing—it will remain a crisis among the upper intellectual types, the soft heads, our own too—Republicans—and the Democrats and the rest. Average people won't think it is much of a crisis unless it affects them."

He never understood that he could trust those average people, just as they had finally trusted him.

In time, the truth began to emerge. Slowly, inexorably, the governmental-political-judicial-public opinion processes began to grind on toward the end.

Richard Nixon, who had been in politics so long and who had supposedly profited from so many critical battles, had made a massive miscalculation. As his transcripts show, he continued to believe that people weren't that troubled by Watergate. It would all blow over and be forgotten in time. He and his aides approached it as another problem to be manipulated rather than solved. A public relations blitz, a PR counterattack, would do the job.

By failing to act decisively, by attempting to conceal and thwart, by putting loyalty to aides above loyalty to the people, by treating a moral issue in an amoral way, his fate was sealed.

It was a pathetic ending for someone whose greatest ambition had been to become an engineer on the Santa Fe Railroad and for whom the train whistle beckoned to faraway places and eventually to meetings with Germans and Italians and all those others who were "the sweetest music I ever heard."

"Crises may indeed be agony," Richard Nixon wrote nearly 14 years ago, "but it is the exquisite agony which a man might not want to experience again—yet would not for the world have missed."

Now he has taken himself through the ultimate "exquisite agony," and carried America and the world along with him. We will all be picking up the collective pieces for years to come.

CHAPTER THREE

HIGH DRAMA AND FLAWED CHARACTER IN A THEATER TOO ACCUSTOMED TO TRAGEDY

By William Greider

William Greider, a national correspondent for The Washington Post *covered the Senate Watergate hearings and the subsequent impeachment developments.*

Our king was ruled by troubled sleep, undone by the ghosts of his secret self.

The nation trembles at this awesome drama which is now complete, the fall of Richard Nixon. It was an ancient epic retold in the brutal poetry of modern life, more gripping than the classics because the stage was real, the theater was our own democracy.

He seemed so bold and powerful in the sunlight days of his presidency, capable of great moments. Yet, in his private darkness, he was merely weak, nursing old wounds and fears, feeding the stale resentments which wiser men put aside. Americans and the world knew the first, the public leader of commanding stature. The unfolding drama taught them about the second man and his fatal flaws.

"Let's make the next four years the best four years in American history," the President proclaimed in his hour of triumph. He was surrounded by affectionate crowds, saluted by drums and the flourish of trumpets. No one could pull down a leader endorsed so over-whelmingly by the people, supported by 61 per cent of the voters and 49 of the states.

But Richard Nixon's unprecedented victory did not heal his dark wounds or completely satisfy his need for vengeance and vindication. In the privacy of his Oval Office with his re-election assured, he talked of getting

22

even. "I think we are going to fix the son-of-a-bitch," the President told his applauding courtiers, referring to Edward Bennett Williams. "Believe me, we are going to."

At the inaugural podium, he spoke of higher ambitions, a pious vision of his public purpose. "We shall answer to God, to history and to our conscience for the way in which we use these years," he promised the cheering masses before him.

Yet his whispered thoughts in private were of revenge, a battle to be fought and won, no quarter given. "We are all in it together," he reassured his lieutenants. "This is a war. We take a few shots and it will be over. We will give them a few shots and it will be over. Don't worry. I wouldn't want to be on the other side right now, would you?"

And so the stage of American political life was set for high tragedy. Power blinded by pride, unable to confront weaknesses.

His loyal friends, a shrinking circle of the faithful, saw Richard Nixon as a modern-day King Lear who raged magnificently at the storm around him. But Nixon lacked Lear's grandeur. Nixon's enemies cast him as Richard the Third, the King who was crippled by his own malevolence. But Nixon did not have the eloquence of that other Richard or his purity of evil purpose. Nixon was confused. Like Macbeth, who listened to the witches' prophesies and found comfort in their riddles. He was both brave in facing his peril but doomed by his blindness to it.

Shakespeare wrote the curse:

> He shall spurn fate, scorn death,
> and bear
> His hopes 'bove wisdom, grace
> and fear;
> And, you all know, security
> Is mortal's chiefest enemy.

For Richard Nixon, the false security was that "mandate of '72." He carried it with him like a shield, as though its magic powers would protect him from any attack by his enemies. As in the tale of that ancient Scottish king, it persuaded Richard Nixon that his throne was safe.

"People who did not accept the mandate of '72," he declared confidently, "who do not want the strong America that I want to build, who do not want the foreign policy leadership that I want to give, who do not want to cut down the size of this government bureaucracy . . . people who do not want these things naturally would exploit any issue, if it weren't Watergate, anything else, in order to keep the President from doing his job."

Lady Macbeth said it more succinctly: "What need we fear who knows it, when none can call our power to account?"

Now that his flaws are so evident, some in the audience indulge a certain self-righteousness at his fall. It seems just and satisfying and such good theater. But in this drama the spectators are victims too. The tragic awareness has settled not just upon the man, but upon the nation and its own sense of itself.

He was, as he liked to remind everyone, chosen overwhelmingly by all of us. And he won that remarkable election victory by espousing the popular values so common to our nation and its past. Hard work and ambition. Civil piety. A pugnacious sense of patriotism. A zest for rugged endeavors. Winning. He used public friends as emblems of what he believed—Billy Graham and the Washington Redskins, Bob Hope and John Wayne and General Patton. His lovely family, a perfect expression of virtuous striving.

And, of course, Richard Nixon has himself the ultimate example of how the tough-minded and talented can struggle upward in America, from the humblest home to positions of wealth and fame. He talked about that often in public and the familiar story of hard work rewarded became part of what we knew about the man.

Then suddenly it seemed he was saying different

things about himself, denials which sounded like unintended confessions.

"I made my mistakes," he said as fortune soured for him, "but in all of my years in public life, I have never profited, never profited from public service. I have earned every cent. And in all of my years of public life, I have never obstructed justice. And I think too that I could say that in my years of public life, that I welcome this kind of examination because people have got to know whether or not their President is a crook. Well, I am not a crook."

People listened to the quavering voice and the feeling spread that, of course, he was.

Now that it is over, the climax seems so natural and inevitable. But it never looked that way as the drama unfolded. On the contrary, at a dozen different junctures it seemed that the President might save himself. Again and again, he was challenged by his enemies and begged by his allies to clear up the matter, to provide the complete factual explanations which would put it to rest. It was the one stroke which was beyond his vast power.

Each time he tried to slay the dragon, it grew another head and came charging back with new fire. Each of his solutions provided an added weapon against him. At one point, Nixon's despair and confusion produced a kind of desperate soliloquy recorded in the White House transcripts. "I don't know. Am I seeing something (unintelligible) that really isn't (unintelligible) or am I?"

Belatedly, he came forward in the spring of 1973 to announce that there was a stench in the White House— weeks after it was already obvious to the world. His disclosure was too late and not enough. In the fall, he arranged what he thought would be a final gesture of compromise turning over the tape-recorded evidence to his own selected arbiter. When that scheme ended in the dismissal of Special Prosecutor Archibald Cox, the move to impeach began in earnest.

A month later, Nixon made another drastic miscalculation of his own invincibility. By releasing his own income-tax returns, he thought that issue would be settled. But his tax returns only deepened the ugly portrait which events were drawing of him and propelled Congress one more step down the road it didn't want to take.

In the spring, the President made another miscalculation, perhaps the fatal one. Hemmed in by courts and congressional investigators, he chose the bold alternative of releasing to the public the transcripts of his frank private conversations, in which he plotted his survival with his closest aides. The coarse cynicism was too much, even for many of his friends.

The episode was like a classical moment of truth telling, in which the hero's illusions are confronted by reality and are overwhelmed by the contradictions. In public, he insisted on a pious view of himself. "I reject the cynical view," he declared at one point, "that politics is inevitably or even usually dirty business." Yet in private he thought it was naive to believe anything else. "Goldwater put it in context," Nixon told John Dean. "He said, 'Well, for Christ's sake, everybody bugs everybody else. We know that.' "

In public, he spoke of his ordeal as a fine period of testing, the crisis decision-making, which he relished throughout his turbulent political career. "I shall always remember this group tonight," Nixon told a Republican fund-raising banquet as the crisis deepened. "Remember that when the going was tough, you hung in there. Remember that when the challenge was greatest, you didn't lose your faith. And if some of you think that, why does this challenge have to come to us, why do we have to endure, let me remind you that the finest steel has to go through the hottest fire. And, I can assure you, my friends, this room is full of fine steel tonight."

But in private this man of steel turned out to be malleable and tarnished. He did not sleep well during this period. He made late-night telephone calls to his two trusted mastiffs, Haldeman and Ehrlichman, seeking their reassurances. His family heard him playing the piano, alone, past midnight. His closest pal, Rebozo, took him on high-speed drives along California thruways for diversion.

"I'm so sick of this thing," the President confessed in a private moment of torment. "I want to get it done with and over. And I don't want to hear about it again."

While destiny closed on the king, his tragedy was enriched by the cast of minor characters around him who also fell. They included slick and cynical men grasping for a share of authority. Haldeman and Ehrlichman, crudely manipulating Nixon's presidential words and gestures like two Madison Avenue Pygmalions. John Dean, the facile scorpion whose poison served the President, then stung him. John Mitchell, smug and belligerent, a law-and-order man concealing his contempt for both. Ronald Ziegler, the comic mouthpiece who occasionally got confused himself about which was truth and which was lie.

When Nixon turned for help, these were the men who gathered for his inner councils, who, each in his own way, helped undo him. They were his friends of choice, men he selected because they shared his qualities or perhaps because he wished he shared theirs. The real enemy, it turned out, was all around him.

Beyond the inner circle, the subplots unraveled in a medley of personal disasters, muted moments of self-awareness for glib and purposeful young men whose opaque sense of values was shredded by Watergate.

Charles Colson, White House tough guy, became a latter-day witness to Christ: "You've got to put your trust in other things than simply retaliating when you're hit."

Jeb Magruder, the loyal organization man who perjured himself to conceal the organization's crime, mused about the values which led to prison: "I would never say the country caused Watergate. Specific individuals are to blame. But there are certain values, certain characteristics and habits in this country—a desire to get ahead, impatience. Our overwhelming legal struc-

27

ture creates in the average businessman, the average worker, a feeling that he has to do his share of shaving, whether it be on his income tax or his expense account."

And Egil Krogh, whose flinty sense of idealism produced a celebrated burglary, came to believe that the whole devastating scandal might be good for America, in the long run, even though it meant torment for him: "I have great hope that what is actually being done is a wonderful healing process whereby what this country represents and what it means are going to be more clearly understood."

As it happened, these minor players described their leader's flaws more clearly than he could himself. His last flourish was brave. Even his enemies conceded that. But it did not illuminate a character who had come to self-realization.

"They have tied me to a stake, I cannot fly," Macbeth roared as Macduff closed in with death. "But, bear-like, I must fight the course." So Nixon said stoutly: "I did an awful lot. I cut off one arm, then the other arm . . ." And he fought on.

Might he have saved himself, at one point or the other, simply by telling the whole truth? Early on, the public might have been forgiving, but his character would not allow it. His harshest critics insist that he could never afford to tell the truth because he was always guilty.

But Nixon's character dilemma rested on a more subtle problem than that. To tell the truth meant to reveal his weaknesses, to confess the White House fears and insecurities, to cut away the petty hatreds and tribal loyalties which led him deeper and deeper into the muck. How can a strong king confess that he is so frail? Indeed, each time the President showed a larger glimpse of his private self, it only made matters worse. People were repelled by what Nixon's men had done, but people were horrified when they saw the private man whom those men worked for.

"The thing that is completely misunderstood about Watergate," said Charles Colson, "is that everybody

28

thinks the people surrounding the President were drunk with power . . . But it wasn't arrogance at all. It was insecurity. That insecurity began to breed a form of paranoia. We over-reacted to the attacks against us and to a lot of things."

A tale of small men who did not belong in high places, who perhaps knew down deep that they did not belong, who wanted desperately to prove that their secret insecurities were wrong.

So the high tragedy is done, but only insensitive partisans can be self-righteous about the outcome. There was no moment of catharsis for the hero, no climactic scene when his rage dissolved into self-awareness.

That moment of truth is for the nation itself, the audience which learned so painfully about its leader and, thus, about itself. If Richard Nixon was so evil, after all, can the rest of us be so good? If he was a mean-spirited leader, then who chose him?

Nixon's tragedy asks the most serious questions of democracy. If Nixon reflected authentic popular values, then perhaps he showed Americans a coarse picture of ourselves, one we would rather not face. Or, if he misled us and deceived us in his climb to power, then our democratic process failed at the most serious level.

"I think our country sinks beneath the yoke," Malcolm said of Macbeth's reign. "It weeps, it bleeds, and each new day a gash is added to her wounds."

What do we really know about the leaders whom we choose? What do we truly know about ourselves? The spectators depart with complicated feelings, a troubled mixture of satisfaction and self-doubt. They are hopeful that Richard Nixon's disgraced presidency has defined a new standard of public honor, but none can be entirely convinced.

CHAPTER FOUR

A PASSION FOR THE COVERT: THE RESPONSE TO THE THREAT OF DISCOVERY

By Carl Bernstein and Bob Woodward

Carl Bernstein and Bob Woodward are metropolitan staff reporters for The Washington Post who have covered the Watergate story since June 17, 1972. They are the authors of All the President's Men, *a narrative of the Watergate episode.*

Vice President Richard M. Nixon had been defeated in the closest presidential election in American history. "I have never seen a man take such defeat with such grace," Herbert G. Klein, his press secretary told reporters the morning after. "Even in defeat, Mr. Nixon goes down in history as one of the truly great champions of our country."

A few hours later, clearly under strain, the Vice President arrived in the ballroom of Washington's Mayflower Hotel to thank several hundred campaign workers. In the front lines of those who had helped bring him so painfully close to becoming the nation's 35th President were an obscure advertising executive from Los Angeles and an equally unknown attorney from Seattle. Their names: H. R. Haldeman and John D. Ehrlichman.

In Kansas City, the returns of the 1960 election had been followed closely by a 26-year-old paper pulp salesman who temporarily quit his job that fall to serve as a ward chairman for Richard Nixon's campaign. His father, an ardent Civil War buff, had named him for the famous Confederate cavalry raider. He was: Jeb Stuart Magruder.

In Washington, the administrative assistant to Sen.

Leverett Saltonstall of Massachusetts had seen his party's national prospects grow dim as the hopes of election eve turned to the morning's hard reality. His name: Charles W. Colson.

In New York, a senior partner in a law firm specializing in the sale of municipal bonds viewed the presidential campaign as far removed from his secure existence on Wall Street. His name: John N. Mitchell.

In California, another lawyer was in the process of building a lucrative real estate title practice in the seaside Los Angeles suburb of Newport Beach. His name: Herbert W. Kalmbach.

Others then unknown to the public were scattered around the country in various stages of their careers. At the headquarters of the Rand Corp. in California, Daniel Ellsberg was pioneering the application of game theories to war.

At the University of Southern California, Donald Segretti was helping manage the campaign of his classmate, Dwight Chapin, for the presidency of Sigma Chi. At a law office in Connecticut, L. Patrick Gray III, a retired submarine skipper, was beginning a new practice in drawing up wills. At a "safe" house in Havana, E. Howard Hunt Jr., recently retired as the CIA station chief in Uruguay, was on a secret mission observing Fidel Castro's Cuba and recommending to superiors that Fidel be assassinated. At the FBI headquarters in Washington, G. Gordon Liddy, a young Fordham law graduate, had finally realized his boyhood ambition of becoming a G-man.

And in Ohio, a bright, sandy-haired student at Wooster College was dating attractive co-eds and hoping his good memory would get him into law school the next year. His name: John Wesley Dean III.

Twelve years later, on June 17, 1972, the lives of all these men became entangled in a web that would become known as Watergate. The beginnings were simple enough: a bungled burglary and bugging at the headquarters of the Democratic National Committee; five men arrested, among them the security coordinator of the Committee for the Re-election of the President. The President was Richard M. Nixon.

And, on June 17, 1972, Richard Nixon was approaching the kind of triumph that always had eluded him. Three months earlier, he had returned from his historic visit to China. This coldest of Cold Warriors had visited the Soviet Union and initiated a thaw heralding the possibility of a generation of peace. In Vietnam, American boys were being brought home by their Commander in Chief from the most divisive war in the nation's history.

Now, less than a month before the Democratic National Convention, the President stood ahead of all announced opposition candidates by no less than 19 points in the polls. Richard Nixon's vision of an emerging Republican majority that would dominate the last quarter of the century, much as the Democrats had dominated two previous generations, appeared possible. The Democratic Party was in disarray as a brutal primary season approached its end. Sen. George McGovern of South Dakota, considered by the White House and Democratic Party professionals alike to be Nixon's weakest opponent, was emerging as the favorite to win the Democrats' nomination for President.

The morning after the arrest of five men inside the Watergate, a front-page story in The Washington Post noted: "There was no immediate explanation as to why the five suspects would want to bug the Democratic National Committee offices, or whether or not they were working for any other individuals or other organizations."

But at Key Biscayne, where the President was resting, and in California and Washington, where his men were meeting, the meaning of Watergate was all too clear.

It imperiled not only the record of accomplishment of the first Nixon administration, but directly threatened the massive re-election mandate which the President, his aides and the pollsters were confident would be conferred by the voters in November. And not insignificantly, it threatened Richard Nixon's place in history.

Unlike the rest of the nation that day, the President and his men then knew the real meaning of Watergate was not merely a "third-rate burglary," as Ronald L. Ziegler, the White House press secretary, had described it. Watergate—a term that would be hammered into the American consciousness and the soul of Richard Nixon's presidency for the next two years—represented something far more serious. To the President and his men, Watergate meant the potential exposure of the crimes of the Nixon administration—"The White House horrors," as John Mitchell would later derisively call them.

Mitchell, the Attorney General of the first Nixon administration and now the director of the President's re-election campaign, received word in California that Saturday of the arrests. While serving as the nation's highest-ranking law enforcement officer, he had been present at a meeting six months earlier when Liddy proposed to place the Democrats under electronic surveillance.

Now Mitchell dispatched Jeb Magruder, who had also attended that meeting, back to Washington. "The cover-up, thus, was immediate and automatic," Magruder wrote later. "No one ever considered that there would not be a cover-up."

The same day, John Dean, counsel to the President of the United States, arrived in California from a trip abroad and phoned the White House. He, too, had been at that initial meeting with Liddy, and at another as well where plans for illegal electronic surveillance of the Democrats were discussed. Upon learning of the arrests, he immediately flew to the capital. Watergate, he knew, was that "peek into the tent" that could bring the tent down.

But it was Richard Nixon, the hard political realist, who knew better than anyone what the collapse of that tent could do to his presidency. Thus it was the President who took the irrevocable step, six days after the break-in, of ordering his aides to insure that the FBI or the American people never learn what lay underneath: the wiretapping, burglaries, cover-ups, lies, money-laundering, secret funds, enemies' lists, dirty tricks, "plumbers," physical surveillance, forged cables, attempted character assassinations, IRS audits . . . a veritable catalogue of illegal activities and abuses conceived and directed by the President and his men.

As the President himself was forced to gradually reveal, he was the man behind the web of Watergate. It was his passion for secrecy that made the demise of his presidency inevitable. Similarly, it was his response to the threat of discovery that set in motion those forces which finally destroyed him.

The longer the cover-up went on—the more intensely that investigators, lawyers, grand jurors, reporters, and congressional committees pursued the larger meaning of Watergate—the more they found. And, as the cover-up spun out in its myriad directions, the web grew; each misdeed in turn required its own cover-up.

In the end, it was finally possible to trace the repeated miscalculations which Richard Nixon had woven. There was no grand plan—for the illegal activities or for the attempts to hide them. But the single unraveling strand was the character, ideology and insecurity of Richard M. Nixon.

He totally failed to perceive the goodwill extended to any President by the people, the bureaucracy, the military, the press, his political party, Congress and the institutions of justice. Instead of using them as allies—in the tradition of his predecessors—he assumed their enmity. In the process, he eroded their ability to help him.

Perhaps there were times in these past two years when Richard Nixon could have saved himself and spared the people of this country the trauma of his ordeal. At crucial points in the conspiracy which finally brought him down, he spoke of "cutting our losses," of "hang-outs," even of telling the truth.

But, as his own aides have sadly conceded, he never did. Instead, he "stonewalled" to the end, even against his own lawyers, his most trusted aides and his staunchest political supporters in Congress and the country. It was Richard Nixon, observed a member of his staff, who had us wallow in Watergate. Almost, it now seems, from the day he took office and began his miscalculations—and his misreading of history—he made the unthinkable possible: that a president would so abuse his vast powers that he would need to obstruct justice, provoke the reluctant institutions of the nation into action against him, and finally—be pushed from the pinnacle in disgrace.

Re-reading the transcripts of his own tape recordings (which, characteristically contained the seeds of Mr. Nixon's destruction), the tragic pattern of the Nixon presidency becomes more clear.

As the tapes demonstrate, Mr. Nixon came to the White House full of suspicions and phobias and, apparently, a belief that his predecessors had routinely used the nation's highest office like the backroom of some political clubhouse. If he had any faith in the existing institutions of government, aside from the power of the executive, it is nowhere to be found in the tapes. Members of Congress, where he had served 6 years, were "assholes," to be loathed and manipulated; the IRS was a tool of the Democrats, to be turned into an instrument of retribution; the FBI was inept and, worse, unwilling to break the law in pursuing the enemies, real or imagined, of the White House; the nation's newspapers, which overwhelmingly supported his re-election, were after Nixon; the bureaucracy, those nameless, faceless and hidebound civil servants, were Kennedyites, or, little better, paper-pushing remnants of the Great Society; the Republican Party was committed not to Richard Nixon but to some vague ideals that drained off money and energy from the President's own electoral ambitions.

The President's men, as revealed on the tapes, shared the fearsome vision of their leader. Chapin, Dean, Krogh, Ziegler, Magruder, Colson, Porter, Strachan, Huston, Young, Haldeman, Ehrlichman. Willingly, even enthusiastically, they outdid each other with plans to

35

"screw" the White House enemies, to supplant the security functions of the FBI with a squad of White House vigilantes, to undermine the electoral process through disruption of the opposition party's primaries, to "fix" mock elections in high schools, to smear the reputations of politicians and public servants of both parties and—finally—to undermine the administration of justice.

Perhaps significantly, the men closest to the President had never held public office nor sought it. They came from the worlds of marketing and public relations and advertising and real estate and the practice of civil law. They were bright, able and, above all else, zealous. There were others, of course cast from a different mold —schooled in government service, the Congress, the executive departments, the diplomatic corps, the line agencies, even academia: Burns, Rogers, Martin, Shultz, Harlow, Moynihan, Laird, Hickel, Richardson, Finch, Ruckelshaus. But they were the outsiders, barred from the Oval Office by the choice of the President, described contemptuously on the tapes by Mr. Nixon and treated with condescension by the eager patrol of beavers under the control of Haldeman, the keeper of the door to the inner sanctum of power.

In his time of crisis, the President rarely called on those who could have helped him—and then only to manipulate them, the tapes show, not to seek their counsel. Thus, in his unique recorded contribution to American history, President Nixon has left us not so much an index to his own character and those around him, but a remarkable drama of conspiracy and tragedy, sweeping in scope, vainglorious and venal.

Listened to in retrospect, the drama unfolds swiftly, the miscalculations providing the finale to each stunning act:

The decision to hire Liddy ("He must be a little bit nuts huh?" the President asks after it is too late); to engage the CIA in the cover-up; to make the conduct of the press the issue, not the actions of his men; to lie continually ("What really hurts in a matter of this sort is not the fact that they occur," he told the American people, "because overzealous people in campaigns do things that are wrong. What really hurts is if you try to cover it up. . . ."); to invoke the sanctity of "national security" long after the President himself cast that legitimate concern into disrepute; to make the mandate of 1972 for license to undermine the Constitution.

And yet the cover-up continued. As the circle drew tighter, increasingly the President was forced to assume more personal direction of the conspiracy. One of the conspirators cracked, and still the President sought ways to keep the others silent. It was only after his personal aides faced certain indictment that he dismissed them. He agreed to the hiring of a special prosecutor, confident that such an extraordinary office could be manipulated in the same manner as his own discredited Justice Department. Faced with the disastrous consequences of that decision, he fired the prosecutor—and then replaced him with a successor equally independent and aggressive. He defied the courts, only to back down in humiliation.

Forced by the courts to turn over material he knew to be self-incriminating, he relinquished only part of it—but still enough for a grand jury of ordinary citizens to name him as a co-conspirator. Aware that his tapes would be made public, he senselessly released transcripts of his conversations at variance with the originals. His credibility long before destroyed, his explanations became more and more implausible.

Finally trapped, he was stripped of all defenses but one: that he was the embodiment of the presidency—above reproach, above the law, above sanction. But in the end, even those who had pleaded his case for so long found at last the reason to abandon Richard Nixon. He had disgraced not just himself. He had demeaned the presidency. Yet in leaving office, he may have bequeathed a legacy of restoration.

CHAPTER FIVE

THE FORCES THAT FORGED THE FUTURE: "HE DIDN'T WANT TO STAY IN YORBA LINDA"

By Lou Cannon

A member of the national staff of The Washington Post, Lou Cannon has covered the White House and Nixon presidency.

> ". . . Perhaps my major liability is—and this may sound incongruous—that I am essentially shyer than the usually extrovert politician ought to be. This seems to be an inborn trait which I cannot change or alter. I have a great liking for the plain people, but I feel ill at ease with the prominent."
> —Richard Nixon, 1968

Richard Milhous Nixon has occupied a prominent place in our public life and in our consciousness longer than any other American politician, and yet his essential nature remains a mystery.

For middle-aged Americans he exists as a series of stereotypes extending back into our childhoods. Durable Dick and Tricky Dick. The relentless pursuer of Alger Hiss and the ruthless campaign scourge of the Democrats. The man who debated Khrushchev in a kitchen and who made peace with the Chinese Communists at a banquet table. The Nixon of Checkers, the Hughes loan and "I am not a crook." The Nixon who lost to John F. Kennedy in 1960 after a self-destructive television debate. The Nixon "You Won't Have to Kick Around Anymore." The resurrected Nixon of 1968 defeating the only Democrat who had lasted as long as he had. The Nixon of Watergate.

These and a hundred other Nixons torment our memories. Each is a separate portrait; none combines to form a composite picture of the man. After all these years Nixon remains, in the human sense, an enigma to his fellow Americans. But it is a different Nixon—or more properly, a whole Nixon—who is remembered by his friends of yesteryear and by a few close aides in the White House. These friends, like most Americans, are deeply troubled by Watergate and the Nixon taxes and all the rest, although perhaps more ready than most to blame the media for what they regard as magnification of the Nixon scandals. These friends retain a regard and even an affection for Nixon and a desire to explain him to others and to themselves. What follows is an attempt to understand Richard Nixon from the perspective of those who care about him.

Nixon is 61 years old now. Many who knew him as a young man are dead, and others are afflicted with failing memories. Some of those who are alive and robust have had their personal views of Nixon colored, for better or for worse, by the dramatic events of his long public career. Still, there is a common portrait of Nixon which emerges from the recollections of his friends and classmates. All speak of Nixon's shyness, of his quick intellect, of his capacity for hard work. Many also remember his poverty and his consciousness of it.

In American mythology, politicians in general and Presidents in particular tend to exalt the log-cabin aspects of their boyhood.

It is commonplace for famous men, in a country that celebrates humbleness of origin, to glorify poverty they never knew. But Nixon's history defies the mythology, on this key point as on so many others.

Unlike most Presidents, Nixon was poorer than he seems. It is true that the Nixons were relatively well-off, in middle-class terms, when the biographers discovered them in the mid-50s, but the Nixons were dirt poor at the most critical times of Richard Nixon's boyhood. His father, Frank, was unemployed and trying to start a lemon-growing business when Richard was born in 1913. The business failed, and the first five years of

Dick Nixon's life were hardscrabble times for the family. Nixon once recalled that in the five years preceding his older brother Harold's death of tuberculosis in 1933—a period embracing Dick Nixon's entire high school attendance—his mother never bought a new dress because of the medical bills. Nixon has never forgotten those years. People who came to know Nixon after he left Whittier rarely knew of his anxieties about material success, partly because they were hidden by his greater and growing concern for the acquisition of power and partly because he displayed a frequently generous spirit to his friends. Robert Finch recalls that Nixon was almost totally oblivious to the financial arrangements when he was trying to associate with a Southern California law firm after his 1960 defeat. Stephen Hess, a former White House aide in both the Eisenhower and Nixon administrations, learned never to set a fee for speechwriting or other services because Nixon always set a higher one when it was left to him.

But this real generosity of which Nixon often was capable obscured his preoccupation with money and the men who made it. "Get to know the big finance men, that's the key," Rep. John Rousselot of California remembers Nixon telling him in the late 50s at the time when Rousselot was a young conservative aspiring to Congress. And one of the early Nixon supporters, a man who helped drafted him to run in 1946, recalls:

"Dick didn't have any money. He lived in a lousy cottage which Herman Perry (the Whittier Bank of America manager) had got for him. On the one hand, Dick never gave a damn about money and was generous with what he had . . . On the other hand he was the child both of a poor family and the Depression, and he was drawn to people who made a lot of money. He's impressed by them. Money was important to him, not as something to have, but as security . . . That was important to Dick. This is what San Clemente is all about."

Whittier was known as "ye friendly town," but there was more tension than friendliness in the Nixon home.

Nixon's least critical biographer, Bela Kornitzer, describes his father, Frank Nixon, as "tough, opinionated, capricious, argumentative and unpredictable." To people who remember him, this seems an understatement. Orphaned and uneducated at 9, Frank Nixon became a carpenter and a handyman and he was a rough disciplinarian with the Nixon boys. Richard learned to avoid the beatings that his brothers frequently received but at the cost of further repressing an already inward nature. "Dad was very strict and expected to be obeyed under all circumstances," Nixon told Kornitzer. "If he wanted something, he wanted it at once. He had a hot temper, and I learned early that the only way to deal with him was to abide by the rules he laid down. Otherwise, I would probably have felt the touch of a ruler or the strap as my brothers did." Frank, a Quaker by marriage to Nixon's mother Hannah and a sometime Sunday school teacher, also was gifted in profanity, and Nixon did not have to wait until his Navy service to learn the expletive-deleted language of the Watergate transcripts.

However, Nixon also was taught what was customary for his day, which was never to swear around women. And for a long time, there was scant danger of that. The young Richard Nixon was extraordinarily shy and stayed away from girls. Roy Day, the Republican campaign manager when Nixon first ran against Democrat Jerry Voorhis, recalled that at 33 Nixon was so shy that he had to be advised to look women in the eye when he spoke to them.

Nevertheless, Nixon was well regarded by his friends, most of whom thought he would make a career as a lawyer, not a politician. Those who have known him a long time praise his competitiveness, but they speak even more of a considerate nature and of the loyalty he shows his friends. "I never found anybody who knew him who didn't like him," says Hubert Perry, a classmate in high school and Whittier College and the son of the banker who recruited Nixon to run against Voorhis. Already, however, Nixon's remote manner and his tendency to compartmentalize repelled those who never came to know him well.

On the eve of his inauguration Perry was quoted in his hometown newspaper as saying that Nixon would be admired as President but added, "I don't think he is ever going to be loved."

This lack was apparent from Nixon's earliest days. Nixon was the sort of young man who impressed relatives and various teachers by his ability to produce the "right" answers and by his bright, hard-working ways. Nixon's classmates also had high regard for his diligence and capability, but most of them were not drawn to him as a person, and his circle of friends was small even then. Within this circle, Nixon gave and received the kind of loyalty that would become a hallmark of his political existence. Outside his circle, however, his reserve appeared as arrogance, and his aloofness, coldness. He always commanded respect. Rarely did he inspire the human affection that Americans often associate with their Presidents.

This young Nixon, whatever else he may have been or would become, was something of a dreamer. His dreams led him to the world outside. The Santa Fe Railway symbolized Nixon's link between Whittier and the world, and the grownup Nixon would remember how the boyhood Nixon had dreamed of leaving on those trains.

"I see another child," Nixon said in his 1968 acceptance speech. "He hears the train go by at night and dreams of far away places he would like to go." One of Nixon's former law partners, Earl C. Adams of Los Angeles, believes this speech to be among the most personally revealing speeches that Nixon ever made. "He wanted to follow that train," says Adams. "It's not a contrivance at all. He lay in bed and he heard that Santa Fe train go by and he wanted to get on it. He didn't want to stay in Yorba Linda. He wanted to go where he is."

Adams is the senior partner in one of Los Angeles' most prestigious law firms and one of the small group

42

of San Marino and Whittier attorneys and businessmen who recruited Nixon to politics in 1945. He also is the executor of Hannah Nixon's estate and a longtime admirer of Richard Nixon's Quaker mother, whom he regards as the source of Nixon's drive. "A great high ambition is what makes Nixon go," says Adams. "It derives from his mother."

The early recollections make it clear that Richard Nixon, the second son in a family of five, must have been the favorite of his mother, who liked to predict great things for him. "He was thoughtful and serious," she told Kornitzer. "He always carried such a weight. That's an expression we Quakers use for a person who doesn't take his responsibilities lightly."

Despite his brightness, Nixon was never regarded as an intellectual. He preferred games and athletic contests, where his competitiveness ran a constantly losing race with his poor physical coordination. "The sports stuff that Dick always spouts is for real," says one of his friends. "I think there were times he would have chucked everything else if he could have played football well." Instead of playing football, Nixon turned his mental talents to competition. He was not drawn to philosophy or even to its stepchild, ideology, but to the winning of argument and debate. Indeed, his Whittier football coach, an admirer of Nixon, believes he had no thought about whether he was Democrat or Republican until he was recruited for the Voorhis race. Nixon himself always has cited debate as the arena of his first achievements, and his autobiography compresses the mistakes of the 1960 campaign into an agony of second-guessing about his "lost" debate with John F. Kennedy.

"I'd always liked to debate," said Nixon in a 1968 interview with Kenneth Harris of the London Observer. "Even when I was a very small boy, I liked to talk to people, discuss things, make points, cross swords in language, and I came to regard the lawyer as the social functionary who most deployed the art of debate." Debate provided Dick Nixon with the outlet for his com-

43

petitive spirit and for the verbal display of independence denied him in his home. It pleased his mother who wanted him to make something of himself, and it also pleased his difficult father, who regarded rhetorical skill as a demonstration of superior education. Frank Nixon was uneducated and his grammar was poor. "But he always admired educated people," Dick Nixon told Harris. "He was more interested in my education than my career."

Debate developed both Dick Nixon's education and his career, but it broadened him rather than deepening him. He developed a quickness, a facility, an ability to argue all sides of every question. He also developed the dozen little debater's tricks that still mar his speeches, especially the ability to plausibly refute an argument his opponent has never made. "I have met a dozen Dick Nixons on debate teams," says one of his debate opponents of those years. "I didn't do well with a proposition I didn't really believe in. Somehow that never seemed to bother Dick."

Later on, events would reinforce Nixon's early view of the importance of debate. He has always believed, and with some justification, that his debates with Jerry Voorhis helped him to win the congressional seat in 1946. Nixon remained the essential debater when he returned to California to practice law after his loss to Kennedy. Says Earl Adams, his senior partner, of Nixon's California practice:

"He practiced law the way he's best suited to practice law. By temperament, he's not the guy to paw through a file and ferret out all the facts. He likes to have that done by someone else, giving him the opportunity to make the sweeping case."

Debate was not Nixon's only achievement. In school he excelled in geography, history and English. Frequently he has told the children of close White House aides that "geography was my best subject," and his report cards support his recollection. "He wanted to go to faraway, exotic places," says a friend. "He was interested in the world and thought about it when no one else did." Perhaps geography, like the Santa Fe Railway, seemed a way out of Whittier. In any case, Nixon loved the subject and he would spend hours reading books about foreign countries and rolling the names of strange-sounding capitals off his tongue. In Congress it would take a single session on the Herter Committee to make of Nixon a thorough-going internationalist.

The country of Nixon's mind, like the minds of other boys, was inhabited by the heroes and villains of his parents. He revered Woodrow Wilson, another dreamer, and the President his mother most admired. He hated newspapermen, as did his father, who once during a serious illness suggested to his Vice President son that they be thrown out of the house. Let those who trace Nixon's suspicion of the press to the Hiss case or to the Checkers speech consider these words from "Our Privileges Under the Constitution," a prize-winning speech Nixon gave as a high school junior:

"How much ground do these privileges cover? There are some who use them as a cloak for covering libelous, indecent and injurious statements against their fellow men. Should the morals of this nation be offended and polluted in the name of freedom of speech or freedom of the press? In the words of Lincoln, the individual can have no rights against the best interests of society."

Robert M. Williams, classmate of Nixon's at Whittier High School, recalls that Nixon "delivered the speech in much the same way he delivers speeches now—not very well." But Williams was impressed by Nixon in other ways. Both were candidates for student offices on what was known as the "senior ticket" with Williams running for editor of the school newspaper and Nixon for student body president. All of the senior ticket candidates except Nixon won, and afterward Williams named him feature writer for the school paper.

Williams said he selected him because of his good marks in English and his reliability. "I knew I could count on him to meet deadlines," adds Williams. "He always did, too."

Nixon's school newspaper stories, like his speech on

the Constitution, were models of organization. In fact, it probably is not too much to say that organization and hard work always have been the twin keys to Nixon's personal success. In his California days he loved to tell the story of how he had pushed his way through Duke Law School, in part by mimeographing the pages of his law professor's thesis in a hot, airless room. Nixon also valued the statement of a Duke upperclassman in the Earl Mazo biography of Nixon. The upperclassman predicted that Nixon, who was then worried sick about the possibility of failure, would make it because "you've got an iron butt and that's the secret of becoming a lawyer."

When he entered politics, Nixon's organizational abilities served him even better than his debating experience. He also developed a fascination with strategy and a habit of explaining his strategies to people as a demonstration of his analytical powers. It was legal strategy at first, then poker strategy in the Navy, then political strategy.

This habit suggests that it was strategy itself that was paramount rather than any particular objective. When David S. Broder and Stephen Hess wrote "The Republican Establishment" in 1965 they would conclude about Nixon, "He is one of the few politicians . . . whose motives are always questioned."

It is this central suspicion that he is a hypocrite that has plagued Nixon throughout his political life. Its roots go deep into the childhood of a home divided between the Quaker instruction in a higher morality and the teachings of a profane, intolerant, opinionated father who did not lightly accept dissent from equals, much less from his sons. "Dick never liked to admit he made a mistake," recalls a high school classmate who says with understatement that the flaw now seems much larger than it did at the time.

Sometimes this dualist morality of his childhood would lead Nixon to make claims that seemed transparently hypocritical as when, during his third 1960 debate with Kennedy, he criticized Harry Truman's use of language and praised President Eisenhower for restoring "dignity and decency and, frankly, good language to the conduct of the presidency . . .

"What made it silly," said a former Nixon aide, "is not only that Dick swore but that he knew full well that Ike swore like the trooper he was."

The contradiction between what Nixon had been taught and perhaps wanted to be and what he was were nowhere more evident than in his spiritual life. He invited both a Quaker speaker and the Rev. Billy Graham to preside at his mother's funeral, and their presence seemed to symbolize the contradiction between Nixon's early reliance on a personal, inner God and his later celebration of the Lord as a political ally of the United States.

The contradiction has been there for a long time. Loverne Morris, a contemporary of Nixon's in Whittier and a retired staff member of the Whittier Daily news, wrote in 1969: "Those who attended Sunday school, church services and young people's meetings with him said he took his normal part but never seemed particularly devout and certainly not spiritual. They said he observed conventional moralities." Others disagreed, both then and now.

One of those who is convinced of Nixon's basic spirituality is Charles Colson, the former White House aide and convert to Christianity who pleaded guilty to obstructing justice in the Ellsberg case. Late in 1973, before the publicization of his conversion, Colson gave Nixon a book by the Quaker writer Elton Trueblood, "Abraham Lincoln: Theologian of American Anguish," and Nixon read it in those distraught days of a 1973 San Clemente trip when he was so depressed and diverted by Watergate that he walked about alone at night and canceled some of his most important appointments. Writing of Lincoln in words that Nixon has come to claim as his own, Trueblood said: "His only certainty lay in the conviction that God will never cease to call America to her true service, not only for her own sake but for the sake of the world."

The God whom Nixon was taught about in childhood

was a more personal one. There are many evidences that Nixon believed deeply in Him, none more compelling than an awkwardly moving eulogy he wrote at 17 to his youngest brother Arthur, who had died at 7 of meningitis. Arthur was Dick Nixon's favorite. Dick Nixon, who ever since has been especially sensitive to the death of his friends' own loved ones, describes how the dying Arthur called his mother into his room and recited the child's prayer: "If I should die before I wake, I pray the Lord my soul to take." Concludes Dick Nixon: "There is a grave out now in the hills, but like the picture, it contains only the bodily image of my brother. And so, when I am tired and worried, and am almost ready to quit trying to live as I should, I look up and see the picture of a little boy with sparkling eyes and curly hair; I remember the childlike prayer; I pray that it may prove as true for me as it did for my brother Arthur." Years later, Pat Nixon confided to a friend that if her husband hadn't gone into politics he would have chosen the ministry.

Whatever the strength may have been of Nixon's spiritual anchor, he wanted to sever his temporal roots in Whittier. He returned to practice law after graduating from Duke, as his family desired, but friends remember that he talked vaguely of going other places, doing other things. The war gave him a way out. Out of respect for the pacifist sensibilities of his mother, Nixon first took a job with the Office of Price Administration in Washington, which he would afterward stigmatize as the model of bureaucratic ills. Then he slipped quietly into the Navy, which he subsequently described as the "breakpoint" of his life. His naval service gave him a useful campaign line about service in the "stinking Solomons" to use against the civilian Voorhis, and a knowledge of poker, which was as precluded by Nixon's upbringing as was military service.

But Nixon has often been proficient at what he was taught to avoid. He won college office at Whittier on the strength of a promise to introduce dancing, although he did not dance. As operations officer on Green Island,

Nixon organized a commissary known as Nixon's Hamburger Stand, which was renowned for its whisky supply. When he left, the men gave Lt. Nixon a party.

After the war, as in the Navy, he took what was open to him. He talked briefly about becoming a bigtime lawyer and frequently about making a success of himself. He was unsure, at first, about politics, then attracted by the opportunity of becoming a congressman.

"Perhaps it was an accident that he went into politics," says Waller Taylor, a member of the Adams law firm. "Remember, they asked him to do it. And once he was in it, his drive and his ambition and his striving for success carried him. Maybe he could have gone into something else and never wanted to go into politics at all. It's hard to say."

Politics was an option available to Nixon in California as it would have been in few other states. He was not "a party man," as he came to be described, and in truth in California at this time there was really only one party, the incumbent party. The state's unique and since-discarded cross-filing system combined with an absence of party designation on the ballot to allow incumbents to run again and again with both parties' nominations. This was fine with the incumbents, who usually did all they could to see that their own parties put up hacks against their friends who were in the office.

The regular Republican organization had put up a long series of hacks against Voorhis, a onetime Socialist who had become a popular and increasingly conservative Democratic congressman. A few people like Adams and Perry and insurance man Frank E. Jorgensen were tired of the Republican performance and put pressure on the GOP organization to finally come up with a candidate. This is what led to the famous fact-finding committee that selected Nixon. "The Republican organization didn't feel we had any right to do what we were doing," recalls Adams. "They were right. We didn't. We were amateurs."

Dick Nixon was the answer to the amateur's dream. He came into the University Club at Los Angeles on Nov. 1, 1945, wearing his lieutenant commander's uniform, accompanied by his quiet wife. He spoke softly, and with reserve. One of the people at that small meeting recalls that Nixon also raised the question about money and the financing of his campaign, a question that commended him to the prudent businessmen in the room.

For Nixon neither then nor later would get over the business about being poor. It was why his new friends, many of them only beginning to break through financially, would set up the fund for him that became the issue of the 1952 campaign and the Checkers speech. Voorhis came from a moneyed family; Helen Gahagan Douglas had more money than he had. Before Nixon came to talk dynastically of "the Kennedys" he talked of "the Kennedy money." The "theys" on the other side always had more money than he had.

The men around Nixon in those days were young men who would make solid careers for themselves, in business and in law. They liked their prospective candidate immediately, but were hardly in awe of him. (Murray Chotiner, who would mean most to him, was not yet in the picture. Despite what has been written about him, Chotiner had almost nothing to do with Nixon until his 1950 campaign.) Nixon himself was attracted by the offer to run for Congress and he was anxious, as always, to make a good impression on others.

But if Nixon was attracted by his new friends—they had already talked to his mother and approved of his origins—he was also unsure that he would pursue a political career. The center stage simultaneously lured him and made him uneasy. The quotation with which this account began is from an interview with Bela Kornitzer in 1960, in which the retrospective Nixon perhaps revealed more about himself than he realized:

"I don't think any man can judge his own assets and liabilities. From my observations of others in political life, however, I can conclude that perhaps my major liability is—and this may sound incongruous—that I am essentially shyer than the usually extrovert politician ought to be. This seems to be an inborn trait which I cannot change or alter. I have a great liking for the plain people, but I feel ill at ease among the prominent . . . This is perhaps because in my early years I grew up with the same kind of people. One of the assets of a politician is his quality of mingling with the great. Frankly, I'm a terrible mixer and this is considered a major liability in politics."

What was this introvert doing in politics anyway? He had no political ideology as such (in the Harris interview eight years later he would describe himself as a conservative, a liberal, an internationalist and a pragmatist within the space of six paragraphs) and there is much to commend the view of his coach that he did not know his own party. But he had been given a unique opportunity in the California political system, and Dick Nixon had learned from an early age to make the most of his opportunities. When Frank Jorgenson suggested to him in 1950 that he should stay in the House of Representatives and accumulate seniority rather than running for the Senate, Nixon replied: "When your star is high, you better go with it."

Most of Nixon's friends, after 28 years, remain understandably scornful of much that has been written about those first campaigns. Even Nixon's most hostile biographers have failed to verify a single instance of the purported surreptitious telephone calls describing Voorhis as a Communist.

In contrast, the public red-baiting of the Nixon campaign that year was standard fare in California, where both Republicans and Democrats were long accustomed to campaigning against the menace of Communism.

But if Nixon's campaign was unexceptional in this regard, it also was devoid of any ethical considerations. Lacking any real experience in politics, Nixon accepted without question the unstated assumption shared by many Americans that the only questions of campaigning are strategic or tactical ones. This is a doctrine sometimes preached but rarely practiced by professional politicians, most of whom realize that there are unstated boundaries beyond which strategy may not go.

Nixon was not a professional, and he did not realize this. He did not, in fact, really value politics, at least not in the sense that Morton Borden has described— "an institutional cement joining Americans of every persuasion."

What Nixon valued was not politics, but political power and the purposes of statecraft, and he could be high-minded when genuine issues of governance were raised. Despite a variety of urgings from well-connected Republicans in 1960 to pursue the alleged vote frauds that produced the questionable victories of Kennedy in Illinois and Texas, Nixon refused to do so. "The President couldn't govern, not knowing whether he was really President," Nixon told friends in words that would prove prophetic. But that was after the election. "In politics," Nixon would write in "Six Crises," "victory is never total." And total victory is what Nixon desired.

Congress was different from the campaign and Nixon from the first strove to understand its customs and peculiarities and to fit into the mold. He joined the Chowder and Marching Society, that friendly group of Capitol Hill jocks and imbibers, along with the other would-be athletes. But Nixon's friends in the House soon learned that he had little taste for fun and games. He already used the yellow legal pad to sketch long serious speeches. He was insecure when other congressmen talked about "good old Jerry," who was then Voorhis and not Ford, and he expressed a determination to prove himself in the congressional arena.

Nixon succeeded in this aim. As in Whittier, those who became Nixon's friends in Congress came to like him. Later, after Nixon became Vice President, these former congressional friends, such as James Utt, Joe Holt, Oakley Hunter, Edward Hiestand, Bob Wilson and Craig Hosmer, would sometimes have a party at the Nixon house at Spring Valley or meet with him in his third-floor Capitol office for a drink and a discussion of political problems. All of these men were fond of Nixon, but they used to mock his seriousness. One of the apocryphal stories that came out in this group concerned the master of ceremonies who was going to introduce Nixon and called Rose Mary Woods asking for funny stories about him. "There are no funny stories about Nixon," was the reply.

And there weren't many funny stories about him. Everyone spoke well of Nixon, but not too well. He was quiet, studious, hard-working, rarely outgoing. He saw less and less of his old California friends but they were always welcome when they came to Washington. Sometimes, after a scotch or two at parties, Nixon would play the piano.

But the people he became closest to were those who shared his seriousness of purpose. One of these was Bob Finch, then a 21-year-old administrative assistant for a Los Angeles congressman next door to Nixon's office in the Longworth Office Building. Nixon was then 34. "I had lost my father as a young man," remembers Finch. "He was like a father or an older brother to me." Sometimes the two men would talk politics for hours on end.

As with many Americans who grew up in the Depression and served in World War II, there is an intense patriotic streak to Richard Nixon. The view of Robert L. King, a former vice presidential assistant and onetime FBI agent, typifies the attitude of many of Nixon's friends. "Fundamentally, he's a decent, gutsy, intelligent, patriotic guy, an apple-pie, Fourth-of-July patriot, a square," says King. "And this frustrates the hell out of the intellectuals because they don't believe him. And it's his strength."

Nixon had campaigned against Voorhis in his lieutenant commander's uniform, until advised that it was no magnet for the votes of enlisted men. He was genuinely proud of his naval service, which apart from Green Island, had not been without its hazards, and he was a captive of the national mood. "The mood at that time," recalls a congressman of the day, "was intensely anti-Communist and Nixon responded to it, as many others did. But it was nothing personal."

What changed that was Alger Hiss. The liberals and

the Eastern newspapers laughed at Nixon in the early stages of the Hiss case. He has never been able to take that, for all his spunk and competitiveness. When Dick Nixon perceived that Whittaker Chambers, all fat and ugly and terribly bright, was right and that Hiss with all his brilliance and moneyed ways was wrong, it ratified an inner feeling for him. He became Chambers. The Ivy Leaguers, the better people with money were Hiss. In his own autobiography Nixon would write of the Hiss case: "The issue at stake, to put it starkly, is this: Whose hand will write the next several chapters of human history?"

Hiss was a watershed for Nixon, because it ratified the conspiracy view of history that he unconsciously shares with those whom he opposes. That conspiracy is not limited to Communists, but includes the press, the liberals, "the better people." Perhaps it explains why Nixon deals so effectively with the rulers of Communist countries who are apt to share his conspiratorial take-off point, and so poorly with the American people, who do not.

One of the people closest to him in the White House believes that this conspiracy theory, when wedded to Nixon's shyness and preference for isolation, goes a long way in explaining why Bob Haldeman became the Oval Office gatekeeper and why Watergate became possible. "Nobody is our friend," Nixon said to John Dean, "let's face it." And, also to Dean: "We are all in it together. This is a war."

The Nixon who made those statements and who proclaimed that his adversaries "are asking for it and they are going to get it," was also a Nixon capable of great and repeated personal kindnesses. This was as much the real Nixon as the architect of conspiracy theories and, to those who knew him, a more real Nixon.

His friends tell a story of telephone calls to persons ill or dying, of a hundred kindnesses, of birthdays and anniversaries remembered, of thank you notes where none were needed. Herb Klein recalls when Nixon, then a private citizen in New York, rushed down to the morgue on a holiday to perform the distasteful chore of identifying the body of a friend who had died on a trip.

White House special counsel Richard Moore remembers the last weekend of April, 1973, when Nixon fired Haldeman and John Ehrlichman, a weekend that another aide calls "Nixon's dark night of the soul." The President was shaken, as all who saw him that April 30 on television know, but Moore remembers the weekend as one of especial consideration. Nixon had summoned Moore while he was preparing the speech, only to learn from Moore's secretary that he was en route to New England for the wedding of his son. The President left instructions that Moore was to go on to the wedding. And on the same distraught weekend that he fired Haldeman, Nixon remembered to dictate a personal telegram of congratulations to the groom. It would be difficult, his close aides say, to count the personal letters that Nixon has written in the middle of the night. He wrote to old friends and to servicemen and to people he read about, like the Georgia woman who put herself through college while supporting a family on a salary of $3,000 a year. Sometimes he wrote on yellow pads when he had trouble sleeping at night, sometimes he sandwiched in the letters between the dictation of memoranda.

Few of the letters and still fewer of the kindnesses, found their way into print. Nixon did not trust the press to begin with, and he was obsessed as President with the necessity of creating the image of a cool, confident and isolated leader. His press aides rarely reported on the genuine kindnesses, if they knew about them, and they were instructed to issue such inanities as the statement by press secretary Ronald L. Ziegler that the President did not watch television or read the newspapers.

Nixon, who had the greatest public need for communicating his humanity, did the best to conceal it. He was like the unpopular ballplayer who agrees to visit a sick child in the hospital only on condition that no one reports it.

Nixon's idealism had an equally difficult time breaking through the Nixon mask. Even on issues where his

55

idealism was largely accepted, he managed to raise serious doubts about his motives. His endless litany of "peace with honor" about a war that had not ended came to bother even those who celebrated the Vietnam peace agreement which secured release of American prisoners. But his private expressions showed a keener sensitivity. In 1971 he received a poem from a 15-year-old girl, Debra Fisher of Laurel, Miss., whose father was missing in action in Vietnam. He sent her a hand-written letter in reply.

"Dear Debra," the letter said. "At Camp David last Sunday I was reading again the moving poem you sent me with regard to your father. I want you to know that all our men who are missing in action are uppermost in my thoughts each day and that I am pursuing every possible means to secure their release by the enemy.

"Your father must be very proud of you—first because you love him so much and second because you have a rare ability to express your love so eloquently. God has given you a great gift of expression and I hope that through the years ahead many others will have the opportunity I have had to know the poetic beauty of your thoughts. Mrs. Nixon and I will be praying for you and your father."

Rarely could Nixon express his own love for others or for country in a way that similarly aroused the emotions of others. But sometimes, in prlvate, the reserve broke down and the human Nixon came through. Law associate Waller Taylor remembers one day in the early 1960s when he and Nixon were driving in Nixon's Oldsmobile convertible in Orange County and Nixon spontaneously put the top down and drove to Los Angeles at 80 miles an hour, yelling and laughing all the way. "Isn't it great to feel the air of America in your hair," he said. "Isn't it great to feel free."

"And then I remember," continued Taylor, "a couple of times we were flying east and he would start to lecture above the checkerboards of the farms. There, he would say, is the heartland of America, and he would rehash the beginnings of the law in this country where there were 640 acres to a section. 'That,' he would say with a thump, 'is America. That is the heart and strength of America.' "

The most misplaced quality of this private, public man was that he lacked the gift to say on the stage what he saw in his heart. He did not know this about himself, rather imagining himself a better public person than a private one. "In a small group or cocktail party he's not at ease like the ordinary fellow," observes Earl Adams. "But you go to him and say the microphones are all ready and 80 million people will be listening to him, and he's in his glory." He spoke better, of course, in the cocktail party, but then Nixon has only rarely been a good judge of himself. In fact, it may not be too much to say that he was ruined by qualities he perceived as virtues while suppressing the humanity that enabled him to survive. Subordinates could find him compassionate, which is what Ehrlichman meant when he said that he had been privileged to see a side of President Nixon that few others saw. Amidst the squalor of the Watergate transcripts the President tells Ehrlichman that Haldeman is going through "the torture of the damned."

And when Ehrlichman laconically agrees that "the family thing is rough," Nixon responds:

"I know the family thing. But apart from the family thing . . . he is a guy that has just given his life, hours and hours and hours you know, totally selfless and honest and decent. That is another thing! Damn it to hell . . . You get the argument of some [that] anybody that has been charged against, you should fire them. I mean you can't do that."

He was always difficult to work for, because he never relaxed, frequently allowed himself to become angry, always kept up the pressure on himself. He tried to hire people who would work as hard as he did, but he couldn't bear to fire those who didn't. "He's chickenhearted," says an aide from his vice presidential days. "He can't recruit. He can't fire. He doesn't like personal confrontations."

He would have been better off in the White House if he had permitted himself a confrontation or two. But the "last press conference" had taught him not to risk losing his temper. And he was consumed with the idea that he was running out of time.

"They had a five-year plan," says Earl Mazo. "Nixon really wanted to do two days work in one." And a former aide says that Nixon in the White House "really thinks he can go over into that little office in the Executive Office Building of an afternoon and solve a world problem by a feat of concentration and thought . . . And sometimes he can."

This ex-aide recalls the early Nixon days:

"It was like being next to a Bessemer furnace for the staff. The President would have all those notes he had written out on his yellow memoranda pad, and he would say 'Bob, you do this and this and this and I want it done by 9:30. John, you do this and this. Bryce, you do this and so-and-so.' It was toughest for the guys who lived next to the Bessemer furnace, which means Bob and John. It was like getting a hypo in your fanny every day. It was challenging, but it would make your insides boil. He knew so much, he had thought about so many things, he had put down so much on paper. He wanted to do everything he could in the time he had allotted to him . . . If you didn't produce he simply turned to someone else because he didn't fire anyone. Maybe that was one of the reasons the staff grew as large as it did."

The pace was accelerated by Nixon's personality. He never learned to relax, and the White House proved a poor place for learning. As an alternative, he tried to escape whenever he could, preferably to San Clemente or Key Biscayne. "He likes the ocean," says an aide who recalls turning blue while talking with a contented President in the cold current off San Clemente. "It works for him. And he likes to take long walks on the beach." Frequently in those walks he would be joined by Bebe Rebozo, whom Nixon liked because Rebozo respected his privacy. A White House intimate remembers two hours in which Bebe walked with them along a San Clemente beach and said not a single word. He was the perfect companion for the President.

Rebozo and Robert Abplanalp, the aerosol spray king, were Nixon's closest friends in the White House during the first term. They thought him a great President and master politician and he regarded them as the epitomes of self-made men. Less forgivably, their delusions about Nixon's political ability were shared by most people of importance in the White House entourage.

This judgment about Nixon the politician was not the view on Capitol Hill, where Rep. John Rhodes' belief that "Richard Nixon's supposed political acumen is one of the most overrated qualities in Washington" was widely shared by Republican congressmen. Many of them believed that Nixon had lost one election he should have won and lost another race he should never have entered. They knew that he had never learned to deal with Congress. But these views were rarely, if ever, expressed to the President's face. Long after the firing of the first Watergate special prosecutor, Archibald Cox, Nixon nourished the belief that he was a better politician than his adversaries.

What Nixon really was, rather than a master politician, was a master student of politics. He learned diligently but he never demonstrated the natural inclination for politics of his immediate predecessors in the White House. In Nixon's case the learning was mechanical and politics was an acquired rather than a natural skill.

He credited his beloved debates with Voorhis for his victory in 1946 and this in turn prompted him to challenge Kennedy in 1960. After his disastrous experience with JFK, he refused to debate Hubert Humphrey in 1968, and he even quit campaigning too early in order not to repeat the mistake he had made against Kennedy of tiring himself out. The success of the 1968 campaign in turn became the basis for Nixon's non-campaign of 1972. Always, Nixon made judgments on the acquired wisdom of the past campaign rather than the requirements of the new one.

"I contend that Nixon is a person to whom the ends justify the means, and the ends were the presidency so the means had to be political, and he learned the rituals of politics," says Stephen Hess. "But it wasn't instinctive. And when one doesn't learn something instinctively, it is easier to unlearn it."

As always, there was another side to Nixon.

Hess remembers the day in California during the 1962 gubernatorial primary when he prepared a position paper on a flagrantly unconstitutional ballot proposition that would have outlawed the Communists. The issue was a touchy one because Nixon was opposed by a hard-right conservative named Joe Shell, and Hess' paper for Nixon skillfully skirted any definitive stand. "He read the statement," remembers Hess, "and he's got a little john in the office, and he's got to go out and make a speech and he goes into the john to shave, and he says I can't do this. I have to be against this thing. I have to look at myself in the mirror."

Nixon's decision to run for the governorship was a shock to his old friends in California, many of whom regarded the office as a trap from which no politician could rise to the presidency. Some of these friends still are puzzled as to why Nixon decided to run, but there are some suggestions that he was thoroughly bored with the practice of law. One day on a Saturday soon after he returned to California, Nixon was working in the Los Angeles law office alone and he called his old friend Patrick Hillings at poolside to ask him to come down and keep him company. Hillings came after gently reminding Nixon that he was supposed to be living the good life now and didn't have to work on Saturday. It was too late to tell Nixon that. He was so used to a 14-hour workday that he found living too easy for his tastes in Southern California. After his defeat in 1962, he quickly accepted an offer to practice law in New York, and Dick Moore and other attorneys remember that it was the challenge which lured him there.

"He turned his back, if you'll pardon me, on the easy way," says Moore. "He really lives his own philosophy."

But it did not work out for Nixon in New York. In

Los Angeles, at least, he was accepted for himself, perhaps because rootlessness itself provides a certain kind of roots in Southern California. He was not similarly accepted in New York. One person who knows him well from those days is convinced that Nixon was snubbed in the "best circles" of the legal profession and the swankiest clubs. "He was very sensitive to that sort of thing, and once talked about 'Ivy League bastards' and other things of that sort," says this friend. "He felt he was as good as anyone but here he'd been Vice President for eight years and all that and he wasn't quite an equal. . . . I think Dick got the idea he was laughed at sometimes, even though he did brilliantly as a lawyer, and he couldn't stand that. Maybe that's why he was drawn to John Mitchell, who never snubbed him. It was a class thing."

When Nixon left California he pledged in writing to his wife that he would never enter politics again. There is every indication that this was one time when he said what he meant and meant what he said. But the lure of the public arena often is irresistible to men who have climbed as close to the pinnacle as Nixon had. With a few exceptions—notably a historic right-of-privacy case involving Life magazine which Nixon ably argued before the Supreme Court—the law was less challenging than public life. Nixon had lost the presidency by the narrowest margin in American history. After the disastrous defeat of Barry Goldwater in 1964, Nixon's old friends began to tell him that he could make it again.

New York, however, had changed Nixon's style. Or perhaps it is more accurate to say that Nixon changed his style in New York by a direct and difficult act of human will. He had been deeply embarrassed by the results of the 1962 campaign and by the reaction to his "last press conference," and he was unwilling to again expose himself to ridicule.

When he said you weren't going to have Nixon to kick around anymore, he really meant it and he wasn't going to put himself into a position where he could be hurt anymore."

In Finch's view this desire not to be hurt led directly to Nixon's change from a politician who had been accused of being his own campaign manager into a prospective candidate, later a President who celebrated his own isolation and wanted to "staff everything out." From now on, others would risk the firing line. Nixon would be within—cool, reserved, totally in command. From his decision in New York came Haldeman, the great staffer-outer. From his decision also, Finch suggests, came Watergate.

Watergate, of course, derived from more than one decision alone or even from the series of decisions which arose from the unfortunate choice of Haldeman as chief of staff. The roots of Watergate go deep into the character of Nixon himself, that shy, suspicious character of a man who believed his enemies had tried to destroy him and who could never forgive them for it. "Bigamy, forgery, drunkenness, insanity, thievery, anti-Semitism, perjury, the whole gamut of misconduct in criminal activities—all these were among the charges hurled against me . . ." Nixon had written in 1962 in describing the campaign against him after the conviction of Alger Hiss. Now he was more certain than ever of the purpose of his enemies but he knew that he could never again after the "last press conference" risk another public display of temper. Haldeman permitted Nixon to retreat into the isolation he preferred and, for a time, to screen his own vengefulness from public view. Haldeman became, in some important ways, an extension of Nixon's own character.

His old friends in California and in Congress perceived this change dimly, if at all. They had been Nixon's friends when he did not have the option of isolation and it had been possible for some of them to protect Nixon from himself by making him more accessible than he wanted to be and by talking and arguing as equals.

"And then," says one of his former top aides, "he outpaced his friends and went to the Senate and to the vice presidency. In all these transfigurations he left behind him a small band of confidants, creating a mutual bond and a mutual dependency. It is easy to degenerate into all for one and one for all. And then you are at a new level with a new group of confidants who may not know as much, and you are still mutually dependent. You are President now. You depend on the bad advice of these confidants to rescue you from the bad advice they gave you."

It might be more accurate to say that in the crisis of his presidency Nixon relied on no advice at all. The names of Finch, Klein or Melvin Laird are conspicuously missing from the Watergate transcripts. The transcripts show that when Bryce Harlow is suggested by the President for an unsavory task, Haldeman sneers that Harlow would be unwilling to perform it. Nixon accepts the judgment without comment, and Harlow is never called.

Perhaps this unwillingness to rely on those who might have advised him better is the single most important flaw in Nixon's character. He did not like confrontations, and he consistently relied on those who mirrored his own limited views of his enemies' intentions. "He doesn't really trust himself," says one Republican who has been close to the White House. "He doesn't really have the traits he admires in other men, which is to say he's not strong physically, graceful, coordinated, handsome. He is impressed by people who appear to be tough or know the answers, like the pipe-smoking Mitchell or the decisive Haldeman."

One former White House staff member recalls that Nixon always watched John Connally in Cabinet meetings to see how Connally reacted to what he was saying. "Connally seemed so sure of himself," says this aide. "The old man liked that. He wanted to be like Connally."

The contrary manifestation of Nixon's need for self reassurance was his increasing reliance on younger, inexperienced men. Some of Nixon's friends had noticed this as long ago as the 1962 campaign, when Haldeman began to bring in people like Ron Ziegler from his ad-

63

vertising staff. The young men treated Nixon with respect and with awe. They were, said one Nixon friend, "loyal to the notion of loyalty," which is not quite the same as being loyal to the President or even to Nixon.

"Nixon wanted to have people around him who were his own temperament and who would do pretty much what he wanted them to do," says Earl Adams. "But loyalty is more than doing what someone wants you to do. The truly loyal person will tell you when you're going to do something wrong."

Nixon had no such person around him—at least no one that he would listen to. His need for reassurance was too great. Unsure of his own resources and his own goals, he tried to convey a toughness he did not possess.

Ultimately, then, Nixon was defeated not by his friends but by his own conception of himself. There is much to commend the view of Douglass Hallett, the former Colson aide, that Nixon "always wants to be a Kennedy" and that for all the administration's dislike of the Kennedys and their ways it became "their most fawning mimic."

But the Nixon tragedy goes beyond the imitation of Kennedy. From his first political utterances, Nixon has always seen himself in terms of some historical figure other than himself. He wanted to be a Lincoln, an Eisenhower—most of all a Woodrow Wilson—and he has usually been most comfortable when clothed in the oratorical robes of some dead President. "Nixon is still trying to please his perceived betters," observes former Nixon administration aide Howard Phillips. "Gaining their approval and regard is important to his self-esteem. In order to get that approval he seems to go through a process of redefining himself to be someone of whom they will approve. In doing so, he denies the worth of his true self which has been lost and layered over. Furthermore, he becomes the pragmatist and relativist whose values, beliefs, and 'norms' of behavior are externally derived. Thus, he leads by following, seemingly more conscious of 'what will play in Peoria' than what he thinks is right."

Nixon must have known that his own character

would be the determinant and that there were ways in which it was found wanting. That is the message of the important introduction to "Six Crises," where Nixon, writing about himself, said, "We must spare no effort to learn all we can and thus sharpen our responses."

He did not learn enough. Though intellectually he was at least the equal of his predecessors, he never overcame the desire to please others that had been inculcated in boyhood and which had carried him further than the boy listening to those train whistles in Yorba Linda had ever dreamed. It had, in fact, carried him too far.

"A long time ago he was an underdog," says a Republican who has observed him closely, "and he still behaves like one. He has all the classic sociological traits of an underdog even when in the majority position. As President, he still acts like a minority. And when people oppose him, it's like when he was on the third-string football team every afternoon and had to let the first string run over him. It's like when his family was broke. Even when he had achieved the ultimate success he could never be quite secure in it or believe fully in it. It's a damn shame."

CHAPTER SIX

THE PROSECUTORS: FROM "A THIRD-RATE BURGLARY" TO "THE SATURDAY NIGHT MASSACRE"

By Lawrence Meyer

Lawrence Meyer, a metropolitan reporter for The Washington Post, covered the Watergate trials and Senate Watergate hearings.

Had it been almost any other office and any other burglars, the June 17, 1972, break-in would have been the kind of crime a prosecutor and a defense attorney settle over a cup of coffee.

Five men wearing surgical gloves were caught with burglary tools by three metropolitan policemen inside the prestigious Watergate office building. The burglars had made a forced entry. They were on the premises without permission. Open and shut.

But this was no ordinary burglary and these no seedy second-story men despite the mocking refusal two days later of the presidential press secretary to comment on "a third-rate burglary attempt."

The five men had broken into the office of the Democratic National Committee. One of them was the security chief for President Nixon's re-election committee, James W. McCord, Jr. Four had had contact with the Central Intelligence Agency at some point in their lives.

In its initial stages, however, nothing about the case suggested that it was the first chapter in the unfolding of the greatest political cause celebre in American history. Before the investigation had run its full course, the promising careers of men at the pinnacle of power in the American democracy would be devastated, the executive branch of government would be seized by paralysis as the trail led first into the White House and then into the Oval Office where the Chief Executive himself would be implicated in a massive obstruction of justice.

The men who tried to cover up the truth feared the worst for themselves and their President, and in the end their worst fears were realized.

But all of this was to come later as the investigation first creaked and groaned along, snaring seven unknowns before the sheer weight of the cover-up transformed the probe into an avalanche whose momentum toppled men and institutions from their secure positions.

Washington is a town with two principal industries —politics and government. If the White House could afford to scoff at a "third-rate burglary attempt," the U.S. Attorney for the District of Columbia could not.

On the first day, principal Assistant U.S. Attorney Earl J. Silbert was assigned to the case. Silbert, a trim, athletic man with olive skin and thinning black hair, is a graduate of Harvard College and Harvard Law School. He had spent his entire professional career working for the Justice Department, beginning in 1960 when Dwight Eisenhower was preparing to step down from the presidency.

By 1972, Silbert—despite his bookish appearance, formal manner of speech and Ivy League background— had developed a reputation for toughness in the law-and-order mode so admired by the Nixon administration. A protégé of Attorney General John Mitchell in the Justice Department, Silbert had played a principal role in drafting the Nixon administration's no-nonsense criminal reform bill for the District of Columbia with its provisions for "no-knock" entry by policemen and preventive detention for suspected criminals.

As principal assistant to U.S. Attorney Harold H. Titus Jr., Silbert already had handled some sensitive cases, but none as delicate as the one he was undertaking.

To assist him, Silbert chose two other veteran prosecutors, Seymour Glanzer and Donald E. Campbell.

At 46, Glanzer was the oldest of the three. A nervous, mercurial man with a habit of chewing his fingers while engaged in passionate argument, Glanzer was chief of the office's fraud unit. He had earned a national reputation for his prosecution of white-collar crimes. Although a graduate of the Juilliard School of Music, Glanzer had later decided to attend New York Law School. When he became part of the Watergate prosecution, he had earned the respect of fellow lawyers for thoroughness in preparation and mastery of the law.

Glanzer's participation in the case began as a part-time affair, as Silbert and Campbell first sought his advice in tracking down and securing documentary evidence. As the case progressed, however, Glanzer's time became increasingly tied up with Watergate and by December it was monopolized to the exclusion of all other considerations.

Campbell, 34, was the only local person of the three prosecutors. A native of Lynchburg, Va., Campbell had attended the University of Maryland for his undergraduate work and for law school. Prematurely bald, Campbell had been a member of the major crimes unit assembled in the U.S. Attorney's office to fight organized crime in the nation's capital, especially gambling and narcotics. Campbell, the youngest of the three, was also the most easy-going, affable and relaxed in conversation, with an ability to laugh at himself despite the gravity of the task that had been thrust upon him.

On the face of it, the prosecutors did not have a difficult task. The day the crime occurred they already had five suspects—caught in the act—under arrest.

What made the case more than a burglary was the wiretapping and eavesdropping equipment that the men had with them when they were arrested. Since the wiretap operated through a tiny radio transmitter, it was reasonable to assume that a listening post was nearby.

Two days after the burglary, the FBI found the listening post. It was across the street from the Watergate office building in the Howard Johnson's motel. A hotel clerk, seeing McCord's photograph in the Sunday paper, had called the FBI to say that McCord had rented rooms in the hotel for the past several weeks.

The trail led the FBI from the Howard Johnson's to Alfred C. Baldwin III, a chunky former FBI agent who had been hired by McCord as a bodyguard for Martha Mitchell, whose husband had resigned as Attorney General in March, 1972, to direct President Nixon's bid for re-election.

Two notebooks found while searching two hotel rooms used by the burglars in the Watergate hotel—adjacent to the offices that housed the Democratic headquarters —turned out to belong to two of the men under arrest— Bernard L. Barker and Eugenio Martinez, both of Miami.

The address book contained two entries of special interest to the investigators—one for a Howard Hunt, with notation "W. House" and the other for a "George," with a phone number that turned out to be George Gordon Liddy's number at the Finance Committee to Re-elect the President, where Liddy was employed as general counsel.

With assistance from Baldwin, who had a promise from the prosecutors that charges would not be pressed against him if he cooperated, the investigation had taken shape. Using photographs, Baldwin had identified Hunt and Liddy as two men introduced to him by McCord who had been part of the scheme to bug the Democratic headquarters.

By mid-July, the FBI had traced $114,000 that had passed through Barker's Miami bank account to the Nixon re-election committee. Of that sum, $89,000 had been "laundered" through Mexico in an elaborate attempt to conceal the source of the funds.

But when the prosecutors tried to go beyond Hunt and Liddy to higher officials in the campaign structure and the White House, they ran into a stone wall. Hunt, who had worked for the CIA before retiring in 1970 for a career in public relations, would not talk. Liddy, a former FBI agent and Dutchess County, N.Y., prosecutor, also refused to cooperate. McCord, another former CIA employee, rejected any deal with the prosecutors. The four other men, all from Miami, were also steadfast in their silence.

From the day they began their investigation, the prosecutors knew that the case was a no-win proposition. If they turned up no conspirators above Hunt and Liddy, they would be condemned for not pressing hard enough. If they pressed harder, but turned up nothing, they would be condemned for head-hunting by the administration. If they went further and struck paydirt, they would he heroes, but the risks—personal and professional—were great.

From the outset, though they did not discuss it, the prosecutors followed some basic rules. None of them ever interviewed anyone without another member of the team present. They wanted to hear everything first hand. But more important they harbored a concern that sooner or later someone would apply pressure on them and they wanted two witnesses to every interview for corroboration.

In those early months, however, the prosecutors felt little pressure. One exception occurred when they subpoenaed former Commerce Secretary Maurice H. Stans, finance director of the Nixon campaign, to appear before the federal grand jury. Stans informed President Nixon's top domestic affairs adviser, John D. Ehrlichman, who made an irate phone call to Assistant Attorney General Henry E. Petersen to demand that Stans be accommodated. In the end, Stans was allowed to give a deposition at the Justice Department away from the prying eyes of the reporters who lurked around the grand jury room in the federal courthouse, according to Silbert's justification of the decision.

But the investigation stalled at Hunt and Liddy. Liddy, the prosecutors were told, had been given almost $200,000 to fashion an intelligence gathering apparatus designed to infiltrate radical groups as a means of monitoring plans for violence at the 1972 Republican National Convention. The story, given initially to the prosecutors by deputy Nixon campaign director Jeb

Stuart Magruder, was corroborated by Herbert L. Porter, scheduling director of the Nixon campaign. The prosecutors were also told by Hugh W. Sloan Jr., who had resigned mysteriously from the Nixon campaign in July with the public excuse that his wife was pregnant, that Magruder had tried to convince him to perjure himself by misrepresenting the amount of money Liddy had been given. When confronted by the prosecutors with Sloan's charge, Magruder denied it and a lie detector test sustained him.

In a memo to the Justice Department, the prosecutors stated their doubts about Magruder which were shared by the grand jury. But Magruder's story held together, supported as it was by Porter and by Mitchell, who made a convincing witness before the grand jury.

The doubts persisted. As Assistant Attorney General Petersen later testified before the Senate Watergate committee, he told Attorney General Richard G. Kleindienst, "Nobody acts innocent." The problem was, Petersen said, "We couldn't translate that." The prosecutors lacked proof. "There were a lot of things the three of us heard that we didn't believe," one of the prosecutors recalled later, "but we had to think in terms of things we could prove."

As the investigation progressed, the prosecutors kept Petersen, their supervisor in the Justice Department, briefed on developments. What the prosecutors did not know was that Petersen was, in turn, briefing White House counsel John W. Dean III. And Petersen apparently did not know that Dean was briefing Magruder, Mitchell, Ehrlichman and White House chief of staff H. R. (Bob) Haldeman. This pipeline from the grand jury was an invaluable aid to the participants in the cover-up being conducted without the knowledge of the prosecutors.

The cover-up was pervasive. The prosecutors, with the gift of hindsight, later calculated that at least 20 witnesses who appeared before the grand jury had either lied or withheld information.

Dean stalled FBI agents who appeared at the White House for routine interviews, keeping them waiting for

71

hours until in frustration they called Silbert, who called Petersen, who called Dean to prod him into giving the FBI agents access to the persons they wanted to question.

The prosecutors were vaguely suspicious of Dean but still ignorant of the cover-up. "I never dreamed it," one prosecutor said later. His suspicions of persons possibly implicated stopped with Magruder. "Would Mitchell be involved?" He asked rhetorically, "An Attorney General of the United States?"

If they had presented a theory to their superiors suggesting that higher-ups were involved, he said, "We would have been hung in a public square."

As the investigation continued through the long wilting Washington summer, the public clamor for indictments grew. One Justice Department lawyer later defended Silbert's conduct of the inquiry. "Earl was under the most intense pressure to return indictments . . . before the election—quick indictments and the fullest investigation in history. That's impossible, first off.

"Next they [the prosecutors] offered all the conspirators a deal to talk before the election, but none took it. All the evidence about a wider conspiracy was bits and pieces—nothing any sane prosecutor would dare go into court with."

The indictments were returned Sept. 15, 1972, charging seven men—the five caught inside the Democratic headquarters and Hunt and Liddy—with conspiracy, burglary, illegal wiretapping and eavesdropping.

U.S. District Court Chief Judge John J. Sirica, a crusty, blunt-spoken jurist who at 68 was nearing the end of an undistinguished career on the bench, took advantage of court rules to assign the case to himself.

Privately, the prosecutors bemoaned Sirica's decision. Frequently reversed by the U.S. Court of Appeals, Sirica showed a predilection for the prosecution that had earned him the nickname "Maximum John." The prosecutors wanted a trial free of judicial error, and with Sirica's shoot-from-the-hip manner of ruling, they feared they would not get it.

Sirica, son of an Italian immigrant, was hard-working and persevering. He had pulled himself up by his bootstraps, through law school into a successful law practice and finally to the federal bench. He was a deep believer in the American dream and was offended by the political pollution that the Watergate break-in symbolized.

As career public servants confronted with a dilemma, the prosecutors decided to chart a cautious course. However sound their decision might have been from a legal point of view, it would raise suspicions about their judgment and conduct that they would never be able to explain to the complete satisfaction of their critics.

Whatever doubts they may have entertained privately, in public they gave the impression that they had the case well in hand, that nothing of significance remained to be uncovered.

At the same time, Petersen fed suspicion about the diligence of the investigation with a speech before an assembly of U.S. attorneys in September, 1972, only nine days after the indictments were returned. In answer to a question, Petersen said that "the jail doors will close" behind the Watergate defendants before they would ever reveal further details about why they had broken into the Democratic headquarters.

In private conversation with reporters, the public impression was reinforced. The prosecutors gave no indication at all that they were suspicious or that they thought the conspiracy went beyond Hunt and Liddy.

The prosecutors turned aside suggestions that the trial could be a vehicle for revealing more about the Watergate affair than had already been made public by the Justice Department. They were confined by rules of evidence to prove the charges in the indictment, nothing more, they argued. But they were responsible for framing the indictment and whatever limitations it imposed on them were limitations that they had played a crucial role in drawing.

At the same time that the prosecutors were leaving

the impression that they had traced the conspiracy as far as it went, press reports were suggesting that the Watergate break-in was part of a far more extensive strategy involving high officials both in the Nixon campaign and in the White House.

Throughout the summer and fall, The Washington Post followed the trail of money from the burglars back to the Nixon reelection committee and into the White House. Despite repeated denials from both the White House and the Nixon re-election committee concerning their role in the Watergate break-in, questions were being raised.

A month before the trial began, Sirica let the prosecutors know that he was not satisfied with the narrow course they seemed intent on following. "This jury," Sirica told the prosecutors, "is going to want to know what did those men go into that headquarters for? Was their sole purpose political espionage? Were they paid? Was there financial gain? Who hired them? Who started this?"

It became a litany with Sirica and in time he came to symbolize the anger, frustration and determination of Americans concerned about the Watergate affair to know the truth about it.

But if Sirica expected the trial of the seven men to produce answers about Watergate, his expectations were misplaced. As the trial began in January, 1973, Hunt—whose wife had been killed in an airplane crash while on a mysterious mission to Chicago—pleaded guilty. Hunt admitted his guilt, but under questioning by Sirica, denied any knowledge pointing to the involvement of others in the Watergate affair.

Five days later, the four men from Miami stepped forward to plead guilty as well. Like Hunt, they professed ignorance about anyone else's involvement. And so the trial—with only Liddy and McCord remaining as defendants—droned on for the rest of the month, through the inauguration of Richard M. Nixon, who had won a stunning landslide re-election victory. Magruder, whom the prosecutors were reluctant to put on the witness stand, appeared as a government witness after the prosecutors decided they had to explain the purported purpose for which Liddy had received Nixon campaign funds.

Silbert, who had been dropping broad hints in public that the conspiracy went no higher than Liddy, told the jury that Liddy and McCord "were off on an enterprise of their own, diverting that money for their own uses."

Summoning up the righteous scorn that a prosecutor reserves for a lawyer who breaks the law, Silbert hammered away at Liddy in the final argument to the jury. Liddy, Silbert told the jury, was "the boss . . . the man in charge, the money man, the supervisor, the organizer, the administrator. That was Mr. Liddy, organizing and directing this enterprise right from the start . . ."

When the jury retired to consider its verdict, it had heard 60 witnesses in 16 days of testimony. After less than 90 minutes, the jury was back with a verdict—guilty on all counts.

Sirica, who had been so eager for answers that he had taken over the questioning of some prosecution witnesses, was still intent on his mission. Three days after the trial, he told the prosecutors during a post-trial hearing, "I have not been satisfied and I am still not satisfied that all the pertinent facts that might be available—I say might be available—have been produced before an American jury."

Silbert announced his intention to call all seven defendants before the grand jury as soon as they had been sentenced by Sirica.

In the next seven weeks, the focus shifted away from the U.S. courthouse to the Capitol, a half-mile away, to the Senate Watergate committee. If answers were to be found, it was likely that they would be produced there.

A relative quiet settled on the courthouse. The scores of reporters who had crowded in for the trial departed as did the photographers and television cameramen who had camped outside the courthouse doors.

Silbert turned to administrative problems that had

piled up while he had conducted the investigation and prepared for the trial.

Glanzer returned to the fraud unit and to less spectacular white-collar crime.

Campbell, bored but amused with the irony of his situation after participating in a trial of national importance, was assigned to the pool of assistant U.S. attorneys, and given an armed robbery to prosecute. After the excitement of the Watergate trial, Campbell had difficulty getting interested in his work.

In private conversation, Glanzer was dejected about the effect of the trial on the careers of the prosecutors. "We're frozen," he told a visitor. "If they promote us, it will look like a payoff. If they demote us, it will look like punishment. So we're just like frozen."

When drawn into conversation about the trial, Glanzer railed against any suggestion that the trial had been a disappointment in its failure to throw more light on the conspiracy behind the break-in. We don't have any proof, he would reply heatedly. In a matter of weeks, the trial began fading from public memory.

When criticisms were raised in public about the quality of the Watergate investigation, Justice Department officials were ready with a battery of statistics apparently designed to overwhelm critics with the magnitude of the effort.

Thus, when acting FBI Director L. Patrick Gray III appeared before the Senate Judiciary Committee, which was holding hearings on his nomination to be permanent director, he called the FBI's investigation a "major special" and "a full court press." According to Gray, the FBI investigation involved 56 of the bureau's 59 field offices, four legal attachés' offices in American embassies abroad, 2,698 leads were covered, 2,347 interviews were conducted, 22,403 agent manhours and 5,492 clerical hours were expended.

This defense of the Watergate investigation, however, was about to be rendered obsolete by events.

On March 23, 1973, almost two months after the trial concluded, Sirica's courtroom was again packed with reporters and spectators for the sentencing of the seven defendants. Encountering a reporter in the hall shortly before he went into court, Sirica said, "I think there will be something you'll find interesting." He did not elaborate.

Sirica entered the courtroom with his customary dour expression, nodding to his clerk, James Capitanio, as he trudged up the steps to his seat. Before pronouncing sentence, he told the courtroom, he had two letters to read into the record—both from McCord.

The first letter was addressed to New York Times reporter Walter Rugaber, complaining about some minor details in a story Rugaber had written.

The spectators listened impatiently. The second letter was addressed to Sirica, who had received it three days earlier.

Perjury had been committed by government witnesses during the trial, McCord wrote. "There was political pressure applied to the defendants to plead guilty and remain silent." Others involved in the Watergate operation had not been identified during the trial, "when they could have been by those testifying."

By the time Sirica finished reading the letter, the courtroom was in an uproar. Reporters jumped from their seats and ran to the door, brushing aside U.S. marshals who tried to stop them. Sirica declared a short recess, not to restore order but because he had a terrible stomach ache.

After half an hour, Sirica returned to pronounce sentence, ordering Liddy to serve at least six years and eight months in prison and fining him $40,000. Hunt and the four men from Miami were given provisional sentences of 35 years. Sirica told the five men that he would weigh in his final determination of sentences how fully they cooperated with the grand jury and the Senate committee.

The next day McCord began talking to the Senate committee. Committee chief counsel Samuel Dash called an extraordinary Sunday press conference to tell reporters that McCord was "naming names." That night, the Los Angeles Times reported two of the names

McCord had given the committee—Dean and Magruder.

The next day, Silbert reconvened the grand jury and brought Liddy before the panel for questioning. As expected, Liddy refused to answer questions that day or in any of his subsequent visits.

The prosecutors, however, developed a strategy they hoped would flush out their quarry. Leaving the door to the corridor open, so that reporters could see the doors to the grand jury room and a small anteroom, the prosecutors periodically led Liddy from the grand jury room to the anteroom where they simply shot the breeze with Liddy and his lawyer before taking him back into the grand jury room.

At one point, the prosecutor asked Liddy's lawyer, Peter Maroulis, to tell reporters that Liddy was cooperating. Maroulis, indignant at the suggestion, refused.

As the prosecutors hoped, Maroulis did just the opposite. He insisted to reporters that Liddy was not cooperating no matter what the reporters might suspect from the movement back and forth from grand jury room to anteroom.

Within two weeks, Dean had approached the prosecutors through his lawyers. A tedious process of negotiations began, with Dean's lawyers seeking immunity from prosecution for their client in return for his testimony. The prosecutors insisted on hearing what Dean had to say before making a decision.

When Dean finally talked to the prosecutors himself, in early April, he indicated that he thought Liddy had already told them much of what he was relating. The prosecutors took some quiet satisfaction that their ruse had worked.

But Dean's narration, during which the prosecutors were not allowed by Dean's lawyers to ask questions, was a rambling, disjointed account. Glanzer finally told Dean that before he left the White House, he should get his hands on every document he could to support his story.

On Thursday, April 12, Magruder's lawyers began

negotiations with the prosecutors. Magruder, feeling himself under unbearable pressure, drinking, taking tranquilizers, told his lawyers he wanted to get the ordeal behind him.

On April 13, the prosecutors met with Magruder and his lawyers to hear Magruder's story. That night an agreement was struck—Magruder would plead guilty to one felony count.

The next day, meeting again in the offices of his lawyers, Magruder gave the prosecutors a full account of what he had done. Realizing that more than any other man he had blocked the prosecutors from uncovering the truth the summer before, Magruder apologized to Silbert. Silbert, taking no chances with Magruder this second time around, scheduled two days of lie detector tests to determine if Magruder was telling the truth. Magruder passed.

By the afternoon of April 14, the prosecutors felt that they had cracked the case. Magruder's testimony meshed with Dean's. The time had come, they believed, to let President Nixon know that three of his top aides were implicated in an obstruction of justice.

What the prosecutors knew about the case at that point did not implicate President Nixon. Dean had told them that he met with Mr. Nixon on March 21, had tried to make him understand what was happening but could not.

At 9 p.m. on April 14, the three prosecutors and U.S. Attorney Titus met with Petersen at his Justice Department office and outlined to him what they had learned. The four men discussed how to approach the President, debating whether Attorney General Kleindienst could be trusted. Finally they decided that with the evidence they had they were in control and had to proceed.

In the early morning hours of April 15, Petersen, Silbert and Titus briefed Kleindienst. Later that day, Kleindienst went to President Nixon, who already knew much of what he was told that day about the cover-up.

At the same time, the prosecutors continued their

discussions with Dean, who informed Silbert about Hunt and Liddy's activities in connection with the Ellsberg break-in. Silbert wrote Petersen a memo about what Dean had told him. Petersen, in turn, informed President Nixon who directed Petersen to "stay out" of the Ellsberg matter on the grounds that it involved national security.

Petersen relayed the message to Silbert and the Ellsberg matter was dropped—for the moment at least. Dean's conversations with the prosecutors, however, revealed that Petersen had been giving him information during the previous summer and fall.

The Ellsberg break-in continued to bother Petersen. Finally, he said, he went to see Kleindienst and told him, " 'Look, you are out of the Watergate but you are not out of Ellsberg. I need some help.' " Petersen said he and Kleindienst discussed the matter and decided that the judge presiding over Ellsberg's trial had to be informed about the 1971 break-in of Ellsberg's psychiatrist's office. If President Nixon disagreed, Petersen said, he and Kleindienst agreed that they would resign.

Kleindienst took the matter up again with President Nixon on April 25. After "a moment's hesitation," Kleindienst testified before the Senate committee, Mr. Nixon agreed.

On April 27, U.S. District Court Judge W. Matt Byrne Jr., the presiding judge in the Ellsberg Pentagon Papers trial, added a new dimension to the Watergate affair by disclosing the Ellsberg break-in.

An additional motive for the cover-up had emerged.

In Washington, the prosecutors were continuing their conversations with Dean.

The prosecutors had determined that Dean was a principal actor in the cover-up and could not be given the immunity he was seeking. As a result, if Dean were indicted, Petersen would be a likely witness. Therefore, the prosecutors told Petersen, he would have to get out of the case. Petersen refused, arguing that if he took himself out of the case, he would have to resign as assistant attorney general and then he would be attacked by the press.

In the first meeting, Petersen prevailed. But two nights later, in a nasty argument, the prosecutors told Petersen that they would have nothing more to do with him as far as the case was concerned. "I think if Henry could have gotten his hand on a gun that night," one of the prosecutors recalled later, "he would have killed all three of us."

Dean's lawyers began to raise the stakes, telling the prosecutors that Dean had more information to give if the prosecutors had the stomach to hear it. The lawyers played a cat-and-mouse game with the prosecutors, tantalizing them without actually producing hard information.

Finally, the prosecutors agreed to hear what Dean had to say. Dean told them that President Nixon had discussed raising $1 million to pay the Watergate defendants to remain silent and that he approved the payment of "hush money." The meeting lasted from 11 p.m. until 3 a.m. the next morning.

The three prosecutors left the meeting lonely and adrift with a terrible burden to carry. Their contacts with Petersen were severed. Kleindienst had removed himself from the case. "We were three assistant U.S. D.A.s who were very low on the totem pole," one of them recalled. "We just didn't know who the hell to turn to. That was a very tough time for all three of us."

They discussed their alternatives, considered going to various senators to tell them what they had been told. The problem was, in the Byzantine maze of congressional politics, whom could they trust? They thought about resigning and going to the Senate Watergate committee if necessary to get the story out.

On April 30, the inevitable flow of events solved their problem. Kleindienst resigned, along with Haldeman and Ehrlichman. Dean was fired. Secretary of Defense Elliot L. Richardson was nominated by President Nixon to be Attorney General.

Within a matter of days, the prosecutors knew their time was running out. Pressure was increasing on Richardson to name a special prosecutor. "We knew exactly where we stood at that time," Campbell said later. "We knew the special prosecutor was going to come in."

The prosecutors could not savor their triumph in having opened the case. Under attack by the public and the press, the prosecutors also were under suspicion by the Senate Watergate committee which was considering investigating the investigators.

On May 18, the second day of the Senate Watergate hearings, Attorney General-designate Richardson picked former Solicitor General Archibald Cox to be Watergate special prosecutor. Cox was picked by Richardson after he dickered for almost two weeks with the Senate Judiciary Committee, which was holding up Richardson's confirmation until agreement was reached over the degree of independence the special prosecutor would have.

Richardson's final offer gave the special prosecutor wide latitude to investigate criminal activity and to make public statements. Richardson sealed the agreement with a promise that was to take on critical importance five months later. He promised not to countermand or interfere with the special prosecutor's decisions and not to fire the special prosecutor "except for extraordinary improprieties on his part." Richardson was confirmed May 23.

Two weeks earlier, speaking to a Republican fundraising dinner in Washington, President Nixon had pledged that Richardson "and the special prosecutor that he will appoint in this case will have the total cooperation of the executive branch of this government."

The changing of the guard—from the three prosecutors to Cox—was a painful ordeal for Silbert, Glanzer and Campbell. They found Cox stiff, aloof and insensitive to what they had been through. Cox, still unfamiliar with the case and wary lest his maneuvering room should be limited by commitments to the three, kept them first at arm's length and then insisted that they work under his supervision.

For the three prosecutors it was a bitter pill to swallow. They believed that they had broken the case, only to find the public, the press and Congress dubious not only of their ability but of their integrity as well.

Petersen, testifying in August, 1973, before the Senate Watergate committee, summed up the bitterness the prosecutors felt in an emotional outburst.

"I resent the appointment of a special prosecutor," he told the committee. "Damn it, I think it is a reflection on me and the Department of Justice. We would have broken that case wide open, and we would have done it in the most difficult circumstances.

"And do you know what happened? That case was snatched out from under us when we had it 90 per cent complete with a recognition of the Senate of the United States that we can't trust those guys down there, and we would have made that case and maybe you would have made it different, but I would have made it my way and Silbert would have made it his way and we would have convicted those people and immunized them and we would have gotten a breakthrough.

"I am not minimizing what you have done or the press or anyone else, but the Department of Justice had that case going and it was snatched away from us, and I don't think it fair to criticize us because at that point we didn't have the evidence to go forward."

For the three prosecutors, the experience was especially difficult. On the one hand, Cox criticized the way they had handled the case in the early stages. On the other hand, Cox was also critical of the tactics that they had employed in dealing with the White House when the cover-up began to unravel.

Ironically, one of the criticisms Cox voiced of the three prosecutors arose when they told him that they had subpoenaed tape recordings from the White House that Dean, Haldeman and Ehrlichman had made. That was not the way to deal with the White House, Cox told them, stating his intention to negotiate with the White House to obtain the tapes.

Five months later, Cox would learn all too well that he could not deal with the White House on gentlemanly terms.

On June 29, a month after an abortive attempt to resign, the three prosecutors left Cox's staff to resume their normal duties.

In accepting the resignation of the three prosecutors, Cox wrote Silbert that "I am aware of various criticisms of your earlier conduct of the investigation and prosecution of seven defendants. Lawyers often differ on questions of judgment, and there are points on which my judgment might have varied from yours. Thus far in the investigation, however, none of us has seen anything to show that you did not pursue your professional duties according to your honest judgment and in complete good faith."

Whatever hopes Cox may have been harboring for White House cooperation in the Watergate investigation began to fade on July 16 when former White House aide Alexander P. Butterfield testified before the Senate committee that since 1971 President Nixon had been automatically and routinely tape recording conversations in the White House Oval Office, his Executive Office Building suite and over several telephones.

President Nixon refused a request by both Cox and the committee to turn over certain tapes. On July 23, for the first time in 166 years, the President of the United States was subpoenaed. Two of the subpoenas came from the committee and one from Cox. On July 26, in separate letters to Sirica and the committee, President Nixon refused to comply with the subpoenas. In his letter to Sirica, Mr. Nixon said he was adhering to the precedent established by his predecessors "that the President is not subject to compulsory process from the courts."

The issue was joined.

On Aug. 29, Sirica ordered President Nixon to turn the tapes over to him so that Sirica could determine how much the grand jury should hear. The White House immediately responded that President Nixon "will not comply with the order" and that his lawyers were considering an appeal or an alternative way "to sustain" his legal position.

On Sept. 6, the White House appealed Sirica's decision to the U.S. Court of Appeals. A memorandum issued by the appellate court a week later urged an out-of-court settlement of the matter. On Sept. 20, the court was told that no agreement could be reached after three days of discussions between Cox and White House lawyers.

On Oct. 12, the Court of Appeals upheld Sirica's decision and ordered President Nixon to surrender the tapes to Sirica for use by the grand jury. On Oct. 19, the deadline imposed by the appellate court for the White House to appeal the ruling to the Supreme Court, President Nixon announced that he would turn over a written summary of the tapes to Cox and to the Senate Watergate committee.

The week beginning Monday, Oct. 15, was critical for both Cox and the presidency of Richard Nixon. By the end of the week, Cox was out of a job—along with Attorney General Richardson and Deputy Attorney General William D. Ruckelshaus—and impeachment proceedings against President Nixon began to be pushed in earnest.

Throughout the week, President Nixon's lawyers and his chief of staff, Alexander M. Haig Jr., negotiated with Richardson about a way to satisfy Cox without fully complying with the court order to produce the tapes.

Periodically, the White House suggested to Richardson that he should fire Cox, but Richardson resisted. Cox and Charles Alan Wright a University of Texas law professor retained by President Nixon, exchanged correspondence about the tapes. Ultimately, Cox and Wright were unable to come to terms among indications that the White House wanted to force the issue in order to fire Cox.

On Oct. 19, President Nixon announced his decision to release written summaries of the tapes, to be verified by Sen. John C. Stennis (D-Miss.). Mr. Nixon noted that Cox had not accepted the proposal, but Mr. Nixon said he was ordering Cox, "as an employee of the executive branch," to cease his attempts to obtain the tapes through the judicial process.

The next morning, Cox called a press conference to announce that he would not obey President Nixon's order and that he would instead continue his fight in court to obtain the tapes.

The night of Oct. 20 was one of the moments when one could feel the palpable presence of history. One observer, confined throughout the evening to a downtown office building remarked later, "I kept thinking I should go to a window to see if tanks were in the streets."

Persons out for the evening might have received the first news of the day's extraordinary events when they turned on their televisions to watch what was to have been an NBC special on Cox's morning news conference. Instead, they saw John Chancellor announce, simply but dramatically:

"Good evening. The country tonight is in the midst of what may be the most serious constitutional crisis in its history. The President has fired . . . the special Watergate prosecutor, Archibald Cox, and he has sent FBI agents to the office of the special prosecution staff and to the Attorney General and the Deputy Attorney General and the President ordered the FBI to seal off those offices. Because of the President's action, the Attorney General resigned.

"Elliot Richardson, who was appointed Attorney General only last May in the midst of the Watergate scandal, has quit, saying he cannot carry out Mr. Nixon's instructions. Richardson's deputy, Mr. William Ruckelshaus, has been fired. Ruckelshaus refused in a moment of constitutional drama to obey a presidential order to fire the special Watergate prosecutor. The President has abolished special Watergate prosecutor Cox's office and duties and turned the prosecution of

Watergate crimes over to the Justice Department."

It was a "stunning development," Chancellor said, "and nothing even remotely like it has happened in all of our history."

Chancellor, who had been a newsman more than 25 years, concluded the program by saying, "In my career as a correspondent, I never thought I'd be announcing these things."

Whatever reaction the White House had expected, it apparently did not bank on the shock, confusion and outrage that immediately swept the country. Two days after the "Saturday night massacre," as it was immediately called, Haig referred to the reaction as a "firestorm."

Was it all a horrible miscalculation—the removal of Cox—or a desperate attempt to stop the investigation before it encircled President Nixon? The cost to President Nixon was immediate—the House Judiciary Committee, which had been discussing the matter in the most tentative of terms, began serious preparations for impeachment proceedings against the President for only the second time in United States history.

And on Nov. 1, yielding to public and congressional pressure, President Nixon approved the appointment of a successor to Cox, Watergate Special Prosecutor Leon Jaworski. And the Watergate investigation continued.

CHAPTER SEVEN

". . . I HAVE BEEN PAYING OFF THE VICE PRESIDENT"

By Richard M. Cohen

Richard M. Cohen, a metropolitan reporter for The Washington Post covered the Agnew case and is co-author of "A Heartbeat Away," about the Vice President's fall.

Shortly after the 1968 Republican National Convention, Richard M. Nixon talked this way about Spiro T. Agnew: "There is a mysticism about men. There is a quiet confidence. You look a man in the eye and you know he's got it—brains. This guy has got it. If he doesn't, Nixon has made a bum choice."

Less than five years later it was clear that Nixon had indeed made a bum choice. Three times in the summer and fall of 1973, as Watergate began to consume his own days, the President had to dispatch aides to demand Agnew's resignation, the final time in terms so blunt that Agnew's lawyers protested the treatment and Agnew himself left the room.

It had never been a happy political marriage, and it was an awful time for divorce. The President was forced to pause in the preparation of his own defense because of the Agnew affair. The Agnew resignation itself on Oct. 10, 1973, and the Justice Department's simultaneous publication of the evidence against Agnew, further eroded public confidence at a time when Mr. Nixon craved that trust, at a time when 76 per cent of the American people, according to the Harris Survey, thought "too many government leaders are just out for their own personal and financial gain."

The resignation raised new questions about Mr.

88

Nixon's ability to choose men. He had been wrong with Agnew, wrong with John W. Dean III, wrong with L. Patrick Gray III, wrong with H. R. (Bob) Haldeman, with John D. Ehrlichman, with Charles Colson and with a host of others who left the White House under a cloud and, in some cases, were later convicted of crimes. And, perhaps most fateful of all, the Agnew resignation helped clear the path for the President's own demise, preparing the country psychologically, demonstrating that it could survive such a shock.

Despite his obscurity when he was first picked as the Nixon running-mate, Agnew had become the Republican Party's best performer, an accomplished partisan brawler who could have rallied his own constituency to Mr. Nixon's cause. Agnew, the seemingly indefatigable Nixon point man, had become the spokesman for that vast range of American beliefs and life-styles known as Middle America. He spoke for its values, for its prejudices, for the President and against his enemies—the students, the press, the intellectuals.

So secure was Agnew in his role as spokesman for these people that Mr. Nixon's hopes of substituting him on the 1972 ticket with John Connally of Texas vanished in the political reality of Agnew's clout. The once-time zoning lawyer from Towson, Md., was suddenly the front-runner for the 1976 Republican nomination, his credentials certified by George Gallup.

In April of 1973, Agnew was the choice of 35 per cent of Republican voters for the nomination, the Gallup Poll reported. His nearest rival, Gov. Ronald Reagan of California, was 15 per cent back with the support of just 20 per cent of GOP voters. Gerald Ford was not even on the list.

Ironically, Agnew's standing was enhanced initially by the very Watergate scandal that brought Mr. Nixon down. Almost alone among the Nixon administration's highest officials, Agnew was unblemished by any connection with either the burglary or the cover-up. His reputation for integrity remained undiminished and, had not events intervened, he could have thrown it into the fight to save the man who named him to the ticket in 1968 and made his name a household word.

Richard M. Nixon, a two-term Vice President himself, had definite ideas about the vice presidency in 1968.

His vice presidential candidate needn't be a man of great stature; the media would soon fix that. His vice presidential candidate needn't be someone he knew personally; Eisenhower had been a virtual stranger to the man he had picked. His vice presidential candidate need only to offer something to the ticket—an identification with the South's border area, a hard line against civil disruption, the general demeanor of a no-nonsense son of suburbia.

Agnew, then governor of Maryland and formerly executive of Baltimore County, had risen fast in the political world, winning both offices with the help of schisms in the county's and later the state's dominant Democratic Party. And by 1968, he had shed his once liberal image.

In the spring of 1968, while Nixon was mulling his vice presidential choice, Agnew dealt toughly with three major incidents involving Maryland blacks—a student boycott at Bowie State College, a sit-in outside his office, and the Baltimore riots after the assassination of Dr. Martin Luther King Jr. One of Nixon's aides, Patrick J. Buchanan, gave newspaper clippings to Nixon about Agnew's handling of the incidents.

The clippings, it soon became apparent, had an impact. The two men met, seemed to hit it off and Agnew, to the surprise of almost everyone, was Nixon's choice.

Agnew, Mr. Nixon said, was to be a prime adviser on domestic policy. To prove it, the new President installed his Vice President in the White House itself, the basement, to be sure, but still the White House. It was there that Agnew received some of the kickbacks from Maryland contractors who still felt honor-bound to continue the payments.

But as it had been for Nixon under Eisenhower, the

vice presidency for Agnew was devoid of a policy-making role. Instead Agnew became the administration's evangelist, a perpetually airborne speaker on the political Chautauqua circuit where he lambasted the press, criticized students and skewered Mr. Nixon's critics in alliterative phrases that became his trademark.

It was always a dry, starchy performance with even the prologue of Bob Hope-like one-liners delivered with the flatness of a reading clerk in a legislature. But it caught on. The laughter and mocking derision gave way to respect. His audiences liked what the man was saying and the way he was saying it.

In the 1970 congressional elections, Mr. Nixon again opted for the Eisenhower pattern. While he largely stayed in the White House, Agnew took to the road—the low road, in the view of many. It was the campaign of the "radiclibs," the "impudent snobs," the attack on Sen. Charles Goodell, the maverick Republican from New York, whom Agnew characterized as "the Christine Jorgensen of the Republican Party."

Although White House speech writers were assigned to Agnew, the delivery—and even many of the words —were Agnew's. The style had even developed back in Towson and Annapolis and was recognizable to Marylanders. Although Agnew seemed to be a puppet of the White House, there is no evidence that he undertook his attack on the press, for example, as a result of presidential orders.

Instead, it appeared that Mr. Nixon was right. Agnew and he thought alike, shared the same view of the world that struck a responsive chord in both the party and large segments of the public. Agnew, by the 1970 campaign, was the party's second biggest draw. Only the President could fill a hall better, and the President was mostly staying in the White House.

During that campaign, Agnew brought an estimated $3.5 million into party coffers. He campaigned in 32 states, traveling 32,000 miles. But when the campaign was over, the results were uneven. Goodell had lost; so had two Senate Democrats, Albert Gore of Tennessee and Joseph D. Tydings of Maryland. But the

GOP had only picked up a net total of two Senate seats while losing nine House seats and 11 statehouses. Agnew called the election results "bittersweet."

It was, in fact, a serious blow and Agnew, as the administration's foremost campaigner, began to feel the scorn of outraged Republican moderates, many of them governors. At the same time, Connally began to be mentioned as a possible Agnew replacement on the 1974 ticket.

Agnew, in several interviews at the time, talked about returning to the practice of law, possibly writing a political column or maybe taking a job in television. He assumed a low profile. The speeches were muted.

But he retained one attribute: loyalty to Richard Nixon. When the Young Americans for Freedom endorsed Agnew for President, he curtly reminded them that he served Richard Nixon. When Rep. Paul N. (Pete) McCloskey of California challenged Mr. Nixon in the New Hampshire presidential primary, Agnew remarked that McCloskey was in such a financial bind that he had to sell his favorite painting—"Benedict Arnold Crossing the Delaware."

Even with the Connally rumors floating around, Agnew made no move to enhance his standing in the party. He did not, as Mr. Nixon did in 1956, attempt to rally county and state GOP chairmen to his side. The President was supreme, he said, and "must select the most powerful and potent Vice President he can find."

That turned out to be Agnew, and the 1970 pattern was repeated. Agnew did the hard campaigning. Mr. Nixon, for the most part, stayed in the White House, letting Agnew, his surrogates and George McGovern win the election for him.

The Nixon-Agnew landslide, as had been expected, materialized in November. Yet five days before his second inaugural, Spiro T. Agnew was a doomed man.

On Jan. 15, 1973, Lester Matz, a Baltimore County engineer, visited his lawyer and announced his plight: His books had been subpoenaed in the Maryland U.S.

attorney's probe of political corruption in Baltimore County. The books would prove that he had been generating cash in order to kick back 5 per cent of his fees to the county executive, Dale Anderson.

Tell everything you know, was the lawyer's advice. The government is not interested in prosecuting you. You will be offered immunity in exchange for information on higher-ups.

"Do I have to tell them everything I know?"

Yes, Matz was told. In that case, he responded, he could not cooperate. The lawyer asked why. "Because," Matz blurted out, "I have been paying off the Vice President."

Relentlessly, the prosecutors in Baltimore—George Beall, the U.S. attorney, and his assistants, Barnet Skolnik, Russell T. Baker Jr. and Ronald S. Liebman—applied pressure to engineers like Matz, unaware of their dark secret.

Agnew, though, was aware, and slowly through the late winter and spring he prepared for the coming investigation. He talked to the Attorney General, Richard G. Kleindienst and complained that the investigation of Anderson had the potential to smear him. He was, after all, Anderson's predecessor. He sent his own lawyer, George White, to visit Beall and also to complain about the potential for damaging publicity.

Privately, he made other moves. He had an aide prepare a log of all the times the engineers and their intermediaries had visited him in either the White House, where he first maintained an office, or in the Executive Office Building. And he retained a lawyer.

The law firm chosen, Colson and Shapiro, was a Washington political powerhouse. One of its partners was Charles W. Colson, former special counsel to the President, who retained entry into the Oval Office. Agnew was apparently hoping that the power of the White House would help him.

In April, Agnew informed Mr. Nixon of the investigation—dismissing it as amounting to nothing much.

He was innocent of any wrongdoing and he had nothing to fear, he said. But he sent his new lawyer, Judah Best, to Baltimore anyway—just to stay in touch.

On June 21, the dam burst. With the pressure on Matz increasing—he was facing multiple indictments—two of his lawyers, Joseph H. H. Kaplan and Arnold Weiner, went to see Beall and his assistants. In minute detail, they laid out what their client would be prepared to say before the grand jury: Agnew had taken kickbacks.

The payments had begun when Agnew was executive of Baltimore County and continued while he was governor of Maryland. In general, they amounted to 5 per cent of the worth of the contracts the county and later the state awarded Matz's engineering firm.

But the payments, the prosecutors learned to their consternation, had continued during Agnew's term as Vice President. Some represented money Matz thought he still owed Agnew for contracts awarded in the past. One payment—for $2,500—was for a stray General Services Administration contract that happened to come Agnew's way.

Other witnesses came forward, adding more and more detail. In the end, four persons—three engineers and an intermediary—signed sworn statements saying they had participated in a scheme to kick back money to Agnew—as county executive, as governor and as Vice President. Two of the witnesses underwent lie detector tests and passed.

On Aug. 1, Beall formally notified Agnew that he was under criminal investigation. The news came in the form of a letter handed to Agnew's lawyer, Best, in Baltimore and delivered to the Vice President that day. The letter set out in general terms the areas under investigation—bribery, extortion, tax evasion and conspiracy. Within a week the news was public.

Agnew, true to his reputation, fought back. The charges, he said at a press conference, were unfounded. He was innocent and would prove it. He would not resign. The President had not asked for his resignation. He would remain in office.

The Vice President was exercising poetic license with the truth. Mr. Nixon had not asked him to resign. But Gen. Alexander M. Haig Jr., White House chief of staff, had. It was just the first of those requests—and the first time Agnew failed to take the hint.

Against Agnew was aligned a solid administration front. The President, for all his protestations of neutrality, wanted him out. Agnew was severely complicating life. He was saying he could not be indicted because he was Vice President—an issue the President did not need to have tested in the courts. Later Agnew attempted to have impeachment proceedings started against him in the House, another route the White House viewed with horror.

But the White House was in a dilemma. Mr. Nixon's own political standing was at an all-time low (although it would soon sink lower). He could ill afford to take on Agnew publicly and risk alienating the Vice President's constituency. The President needed every vote, and a large number of them were tied to the fortunes of Spiro T. Agnew.

In the Justice Department, the new Attorney General, Elliot L. Richardson, also viewed the Agnew case with horror. A man he was convinced was a criminal could succeed to the presidency at any moment. The President was under extreme pressure. He had, in fact, been hospitalized in July for viral pneumonia, a disease Richardson thought improbable. Might it have been a stroke, or something else?

And, of course, there was Watergate. Mr. Nixon had indicated he might not honor a Supreme Court order to turn over tapes of presidential conversations. That could provoke an unparalleled constitutional crisis, possibly impeachment. How could there be impeachment when the No. 2 man might himself be under criminal indictment?

So together the White House and the Justice Department—each suspicious of the other—strove to effect Agnew's resignation. One by one, Agnew's possible avenues of escape were closed off—impeachment, a suit over possible leaks coming from the Justice Department or even Agnew's attempts to say he, like the President, was immune from criminal indictment.

Through it all, Agnew continued to look to the White House as his possible savior. When he attacked, when he attempted to rally his constituency, he lashed out not at the White House but at the Justice Department. He drew a fine line between the President and the men he appointed.

The attack came Sept. 29 in Los Angeles in a speech before the National Federation of Republican Women. It began routinely enough. But then Agnew reached into his pocket for the notes he had scribbled on the plane coming up from Frank Sinatra's home in Palm Springs.

"In the past several months I have been living in purgatory," Agnew said. Then he launched into an unprecedented attack on the Justice Department of his own administration, singling out for severe criticism "the chief of the criminal investigation division," stopping short only at using his name—Henry Petersen. He called Petersen's conduct "unprofessional, malicious and outrageous."

Agnew, who earlier in the speech had reiterated his innocence, ended by declaring, "I will not resign if indicted. I will not resign if indicted." As expected, the speech brought down the house. The Republican women, long-time Agnew supporters, stood on chairs to applaud the Vice President. He strode from the hall in triumph.

The triumph, however, was short-lived. That speech, more than any other single event of Agnew's term as Vice President, demonstrated how little he knew about the White House, and especially about Richard Nixon. He apparently did not know what the transcripts of presidential conversations were later to reveal—that the President had a close relationship with Petersen who was acting as a sort of intermediary between Mr. Nixon and the Watergate grand jury.

Shortly after the speech, Mr. Nixon sent Agnew a

message which loosely translated said: Quit playing demagogue or there will be no deal. Without a deal, Agnew faced an almost certain trial and a likely jail sentence. It was time, Agnew concluded, to concentrate on the bargaining table and see if he could strike an agreement with the Justice Department.

The speech was important for another reason, too. It had been a bold declaration of innocence coupled with a solemn vow not to resign even if indicted, and it was believed. When Agnew did resign within 11 days of the speech, it was yet another blow to the standing of all public officials, and especially Mr. Nixon's.

No longer would a ringing declaration to remain in office be accepted at face value. Mr. Nixon's own vows, the public could later conclude, were no different.

Soon Agnew's lawyers—Jay Topkis, Martin London and Best—were back at the bargaining table with Richardson and others from the Justice Department. One series of plea-bargaining sessions had been broken up when news of them was reported in the press. Now, in a motel room in Alexandria, the two sides attempted again to hammer out the deal that would remove Agnew from office.

The bargaining itself was unprecedented, a break with the Justice Department's standard procedure. Prosecutors do not bargain with the chief target of their investigation, and they certainly do not bargain with recalcitrant targets. Agnew was both.

But Richardson and his aides in the Justice Department, and the President and his men in the White House, were intent on clearing the line of succession. Agnew, they concluded, must go. The White House, as was its custom in the case, played middleman, bringing together the two sides and mediating some disputes.

The deal was the essence of simplicity. Agnew was willing to resign only if guaranteed that he would not face a jail term. The Justice Department insisted on releasing its evidence to disprove Agnew's claims that the investigation was a concoction of perjury and fantasy.

And so, at 2 p.m. on Oct. 10, 1973, Spiro T. Agnew rose in a courtroom of the federal courthouse in Baltimore and pleaded nolo contendere—no contest—to a single count of tax evasion. At the same time, a lawyer from the firm of Colson and Shapiro in Washington handed Agnew's resignation to Secretary of State Henry A. Kissinger.

U.S. District Court Judge Walter Hoffman, after noting that a no contest plea was tantamount to a guilty plea, imposed a $10,000 fine on Agnew and sentenced him to a three-year term—suspended. Within moments Spiro Agnew, private citizen, left the courthouse and the 40-page exposition of evidence was distributed to the press.

Ten days after the resignation, the men who were the architects of the deal were gone. In a dramatic Saturday night shuttling of limousines between the Justice Department and the White House, Richardson, his deputy, William Ruckelshaus, and the Watergate special prosecutor, Archibald Cox, were gone. The nation again was in the throes of the Watergate story and the Agnew episode of petty corruption was quickly shelved.

As for Agnew, he paid his fine, cleared up his paperwork in an office provided by the government and sold a novel to Playboy Press. For the most part, he refused all interviews and kept his mouth shut while the man who saw so much by looking him in the eye slipped from office himself.

CHAPTER EIGHT

PAT NIXON: A FULL PARTNER IN THE AMERICAN DREAM

By Donnie Radcliffe

Donnie Radcliffe is a staff member of the Style section of The Washington Post.

Of all Richard Nixon's advisers, only one at the end had been there at the beginning, and not until she conceded it was all over would he finally believe it, too.

"No," Pat Nixon had said in May when asked if she would let her husband resign. "Why should he? There's no reason to." Even in the twilight of Richard Nixon's presidency, Pat Nixon was determined to ward off his destruction, knowing it was her own as well as his and, in legacy, that of their children.

Her sustenance, she had said, was "the truth . . . When you know the truth you have nothing to fear." Truth, for her, was "great faith in my husband . . . an honorable, dedicated person"—not what he had done but what he had meant to do.

She held to the "positive outlook" through her almost daily readings of a word, a look, a handshake—things she could later describe to her husband. There were teas and luncheons and receptions, and old friends and new friends, and in the crush she listened for their versions of "the truth" as evidence of unlagging support.

"You'd think that every day reading the paper, seeing some negative things and some positive things, but most of the time negative, it would get you down," Julie Nixon Eisenhower said in describing her mother's emotional state. "But she seems to be able to weather anything, and I really admire her for it."

Pat Nixon's strength, said this loyal daughter, issued from a combination of love for and belief in her husband, the "very philosophical" ability to take things with "a grain of salt."

If Mrs. Nixon despaired in private, she did not say so. Only her face betrayed her in deepening lines around the mouth and an unnatural puffening about the eyes. What she seemed to have been spared so long, for 62 years, was cruelly catching up at last, yet another indignity to be suffered in an unending succession of them. "You live one day at a time," she said, renewing a lifelong creed she had clung to as a tormented bride of crises.

But while Richard Nixon watched his dreams crumbling, she averted her eyes from her dreams by searching endlessly for one more reassurance that as First Family they were still what they seemed to be.

"You can't live by criticism. You must do what is right," she once told an interviewer. But she could live by small talk and did, wringing out some meaning from the banalities mouthed by the awestruck, the fatuous, the curious.

The campaign—there was always a reason to campaign—had never ended. She listened for the cheers, her sanitized smile apparently undisturbed by the chants and placards calling for the impeachment of her husband. What she looked for she saw, her defense against what she did not want to see or hear. She blotted out Watergate by refusing to discuss it.

"No," she interrupted a reporter traveling with her from South America in March. "I really don't wish to speak of it. It's just a personal thing and why bring that into the trip?"

Eyes suddenly steely and voice stern, she rebuked her press corps further: "You all who follow me day after day know how positive I feel about everything and I really have faith in the judgment of the American people and the press people. I'm not going to rehash an innuendo and source story in repetition . . ."

Whatever her rationale in reaching "the truth" about

100

her husband's Watergate role, she arrived at it after 28 years in Richard Nixon's philosophical and political shadow.

In March, 1974, Watergate was so unimportant, she said, that Latin American newspapers did not even bother to report it. "It's only covered in (U.S.) metropolitan papers," she informed reporters on that South American good-will mission. "Even out in the country in the U.S.A. it isn't."

It seemed as if Pat Nixon was determined to see only the bright side. During antiwar demonstrations in 1971 when placards and picketers glared from Lafayette Park, she told of working on "the other side of the house. I can see the Washington Monument and Jefferson Memorial outside my windows. The view inspires me." At a 1972 press conference, she hardly hesitated before answering that in all her years of public life, "I don't believe I have had any disappointing moments."

Despite published reports to the contrary and even Richard Nixon's own words, she denied they had ever discussed quitting politics after his unsuccessful 1962 race for governor of California. "We just got interested in other things—law, New York, a trip to Europe with the girls. It wasn't a time for depression."

Even her view of angry anti-American demonstrators threatening her and Richard Nixon's lives in Caracas, Venezuela, in 1958, is a charitable one. "There were only a few radicals, terrorists really," she recalled 16 years later of this "fourth crisis." "The majority of the people were gracious and nice, and for that reason I say that I remember the trip with pleasure rather than fear."

Legendary by the time she reached the White House in 1969 as the once reluctant political helpmate, she had learned that "you can do anything you put your mind to. You can adjust to anything if you want to." And she had long before adjusted herself to Richard Nixon's career in politics because it was what he wanted "and there was a part for me to play."

No one knew that better than Richard Nixon himself,

and her stage became the campaign arena where she soared to stardom as one of his most attractive political devices. He was repulsed by the tactics of some who dragged an opponent's personal life into the fray. ("I don't believe, for example, that a candidate's family is fair game," he told author Earl Mazo in 1959.) But he was not averse to trotting out his own.

Never modest about her way with people—"I hate to brag," she once replied when asked who was the family's best campaigner—Mrs. Nixon said her secret of success was, "I always look the person in the eye. I feel when you meet the eye a friendship is started."

If there ever was a real Pat Nixon, history will have to look earlier to when she was Thelma Catherine Ryan, a resolute little girl of solid if humble origins. "I may have been born in a tent," she said years later.

The American Dream was accessible to all, and she dreamed it often while growing up as a truck farmer's daughter in that California community called Artesia. Motherless at 13, fatherless at 17, she overcame limited means and meager opportunities because she worked hard.

"I know my life has been really a great one," she would say by 1968. "I'm a self-made person, and in my own way, I've tried to help others. I just don't believe in making a public show of it."

Her years as a poor farm girl, a $7-a-day movie extra earning her way through college and ultimately a $190-a-month school teacher led to struggling young lawyer Dick Nixon and his political calling. "I could see it was the life Dick wanted," she said in those interminable interviews that began in 1946, when, rising from her first bed of childbirth, she became his "white glove" fund-raiser, stand-in and campaign office manager.

Ever the good scout, her devotion to husband seemed to preempt that to self in a kind of Catholic view of marriage from which escape was unthinkable. She was not Catholic, though her father had been, but she was a worthy understudy to Richard Nixon's mother, canonized forever in his supposedly Quaker mind.

As self-made man married to self-made woman, they combined American Dreams, rising from a Whittier garage apartment, to Parkfairfax togetherness of young congressional Washington-on-the-make, to stately Wesley Heights tudor befitting a Vice President, to fashionable Park Avenue apartment of wealthy Manhattan lawyer, to the White House. And, with the White House, seaside estates at San Clemente and Key Biscayne.

Though uncaring, she said, of "creature comforts," Pat Nixon set about refining her dream house. In 1969, as she showed off the results to White House reporters, she told of "trying to be economical" and working on a "sort of" budget.

Leading us through her 14-room Spanish-style hacienda overlooking the Pacific, she called our attention to new wallpaper, fresh paint, new windows and new landscaping. "I took some big bushes out so we would have a better view," she said, motioning to the living room windows. In the President's study atop the house, reached by an outside stairway from the inner courtyard, she again called attention to the view by explaining that "all the windows were too high so I had them lowered."

Though the Secret Service would later insist that such landscaping and remodeling had been for security reasons, Mrs. Nixon was proudly taking credit that evening in 1969. "If you'd seen this house before, you'd know you had to have imagination to change it," she said, escorting us back to the swimming pool.

The Nixons were courting the press in those days, or at least hiding the bitterness of the 1960 and 1962 campaigns. Like properly brought-up guests, we brought a thank-you gift—a 150-year-old antique Imari ashtray intended to play along, in a way, with Richard Nixon's gag a few days earlier that he would have to hide the ashtrays the night of the party.

The presentation was brief but the presidential bon mot of thanks caused even Mrs. Nixon to wince. "The way you know it's an expensive gift," he said, weighing the package in his hands, "is it's so light."

"My," said Mrs. Nixon, standing near me, "how grateful."

She winced again a few days later in Humboldt County where the Nixons and the Lyndon Johnsons had flown to dedicate, on Johnson's 61st birthday, the Lady Bird Johnson (redwood) Grove.

"President Johnson and I have much in common," Nixon told the crowd as sunlight filtered through those thousand-year-old trees to spotlight the heads of the official party, among them the wife he neglected to introduce. "Both of us were born in small towns, both of us served in the House, both in the Senate, both were Vice President, both were elected President. And both of us were very fortunate in the fact that we married above ourselves."

When Johnson's turn came, he extemporaneously took another view, recalling that Harry Truman, on his 61st birthday wrote his mother that Presidents were lonely people. " 'The only ones they are really sure of all the time are their women folk,' " Johnson said. "President Nixon and I have another thing in common. We can always depend on our women folk."

Richard Nixon, of course, knew that. In his Checkers speech of 1952, he told a nationwide television audience that "Pat is not a quitter. After all, her name was Patricia Ryan and she was born on Saint Patrick's day and you know the Irish never quit."

He would later reveal of that crisis and pressures on him to resign, "Pat reacted with fire in her eyes. 'You can't think of resigning. If you do, Eisenhower will lose. He can put you off the ticket if he wants to but if you, in the face of attack, do not fight back but simply crawl away, you will destroy yourself. Your life will be marred forever and the same will be true of your family and particularly your daughters.' "

By Jan. 20, 1969, fulfillment of the American Dream was at hand. She seemed to know exactly where she was going that crisply cold morning as a bipartisan congressional group, invited to the White House for coffee broke up to leave for the Capitol. Striding out of the Red Room, Lyndon Johnson quickened his pace to the limousine outside. Behind him, hurrying to catch up, was Richard Nixon. Looking first at his own feet then at Johnson's, Nixon shuffled into step and moved to Johnson's left.

"I've got my protocol right this time," he said, to himself as much as to Johnson. "The President is on the right." Behind them, in proper order, were Lady Bird Johnson and Pat Nixon, both looking straight ahead.

On center stage as First Lady, Pat Nixon charmed thousands, assuring them that "I'm taking good care of your home" as she smothered their hands with hers, looked them straight in the eye and, miraculously sometimes, even remembered where they might have met.

Behind the scenes she was the devoted mother and confidante and presidential consultant. In 1972, she told reporters that she often read presidential documents and statements and in their discussions together, only foreign policy seemed out of her realm. "He knows more," she said.

"Oh, no, indeed," his advisers never had to brief her, she claimed. "I have my own ideas. I've been in this field so long I don't think anyone could brief me. They very often ask for my advice—they find I have lots of experience."

In pre-Watergate days, she viewed her husband's critics as "part of the job. I once read that Lincoln had worse critics. He was big enough not to let it bother him. That's the way my husband is."

Later, after transcripts of the Nixon Watergate tapes were made public, the outrage of longtime Republican friends and erosion of their support stunned her. She confided to friends that then, more than ever, was the time to show solidarity.

Her elder daughter Tricia went into seclusion, more distrustful than ever of the adversary press. Julie, the Nixon women's most eloquent spokesman, longed to go public and did in May, bearing her father's message that he would see his seventh and final crisis through to its constitutional conclusion.

By the end, the fabric of Pat Nixon's life, woven from "good Republican cloth coats," had begun to look threadbare.

CHAPTER NINE

THE POLITICAL LEGACY: A CLIMATE OF CYNICISM, AN ATMOSPHERE OF DISTRUST

By Jules Witcover

Jules Witcover, a veteran political correspondent for The Washington Post, is the author of books about Robert F. Kennedy, Richard M. Nixon and Spiro T. Agnew.

Richard M. Nixon, famed as a master politician, set out in 1969 to change the politics of the country—to make his Republican Party the majority. Instead, in the end, he probably did more than any other President of either party to destroy public confidence in all politics.

With his departure, he leaves behind a political legacy of negativism that far transcends the damage to his own party. By indulging in abuses of power himself, and by tolerating or encouraging them in his subordinates, he raised to an unprecedented level public disenchantment toward all politicians and elected office-holders.

The public skepticism that always had been regarded as a healthy thing in the electorate was escalated in the Nixon years to rank cynicism, tarring the honest and the dishonest politician alike. In a system whose effectiveness is predicated on the informed consent of the governed, this ramification of the Nixon presidency may be more destructive in the long run than any other.

The rape of legitimate political campaign activity demonstrated in the Watergate break-in seemed to trigger the worst expectations among voters, giving rise to the callous view that in politics anything goes—in both parties. There was ample evidence that the break-in and the consequent cover-up were excesses well beyond normal campaign "dirty tricks" practiced in the past by either party. Nevertheless, the acts were taken widely as confirmation that, as voter after voter interviewed said, "both parties do it but only one got caught."

Democratic incumbents complained that it wasn't so, but they—like Republicans who had nothing to do with Watergate and denounced it early and often—cringed in anticipation of voter revolt against incumbents in the November elections.

The upshot of all this cynicism is likely to be, in the immediate future at least, not the sharpening of party lines and identification that Mr. Nixon sought in trying to build a majority party, but a further blurring, as candidates seek to distinguish themselves from the discredited pack of professional politicians. A clear trend toward independent voting patterns and identification was under way well before Watergate; it seems certain to grow in its wake.

Already, more voters consider themselves independents (34 per cent) than Republicans (24 per cent), according to the most recent Gallop Poll on the question.

Nor is it just the parties that have been damaged. In a Senate-financed poll by Louis Harris, the White House ranked the lowest in public esteem of 22 institutions of American life, with only 18 per cent of those surveyed expressing confidence in it.

Similarly, in a survey by the University of Michigan's Institute for Social Research, 2 of every 3 persons questioned felt they could trust government only "some of the time." More than half believed that "quite a few" of those running the government were crooked. Also, the President as the most-trusted public official fell from 42 per cent in 1972 to 24 per cent in 1973.

Congress, too, has suffered in the climate of cynicism. Another Harris Survey that showed only 30 per cent of those surveyed giving the President a favorable rating in February had Congress even lower, at 21 per cent.

But it is the presidency, more than any other political institution, that has been scarred by the Nixon years.

There had grown up in the public mind a respect approaching reverence for men elected to the White House, and a kind of mythology about the high plane on which they conducted the nation's business.

The revelations of the true one of the Nixon presidency, as disclosed in the transcripts of Watergate-related conversations, stripped away those illusions and only intensified the public disaffection.

Some deflation of the presidency, which had grown in the public mind to be an approximation of royalty in the United States, was long overdue. Mr. Nixon inadvertently helped bring about that deflation with the excessive trappings of office he embraced; with the expensive additions to his San Clemente and Key Biscayne homes at tax-payers' expense, and with his own personal income tax troubles.

Also, in his partisanship and the atmosphere of political siege he saw all around him, he subverted the lofty image of the presidency by using the office as a command post for waging political war. He waged it not only against the opposition party, but also against Congress, the press and any segment of the population, like war protesters and student dissenters, that dared be critical of him.

He spoke of ending an era of confrontation in foreign policy and ushering in an era of negotiation, but in domestic politics confrontation was the byword. The presidency was less often heard as a voice of persuasion than as a voice of accusation or intimidation, with resultant alienation of the target group. Under Richard M. Nixon, the public was exhorted repeatedly from the White House to join together for the common good. But the nature of his excessively partisan leadership often caused the public to question whether he himself had the common good in mind.

Politics has been called the art of the possible, and Richard Nixon in his rise to the presidency had been widely lauded as a master of the art. Yet there was seldom in his presidency the essential quality of compromise that is the essence of achieving the possible. Rather, he was a fiercely give-no-quarter politician, driven by failure not to accommodation but to isolation and divisive excess.

From the start of his political resurrection after his 1960 presidential and 1962 gubernatorial defeats, his concentration was on partisanship. From the Republican Party's depths in 1964, when the landslide defeat of Sen. Barry Goldwater led some to predict the party's demise, Mr. Nixon more than any other single Republican leader rallied the troops and returned his party to national power.

As a private citizen in the congressional elections of 1966, he campaigned tirelessly for others and received much of the credit for an impressive 47-seat GOP comeback in the House that signaled the party's rejuvenation. Three Senate seats, eight governorships and 540 state legislative seats also were picked up by the Republicans that fall.

That performance projected Mr. Nixon into the presidential politics of 1968, and although his own narrow victory that year failed to bring in a Republican Congress, the presence of the party's first authentic political practitioner in the White House since Herbert Hoover raised hopes of a party renaissance.

Once in the presidency, Mr. Nixon set out on a mission not simply to bolster Republicanism, but to cleanse it of liberalism and of dissent. As he had done throughout his career, in the White House he played hard-ball politics not only against the opposition party but against those in Republican ranks who dared to differ with him.

With his personally selected Vice President, Spiro T. Agnew, employed as an oratorical battering ram—just as he himself had functioned as Vice President to Dwight D. Eisenhower—Mr. Nixon undertook what Agnew called the politics of "positive polarization."

In his first years the Vietnam war colored all politics, and the President sought to win support for his policies by castigating the motives and the patriotism of those who disagreed with him. Agnew was the chief weapon, but the President himself chimed in. Agnew characterized antiwar youth in 1969 as "rotten apples" to be cast out; Mr. Nixon called them "bums." The objective in each case was the same: to isolate and destroy the opposition.

Mr. Nixon, commenting once about President Lyndon B. Johnson's sniping at him in the 1966 congressional elections, recalled the old adage, "Never strike a king unless you kill him," and converted it into his own political strategy: "You don't hit your opponent unless you knock him out."

That always was the Nixon political style, as a candidate for Congress, for the Senate, for the vice presidency, for governor of California, and for President.

In the 1970 off-year elections, he joined Agnew in a broadside attack not only on Democrats characterized as "radical liberals"—those who criticized his policies— but also on a senator of his own party—Charles Goodell of New York—who openly opposed him on the war.

The attacks on the Democrats, which failed to produce a Republican Senate, were clearly part of Mr. Nixon's strategy to deal a body blow to the opposition party, ushering in an era of a "New Republican Majority." The purge of Goodell indicated he was after not just a Republican majority, but the right kind of Republican majority.

Having already administered a shellacking to the party's increasingly ineffectual left wing in his own 1968 capture of the GOP presidential nomination, Mr. Nixon worked to emasculate it.

In his administration, the liberal voice of the party was stilled to a whisper, and its attempts to have a say in the 1972 party platform were pathetic, so tightly did Mr. Nixon hold the apparatus after four years in the White House.

His New Republican Majority was to be compiled of conservatives and moderates, converted Southern Democrats, plus blue-collar and ethnic voters brought over by appeals to law and order and other concerns of "Middle America," like opposition to school busing. Middle America in this context was more economic and attitudinal than geographical; it was all those middle-class voters who felt they were being ignored as government reacted to the noisy demands for help from minority America, be it poor or black or both, as often was the case.

Deep inroads into the blue-collar and ethnic votes were made by Mr. Nixon in 1972, but they were misleading. They were much more a negative response to his Democratic opponent, Sen. George McGovern, than a positive embracing of Mr. Nixon, or of his party. While the President was winning re-election resoundingly both houses of Congress remained in Democratic hands, as they had been throughout his presidency.

And as the revelations of Watergate and of his personal financial transactions spilled out in the first months of his second term, Mr. Nixon's political dream and his own political power turned to ashes. Fellow Republicans in special elections sought to run on their own and GOP members of Congress looked toward the fall general elections with trepidation that he might be an albatross around all their necks.

When the first serious and concerted calls came for his resignation from Congress, they came, notably from fellow Republicans who were both disenchanted and dismayed by all the disclosures and fearful that in his own destruction their party would be destroyed too.

Ironically, just as in 1964 before he led the GOP's climb out of the abyss, talk is heard again that the Grand Old Party may be on the verge of breaking up. The liberals already have been all but shut out; the conservatives, shocked by the constitutional abuses of Watergate, actively speculate about realignment.

Kevin Phillips, the young analyst with firm lines into the party's right wing, noted in his newsletter earlier this year that such conservative spokesmen as William F. Buckley, F. Clifton White and Gov. Ronald Reagan of California are voicing interest in a new ideological vehicle.

"One overriding concern of conservative strategists," Phillips wrote, is "that great opportunities come and go in history, and that Richard Nixon has flubbed the GOP opportunity. Denied effective political expression through Nixon Republicanism, conservatives are talking about the possibility and timing of a new party."

It is much more likely, however, that just as in 1964, Republicans will address themselves to rebuilding the old, rather than starting something altogether new. A major part of such a rebuilding job must be re-establishing public confidence in the whole party after the ravages of the Nixon years. And that confidence will not be achieved simply through the departure of Mr. Nixon.

It is convenient but not very persuasive for Republicans to paint Mr. Nixon and his arrogant White House coterie as a total aberration, a political barnacle that attached itself to the party along the way.

Actually, the Nixon political operation was an excessive product of GOP organizational politics, always known for its diligence, determination and attention to detail.

The establishment in 1972 of the Committee for the Re-election of the President—a separate campaign arm from the Republican National Committee—was no more than an over-zealous, overfinanced application of a tactic long utilized in presidential campaigns by candidates of both major parties.

As a result of the Nixon experience, it might be expected that from now on the parties will eschew this organizational approach and run future campaigns from within the established national party structure, to achieve greater oversight and to avoid the excesses of 1972.

Indeed, Gerald R. Ford as Vice President in one of his few strongly implied criticisms of Mr. Nixon, blamed Watergate on the establishment of "CREEP," calling it "an arrogant, elite guard of political adolescents" that tarnished the whole party with its stupidity.

He suggested that future Republican presidential aspirants be required to pledge they would run their campaigns through the Republican National Committee, staffed predominantly with veteran professionals.

But presidential campaigns nearly always have been waged by a relatively small group of masterminds around the candidate; the temptation to cut away from the structure and set up a separate command system may prove just as irresistible in the future as it has been in the past.

Limitations on campaign spending and greater accountability requirements, among the positive outgrowths of the Watergate climate, may bring more integrity to presidential elections. For one thing, they are likely to increase the influence of professional campaign organizers and managers, who presumably at least can be expected to reject Watergate-like excesses as potentially self-destructible.

Large corporate givers, burned for their clandestine generosity in 1972, are likely to be more wary, if not more stingy, than in the past, thus forcing presidential candidates to rely on smaller contributors or on federal money that will be available to them through the income tax checkoff for the first time in 1976.

While the 1972 campaign of Richard Nixon will be remembered by the public for Watergate, professional politicians are still likely to study it carefully for the legitimate techniques that helped fashion Mr. Nixon's landslide victory.

Some young functionaries in that 1972 Nixon campaign have boasted with what seems laughable detachment that "except for Watergate, we ran the most effective campaign in history." That exception is, of course, a huge one; like a Christian saying that except for the lions, he had a swell afternoon in the Coliseum.

But if the premise is accepted, it must be acknowledged that the remaining Nixon techniques—voter identification, media manipulation, keeping the opposition on the defensive, astute and tightly controlled exposure of the candidate—were most effective and doubtless will be copied in future campaigns.

But a political legacy consists of more than the passing on of new campaign techniques and mechanics. The Nixon legacy more importantly is one of increased public doubt that voters really can have an effective voice in shaping their own lives through the ballot box. It was bad enough when they believed politicians would say anything to get elected, and then ignored their promises. It is far worse when they believe the ballot box is stuffed or otherwise monkeyed with by campaign techniques of manipulation, deception and—in the extreme —outright criminal subversion of the political system.

Before Mr. Nixon's time of political glory and trial, there had always been a kind of assumption among the American people that politics was unsavory, but within certain limits. Politicians played pranks and cut corners, but at the presidential level at least, the shenanigans did stop short of subverting the system. Watergate and its attendant sideshows seriously assaulted that modestly hopeful assumption.

Compared with other countries where citizens have the franchise, voter turnout in the United States always has been distressingly low. Government by consent of the governed requires citizen participation at the polls once every four years, if nowhere else, or it is a sham. If the Nixon political legacy is the further alienation or apathy of the voter, it will inflict damage on the system far beyond the weakening of one party.

If, on the other hand, the public mistrust toward politics engendered by the Nixon years generates a new awareness among politicians that a more candid and nonmanipulative kind of politics must be practiced to restore public interest and confidence, Mr. Nixon's departure could signal a revitalization of the system.

Already, both parties have been openly in search of candidates who either are fresh to elective politics or carry a distinctively "clean" image. Former astronaut John Glenn, open and still boyish-looking at 52, won the Democratic senatorial nomination in Ohio at least in part on the strength of that kind of image.

Images, of course, even "clean" images, can be misleading. Mr. Nixon's hand-picked first Vice President, Spiro Agnew, nurtured a "Mr. Clean" reputation to within a heartbeat of the presidency before he was exposed as a taker of payoffs through most of his meteoritic political career. Once burned, the electorate is going to be, or should be, more discriminating.

Considering the track record of politicians of both parties through the years, a skepticism among the voters that politics will be cleaner post-Watergate is inevitable, and not necessarily bad. But when public skepticism is driven to cynicism and the voter drops out, the hand and the influence of the manipulative politician is immeasurably strengthened.

Richard Nixon as politician has been one of the foremost practitioners of the art of voter manipulation. It will be among the greatest of ironies if, as a result of his political excesses, voters turn their backs and the system is thus rendered even more vulnerable to manipulative politicians of the future.

It will not be known for some time what the Nixon years have done to the presidency itself—how severely its power has been diminished. That the office has been tarnished in the public eye cannot be denied; the impairment of its power, with a consequent ascendancy of Congress, may depend largely on how the new occupant of the White House conducts himself.

Gerald R. Ford, himself for nearly three decades a partisan Republican politician, embarks on a presidency he never sought amid some hopeful signs. In his short tenure as Vice President, while remaining loyal to Mr. Nixon, he has been a more conciliatory figure. For all the public lack of trust in politicians, he enters the White House with that same general good will that the American people bestow on any individual who assumes that burden, especially in adversity or in national crisis.

He has an opportunity to take his decimated and demoralized party and make what he will of it. More importantly, if he conducts an open and candid presidency and an above-board political apparatus sustained by his personal integrity, he has a chance to convert the good will extended into a rehabilitation of public confidence in the presidency and the whole American political system.

It will take time. The Nixon political excesses have seen to that. But the system has shown itself to be remarkably resilient, and the people optimistic over the long run. Besides, Mr. Ford has no choice now but to try.

CHAPTER TEN

THE DOMESTIC LEGACY: THE NOT-YET-COMPLETE NEW FEDERALISM

By David S. Broder

The political correspondent and columnist for The Washington Post, David S. Broder is a Pulitzer Prize winner whose latest book is The Party's Over.

It was headed by a President whose prime interest lay in foreign policy. It was harnessed to an economy whose rampant forces it never learned to discipline. It was hectered and hampered throughout its life by an opposition-controlled Congress.

For all these reasons, and more, the Nixon administration was about as weak a contender to make a significant contribution to American domestic policy as any government in recent history.

And yet, historians of a future age may look back on Richard M. Nixon's 5½ years in office as a time when a significant turnabout occurred in the way the American people and the American government attempted to deal with their needs and problems.

It was a change designed to shift the initiative in domestic decision-making out of Washington and into the states and communities, the private institutions and individual families of America. It was what Mr. Nixon called New Federalism, or the New American Revolution.

It did not happen during his 5½ years, but if his successor, Gerald R. Ford, and the Presidents who come later find the beginnings made by the Nixon administration sound, it may yet yield him a place of significance in American domestic history.

Seated in his White House office while the President was composing his resignation speech, Domestic Council Executive Director Kenneth R. Cole Jr. mused on what had—and had not—been done in the Nixon years. Both the man and his job said something about the Nixon approach to the domestic situation. Cole is a young advertising executive, one of many from that field recruited to the White House with what they all conceded to be a stunning lack of background in legislation, politics or the substance of social and economic issues.

The organization he headed—the Domestic Council —was a Nixon invention, one of several new White House agencies created to take the direction of domestic policy out of the hands of old-line Cabinet and agency bureaucracies and place it under control of the President and his aides.

That assertion of direct White House authority over domestic policy provoked most of the major political battles between Mr. Nixon and the Democratic Congress. It led many of his critics to assert that he was, at heart, a man who believed as much as any of his liberal Democratic predecessors that the government knows best, and the President knows better than anyone in government.

And yet when Cole was asked what he thought the historians might consider Mr. Nixon's most significant domestic achievement, he gave an unexpected answer: "Ending the draft."

At first glance it seems an odd reply. Yet if one took seriously the line in Mr. Nixon's first inaugural address that "the essence of freedom is that each of us shares in the shaping of his own destiny," it was not illogical to argue that the end to the government's requisitioning of its citizens' time and bodies was, indeed, a critically important change.

Then Cole mentioned a series of New Federalism legislative actions in the fields of transportation, agriculture, manpower training, education, housing and community development—all containing elements of eased federal directions and greater choice for individuals and local governments.

"Each one of these sets a direction for the future that is really a reversal of the past tendencies to make the decisions in Washington and hand them down the line," Cole said. "It will not be easy to continue in this direction, given the forces of opposition in Congress and the bureaucracy, but at least a substantial momentum has been built."

Doctrinally, Mr. Nixon set his goal to reduce the direct role of the federal government in American domestic life from the very start of his administration. "In this past third of a century," he said on that January day in 1969 when he took the oath of office, "government has passed more laws, spent more money, initiated more programs than in all our previous history . . . We are approaching the limits of what the government alone can do."

That message was framed in the classic rhetoric of conservatism. It was a tone that both circumstance and political inclination—his own inbred skepticism toward Washington bureaucracy and the country's weariness with the social programming of Lyndon Johnson's Great Society—made natural.

But the rhetoric collided with the reality of Richard Nixon's Washington—and produced an astonishing jumble of results.

His five years saw a 60 per cent increase in the overall federal budget, a doubling of domestic spending. There was a vast expansion in food and income supplements for the elderly and the needy, a significant budgetary shift from defense to domestic welfare purposes, and even the birth of the first major federal subsidy for the arts.

Even more unexpectedly, this conservative President, who carried to the Oval Office his own personal memories of the paper-shuffling frustrations of the wartime Office of Price Administration, found himself ordering and enforcing a system of peacetime wage-and-price controls which he later described as "discredited patent medicine."

The economy was the bane of Mr. Nixon's existence. An ill-timed recession embarrassed his political hopes for control of Congress in the mid-term election of 1970, and the rampant inflation, consistently underestimated by his advisers, forced him into policies he himself detested.

If the minimal standard of performance expected from a conservative administration is the protection of the dollar and the preservation of a degree of economic stability, then the Nixon administration was a failure.

"The only thing we learned," said Cole, "is that no one here is smart enough to manage an economy as big and complex as this one."

They also demonstrated that despite the rhetoric of law and order that marked the Nixon campaigns, the national government possesses relatively few tools that directly influence the safety of the cities' streets.

And they showed that there is a huge gap between announcing environmental and energy policies and accomplishing a reasonable accommodation between the needs of the nation for reliable fuel supplies and the desire for clean air, water and land.

Only some of these developments in the Nixon years came about because he willed them. Others represented his response—or his acquiescence—to political and economic forces beyond his control. For the same Richard Nixon who asserted his strategic command of the foreign policy area immediately upon taking office was never in 5½ years able to gain that leverage in domestic affairs.

But he had his moments. One of them came almost at the end. Just last month the same Supreme Court that had sealed his fate by forcing disclosure of the devastating June 23, 1972, tape, handed down its decision on cross-district busing.

From the start of his 1968 campaign, Mr. Nixon had pledged himself to oppose busing pupils out of their own communities and neighborhoods for the purpose of integration. He made each of his Supreme Court appointments with that issue in mind—suffering rebuffs from the Senate twice on the confirmation of his nominees.

But in the end, the four justices he appointed comprised the heart of the 5-to-4 majority by which the high tribunal ended its 20 years of consistent pressure for desegregation. In the Detroit case, the court ruled that busing between cities and suburbs was not justified as a general rule, in the cause of integration.

There were other good moments for Mr. Nixon in domestic policy. One of them in particular, at Independence Hall in Philadelphia, on Oct. 20, 1972, may not only prove a consoling memory for the deposed President but be marked as well as a date of significance by the historians.

That day Mr. Nixon signed the general revenue-sharing bill. He had sought it for three years, and finally obtained it from the Democratic Congress. It was the keystone of his New Federalism program.

Its purpose, he told the mayors, governors and congressmen who symbolized by their presence the three tiers of American government, is "to renew the federal system that was created 190 years ago" and to demonstrate that "we believe that government closest to the people should have the greatest support."

General revenue sharing—lobbied through Congress by a bipartisan coalition of local officials—pledged roughly $6 billion a year of no-strings aid for five years to the 38,000 units of state and local government.

By itself, it was not much more than a few drops in the bucket—barely one-seventh of the total federal aid to states and cities.

But the concept, though originated by Democratic economists Walter Heller and Joseph Pechman, represented a sharp break with the underlying philosophy of past Democratic programs—the notion that federal dollars should be targeted to federal priorities and tied down by federal regulations, even if spent by state and local governments.

General revenue-sharing had quite a different premise. The assumption was that the national interest would be better served if the revenues generated by the federal income tax mechanism went back to states and cities. They, in turn, would use them at their discretion for objectives that seemed to them important.

Critics claimed this was a "cop-out" policy, one that would work against those citizens and groups who lacked political power in their own communities. But Mr. Nixon insisted it was the American way to achieve the goal of "returning power to the people."

In his view, this was part of a much larger design for the decentralization of domestic decision-making. He referred to this concept on numerous occasions as New Federalism or the New American Revolution.

Realistically, there was more slogan than substance to his grand design. Administration planners preoccupied with the political problems of maneuvering revenue-sharing through a skeptical Democratic Congress, did not raise the hard questions of which units of local government should share in the federal largesse —or how well-equipped they were to handle their new responsibilities.

Many of the Nixon administration's companion measures to give local officials flexibility in their use of categorical grants-in-aid for housing, health, education and a hundred other purposes were delayed or defeated in Congress.

But as Cole sat in his White House office this week, he ticked off a series of legislative enactments that complement the basic philosophy of New Federalism. Transportation policy has been changed to allow cities some choice on using portions of highway money for mass transit.

The 40 years of direct farm subsidies from Washington were ended by the Agricultural Act of 1973. This year's manpower, education and housing bills contain elements of the kind of decentralization and flexibility that Mr. Nixon was seeking.

But to the extent that New Federalism was part of a grand design for the reorganization and reorientation of domestic government, it was still in its infancy when Mr. Nixon was driven from office.

He had hoped for and proposed the reorganization of the Executive Branch to make it a more capable partner —if a less domineering one—in the federal system. He wanted to merge the old-line domestic Cabinet departments, with their strong constituency interests, into four functional "super departments," addressing human needs, energy, the environment and natural resources, the economy and community development.

Congress and the interest groups were cool to the idea, and Mr. Nixon kept improvising new White House coordinating agencies, in the process building the largest presidential staff in history.

In addition to the Domestic Council and its myriad subcommittees, there came to be a Council on Environmental Quality, an Office of Telecommunications Policy and a Council on International Economic Policy. The old Bureau of the Budget became the Office of Management and Budget—but none of these devices necessarily left the government more manageable than Mr. Nixon had found it.

Similarly, Mr. Nixon was unable to score the breakthrough he had sought in transforming the character of the federal government's relations to individual citizens in need of help in meeting their human needs.

Mr. Nixon came to office with the belief that the turmoil of the 1960s—and particularly the wave of urban riots—had been provoked by the government's habit of promising more than it could deliver.

Moynihan, the revisionist liberal Democrat he recruited for the White House, suggested an escape from this dilemma might be found in the policy of other industrialized nations: supply direct cash assistance, on a sliding scale, to all those who fall beneath a defined standard of income.

After intense debate within the administration, Mr. Nixon in 1969 committed himself to the Family Assistance Plan—a bold and expensive proposal to put a floor beneath the income of every family, in every

state, not just those on welfare but also, and importantly, the "working poor."

The legislation was caught in an immediate crossfire between those who insisted its benefits were degrad-
ingly low and those who argued it was creating additional millions of handout dependents.

It passed the House once in Mr. Nixon's first term,
but the negotiations for compromise in the Senate were
never completed—largely, many participants felt, because Mr. Nixon himself had had second thoughts about
the wisdom of the scheme. One of the White House
tapes shows him telling an aide, "There ain't a vote in
it."

Some associates saw in this off-again-on-again pattern a reflection of Mr. Nixon's own intermittent attention to domestic issues. Others said it was because he
never found among his set of domestic advisers—
Patrick Moynihan, Arthur Burns, George Shultz, Cas-
par Weinberger, Elliot Richardson, Kenneth Cole or
Melvin Laird—the single compatible, systematic approach that he drew from Henry Kissinger in foreign
affairs.

Despite this, the Nixon years did see—partly, or even
largely, as a result of congressional initiatives which he
was persuaded to accept—great increases in payments
to the elderly through Social Security, and a significant
expansion of food distribution to the needy.

While full reform of the welfare system, as envisaged
by the Family Assistance Plan, was not accomplished,
the federal government did take over from the states
full responsibility for the aged, the blind and the totally
disabled.

What else might have happened, had he been given
another 30 months, or had he ever had the cooperation
of a Congress controlled by his own party, is, of course,
a matter of speculation.

At the time of his re-election in 1972, with a 49-
state mandate and a massive popular-vote majority, Mr.
Nixon moved boldly to assert his own concept of domestic policy.

125

He laid down a series of impoundments of congressionally appropriated funds that told the Democratic legislators, in effect, that he would not sanction spending in the domestic field for purposes he did not approve.

He challenged Congress to a "battle of the budget," and seemed, in the wake of the truce in Vietnam in early 1973, to have popular support for pressuring the Democrats to accept his own sense of national priorities.

But that turned out to be but a brief interlude. Within weeks, he was embroiled in the long fight to save his administration and himself from the spreading scandal of Watergate. His energies were diverted from domestic legislation to that battle. The resurgence of inflation, spurred by the Middle East oil embargo, added further to his woes.

Congress and the courts rallied to reject his claims of authority to impound funds or reorganize whole departments.

At the end, he left his successor a Congress newly aware of its own prerogatives and newly equipped with a budget-making mechanism of its own.

He left him a nation more tranquil on the surface, but more disturbed at its depths, than he had inherited in 1969.

But he also left Gerald Ford with the germ of an idea—an idea that the full resources of American institutions, state and local governments, as well as private individuals and institutions, might be mobilized to meet the needs of the nation.

And if that idea proves fruitful, Mr. Nixon may be more kindly remembered for his domestic policies than seems likely now.

CHAPTER ELEVEN

THE ECONOMIC LEGACY: A NON-POLICY TO FIGHT INFLATION

By Hobart Rowen

Hobart Rowen is financial editor and columnist of The Washington Post.

The Nixon years were little short of a disaster for the American economy. To be sure, there were many unhappy economic events out of Mr. Nixon's control, including the worldwide commodities boom that supported inflation and crop failures that helped to drive food prices up.

But the biggest weakness of Mr. Nixon's economic regime was that it never had a genuine policy—or if it did, it was changeable overnight.

Thus, in 1969, when Mr. Nixon came into office, the inflation rate was running around 5 per cent and the level of unemployment was 3.3 per cent. Under Economic Council Chairman Paul W. McCracken, a policy of "gradualism" was adopted to slow the economy down.

And, indeed, it slowed the economy down: We had a recession by the end of 1969 and unemployment rose to 6 per cent, but so did the rate of inflation. And while Federal Reserve Board Chairman Arthur Burns began to suspect that the "old-time religion" of tight money and fiscal austerity might not be as effective as it once was, the Nixon managers barreled ahead, anyway.

The result, of course, was that Nixon, after repeated assurances that he would never adopt controls, had to turn full cycle on August 15, 1971, slapping wage and price freeze controls on the economy to help break inflation (and to give the dollar some additional credibility abroad, a fact conveniently forgotten by critics of controls).

In addition, Mr. Nixon abandoned fiscal austerity and began to pump up expenditures. The sluggish performance of the economy during the congressional elections of 1970 was not one that Mr. Nixon wanted repeated during the presidential election year that lay ahead for 1972.

So far as this observer is concerned, Mr. Nixon's best economic performance came with that decision of August 15, 1971. Coupled with the breaking of the dollar's link with gold—which led eventually to dollar devaluation—the freeze and the subsequent Phase II of controls was a courageous program which may have saved the U.S. and the world economy from collapse.

Mr. Nixon's performance in the foreign economic field was superior to what he did at home. It was necessary to devalue the dollar, although the strong-arm methods he was encouraged to use by John Connally hurt the U.S. in the eyes of the rest of the world. George Shultz deserves to be remembered for recouping some of the damage of the Connally era, and for starting the world on the road to flexible exchange rates in the fall of 1972.

It was also necessary to embark on wage-price controls, and the program cannot be denied a share of the credit for a drop in consumer prices from a 5 per cent annual rate in 1971 to less than 3.5 per cent in 1972, while wage increases slowed from 6.5 per cent to about 5.5 per cent—or to the level of the famous guideposts.

But Mr. Nixon couldn't leave well enough alone. Exuberant after his re-election, he responded to the ideological pressures of advisers like Herb Stein and Shultz, and mistakenly discarded effective controls in January, 1973, for a new Phase III. If the August 15 program was the high mark for good judgment, the January, 1973, program was the low point, a bonehead move without parallel. (A close candidate—in which Congress shares the blame—is the total removal of controls in April, 1974, followed by reinvocation of "the old-time religion," when inflationary forces again proved stronger than administration forecasters believed possible.)

As the second term started, the administration misread the pressures that were developing on supplies. It waited a year too long to call Secretary of Agriculture Earl Butz off his mad adventure in holding down farm output. The Russian grain deal (the Capitalists "shnookered" by the Communists) made things worse.

We know now, thanks to the White House transcripts, that all during this period Mr. Nixon was preoccupied with managing the Watergate cover-up. Moreover, as the June 23, 1972, tape shows, he was bored with economic affairs—and gave both the problems and his advisers (even Shultz) short shrift.

But in the perennial search for a quick fix and a favorable headline, Mr. Nixon tried a second freeze, this time just on prices, in June, 1973.

As soon as the 60-day freeze ended, prices resumed a rapid climb. Controls and controllers were discredited, except for Cost of Living Council Director John T. Dunlop, who managed to keep wages from going through the roof.

The four-fold increase in the price of oil, and the oil embargo itself, of course added to the problem—one of the external factors often cited as beyond the reach of domestic policy. But the administration since its inception had given first priority to protection of domestic oil interests, rather than the expansion of oil supplies, and rejected a Cabinet committee recommendation in February, 1970, which foresaw the potential impact of a cutoff of oil, and which urged Nixon to liberalize import quotas.

In handling the oil crisis, Mr. Nixon took the incredible step of boosting the domestic price of oil, although that merely encouraged oil company profits, not supply. This bonanza surprised even the oil companies, who naturally didn't turn it down.

Another "external" factor often cited for the miserable economic results of the Nixon years is the impetus to inflation from two dollar devaluations. At the time of the first part of the December, 1971, Smithsonian Agreement—which Mr. Nixon called "the greatest monetary agreement in the history of the world"—administration officials flatly denied that there would be an inflationary impact. But, of course, there was: the dollar prices of imported goods rose sharply and, since our goods appeared more attractive, foreign buyers snapped them up with their more valuable currencies, exacerbating shortages here.

Inasmuch as a trade deficit continued in 1972, and the dollar continued to show weakness abroad, a second devaluation was needed in February, 1973. But one of the elements that probably forced the second devaluation was abandonment of the effective Phase II of the wage-price program a month earlier: the world calculated correctly that the enviable U.S. record of price stabilization had been jettisoned by Mr. Nixon.

The stock market made a comparable judgment. Having recovered from the first Nixon bear market in 1970, stock prices had touched a high point in January, 1973, the day that Phase II was junked. They have been depressed ever since.

Where does Mr. Nixon leave us? We are in the second recession of his time of office, with prices accelerating and wages threatening to take off with their own explosion as labor attempts to recover what it lost in real wages during the past year. The economy is stagnant, with fears about the financial system itself. Interest rates are so high that the Government was forced to offer 9 per cent on a Treasury note, the highest coupon in more than a century. Chairman Burns admits that the Fed may have contributed to the mess by being too easy in credit extension in 1972, with a result that a lot of bank debt doesn't look as collectible as it did when the loans were made. The savings and loan associations face massive withdrawals and housing is in its own depression.

So—it's so long to Nixonomics with no regrets. The challenge to President Gerald Ford is enormous, more than can be expected of any man to handle quickly or completely. We trust that we won't get the dose of ineffective and unimaginable policies and weak leadership under another name. But, in the days just ahead, the mere change should provide a sense of relief.

CHAPTER TWELVE

THE DIPLOMATIC LEGACY: ACCOMPLISHMENTS TO BE ASSESSED FOR DECADES

By Murrey Marder

Murrey Marder, diplomatic correspondent for The Washington Post, closely followed the Nixon foreign policy ventures in this country and overseas.

> "I've always thought this country could run itself domestically without a President, all you need is a competent Cabinet to run the country at home. You need a President for foreign policy . . ."
> —Richard M. Nixon, quoted by Theodore H. White in "The Making of the President—1968"

In world politics, which he chose as his highest challenge, President Nixon set out to reverse the national course of total confrontation with communism, recognizing that it carried extreme risk by mutual disaster in a nuclear age of equally armed superpowers.

In doing so, he successfully transformed a strategy he had championed in earlier years. In international terms, he enhanced national security by shifting East-West competition away from a perpetual collision course. The tragedy of his presidency is that his global accomplishments were diminished, if not offset, by the domestic damage his administration inflicted on the nation in the guise of protecting national security at home.

The conduct of foreign policy is not an end in itself; the object is to enhance national well being. Democratic societies can only project externally the strength, cohesion and purposefulness that they possess internally.

President Nixon, in one sense, ended up not unlike

one of his original models, Woodrow Wilson, who could have scored triumphs for peace abroad if only he had not lost the battle at home. President Wilson, however, left office with a frustrated but idealistic glow. President Nixon, on entering office, had identified "a crisis of the spirit" as America's worst affliction. During his presidency, he compounded that crisis, leaving the nation far emptier morally and spiritually than when he arrived.

He set as his "first priority" an "honorable end of the war in Vietnam." Historians are likely to debate for years to come the costs and the consequences of the stratagems used by the Nixon administration in prolonged pursuit of that goal. President Nixon did surmount the Vietnamese war, which drove his predecessor from office, although the nation was severely shaken in the process and the seeds were sown for his ultimate departure from office.

He did not end the war, he de-Americanized it; the struggle for control of South Vietnam goes on. President Nixon extricated a half-million American troops from the battle after four additional years of bitterly divisive involvement, with, he insisted, U.S. honor intact. As recorded by the 1972 election returns, and the shift of public attention away from the continuing war, Americans counted that a major gain for surcease from national anguish.

President Nixon, in his first inaugural address, committed the United States to a new "era of negotiation" after "a period of confrontation," inviting America's world adversaries to "peaceful competition." This was his fundamental innovation.

He fully fulfilled that commitment. As evidenced by summit meetings held, agreements signed, international tension abated, American relations with the Soviet Union were eased considerably. For the first time in a generation, the United States could converse with the population in the People's Republic of China.

"Detente," the imprecise catch-all word for limitation of tension, already has once survived what it was intended to preclude—the threat of East-West confrontation, in the 1973 Middle East war.

The Nixon administration, through the Nixon Doctrine (actually more anti-doctrine than doctrine), acknowledged in 1969 that America could not indefinitely sustain the United States' self-assigned, post-World War II mandate of world policeman.

President Nixon later explained to Congress, in defining the doctrine:

"Its central thesis is that the United States will participate in the defense and development of allies and friends, but that America cannot—and will not—conceive *all* the plans, design *all* the programs, execute *all* the decisions and undertake *all* the defense of the free nations of the world. We will help where it makes a real difference and is considered in our interest."

The message was clear: American resources were not limitless, and the generation-long drive to exorcise communism would bow before that reality, in effect, by redefining American ideology.

". . . The slogans formed in the past century," President Nixon told Congress in 1970, "were the ideological accessories of the intellectual debate. Today, the 'isms' have lost their vitality . . ."

To help reconcile resources and objectives, the President committed himself to reduction of the world "burden of arms." Pursuit of that objective, and of an end to East-West confrontation, brought breakthrough U.S.-Soviet accords on strategic arms limitation (SALT), opening up an entirely new dimension of relationships between adversary nations. The actual reduction of arms spending, however, continued to be an elusive goal.

A world-wide groundswell of rising inflation, intensified in part by the accumulated costs of the Vietnamese war since 1965, demonstrated, by the early 1970s, that economic power, even more than military power, was the determination of the strength in a new world of nuclear parity between the superpowers. The long-heralded "crisis of capitalism," Marxist theorists hopefully proclaimed, was in sight. Western economists scoffed at the claim, but were deeply troubled by the escalating economic instabilities.

The Nixon administration, pledged to maintain "the stability of the dollar" as the essential rock of the world monetary system, was forced to "close the gold window" in 1971, ending convertibility of the dollar into gold, and twice it was compelled to devalue the dollar.

Allied relationships reeled under the multiple shocks of surprise American rapprochement with China, trade rivalry between the United States and Western Europe, the surge of U.S.-Soviet accords, divided policies in the 1973 Arab-Israeli war, and especially the accelerated world energy crisis, speeded by Arab manipulation of oil supplies and prices as a political weapon in the Middle East conflict. Despite the disclaimers of the Nixon Doctrine, American foreign policy was massively engaged globally.

From the beginning of the Nixon administration, the Middle East, not Southeast Asia, was recognized as the greatest hazard for East-West confrontation.

While the Arab-Israeli war reverberated in October, 1973, Secretary of State Henry A. Kissinger plunged into the conflict, first to engineer, with the Soviet Union, a cease-fire, and then to launch the most ambitious American search for peace in the region of the world most resistant to peace.

Overall, the Nixon administration pursued a supremely activist, although not a uniformly balanced, foreign policy, selectively concentrated, with blind spots (such as Africa, and, until 1974, Latin America), and not exempt from strategic disasters (notably the India-Pakistan war of 1971, in which the Nixon administration "tilted" toward Pakistan, the loser).

If measured by instant history, the Nixon administration's world balance sheet shows far more credits than debits, even though the reality cannot match the rhetoric of the President's promised "generation of peace," the shimmering goal he sought to inscribe in the history of his two terms in office.

It is inaccurate, as well as a hazardous illusion for the future conduct of American foreign policy, to credit Kissinger, rather than the President, with initiating the Nixon administration's fundamental shift in U.S. global strategy. "No Secretary of State is really important," Mr. Nixon said in the continuation of the quotation at the head of this review, because "the President makes foreign policy."

The President's pre-inaugural derogation of the importance of Secretaries of State became obviously wrong in the case of Kissinger, as it was in the case of John Foster Dulles and Dean Acheson in earlier administrations. But it is the authority of the presidency that makes foreign policy; without it, any Secretary of State is powerless.

President Nixon prided himself on coming to office more experienced with the world than any recent predecessor. Over a 20-year period, he said in his first inauguration, "I have visited most of the nations of the world. I have come to know the leaders of the world, and the great forces, the hatreds, the fears that divide the world."

Mr. Nixon also entered the White House with something else that few Americans knew at the time: a private, compelling drive for greatness, a determination to stand in world history as one of the boldest, most imaginative, most successful Presidents, who overcame the odds of lower middleclass origin, lack of family wealth or social status, and the sneers of liberals and the "Eastern Establishment," to score a dramatic global record.

The obsession showed through repeatedly on the presidential record. There were references, as offhanded as his withdrawn personality would permit, to Woodrow Wilson, Theodore Roosevelt, Disraeli, Franklin D. Roosevelt, Abraham Lincoln, Charles de Gaulle. In time of challenge, when he needed psychic reinforcement for audacious decisions of high risk, he replayed "Patton," the biographical film of the headstrong World War II American commander of armored forces.

After the disaster in the covert Cuban invasion at the Bay of Pigs in 1961, Mr. Nixon, out of office, criticized President John F. Kennedy for "a Hamlet-like psychosis" of indecision. However, when the United States faced down the Soviet Union in the 1962 Cuban nuclear missile crisis, Mr. Nixon hailed that as President Kennedy's "finest hour."

The living leader whose style President Nixon envied the most was de Gaulle. The French President's mystique, grandeur, his personification of the nation he ruled, his techniques for springing international surprises, indeed, for outfoxing the ultra-rightists who helped restore him to the presidency in 1958, intrigued Mr. Nixon.

President Nixon, at least until he faced the threat of impeachment, apparently never overcame the awe of being President.

A British writer, granted a lengthy interview in February, 1971, wrote:

". . . For a man who has got to the top in politics, he seems strangely unable to realize that he is at the top. Listening to him talking about the role of President Nixon, it was rather as if he was talking about a function and a person that still lay in the future rather than in the present, more as if he was describing how he would fill the role when he eventually reached the White House than how he was actually filling it here and now."

President Nixon often spoke solemnly of the solitude of his decision-making process: alone, pen and yellow legal memo pad in hand; methodically calculating, then unhesitatingly selecting the close, but right, choice.

The most momentous decisions, he indicated, were taken in near-isolation. "The loneliest decision of all," he told an interviewer in mid-May, 1974, was his order for massive B-52 bombing of North Vietnam in December, 1972, which, he said, "brought the war to an end"—meaning the cease-fire accord of January, 1973. His 1970 decision to send U.S. troops into Cambodia, the President said, "had very little support from my advisers."

An inner sense of loneliness, secretiveness, apartness in conducting great affairs of state is also a characteristic of Kissinger.

Kissinger once admitted to an interviewer, and rued it afterward, that his fascination for the public was like that of the "lone cowboy" in American Western dramas, single-handedly circling the globe for multiple "High Noon" showdowns, winning out repeatedly against overwhelming odds.

This helped to explain the Nixon-Kissinger affinity—each was inherently a loner.

And yet, when the White House made public the large volume of presidential Watergate tape transcripts, one disclosure that surprised some of the highest ranking officials in the administration was the inner relationship of the President and his two closest White House aides, H. R. (Bob) Haldeman and John D. Ehrlichman, ousted in the Watergate crossfire.

Their readiness to correct, or disagree with the President and his frequent deference to their judgment aroused speculation about what role Haldeman and Ehrlichman actually played in global decisions. White House loyalists insisted that the Watergate discussions were atypical; that the President, on world issues, made his own decisions without equivocation or responsiveness to his staff subordinates.

Only on one occasion is there any detailed public record of substantial consultation with Haldeman and Ehrlichman on high foreign policy.

During consideration of the 1970 decision to send American troops across the Cambodian border, a White House version published afterward in Look magazine showed Haldeman and Ehrlichman being consulted on what the President might do.

Ehrlichman, "sound(ed) . . . out" by Kissinger, was reported telling Kissinger, "Go ahead, both at the Parrot's Beak and the Fishhook" regions on the South Vietnamese-Cambodian border. President Nixon was described as subsequently meeting first with "(Attorney General John N.) Mitchell, Haldeman and Kissinger" to tell them he was ordering U.S.-South Vietnamese operations into both sectors. The account stated that the chief Cabinet officers concerned, Secretary of State William P. Rogers and Defense Secretary Melvin R. Laird, were informed only afterward of the President's decision, "in the presence of the Attorney General . . ."

The participation of Mitchell, Haldeman and Ehrlichman in the formulation of foreign policy was otherwise discernible only fleetingly, never officially.

Mitchell was a special member of the National Security Council, and a member of the secretive interdepartmental committee that supervises U.S. intelligence operations abroad. The role was not unprecedented; the late Robert F. Kennedy had at least as broad a function in the Kennedy administration. Kissinger once said that Mitchell filled the role of "the President's lawyer" on the NSC, an assignment not otherwise explained.

The White House relationship between Kissinger and the President's pre-inaugural inner circle of intimates was never easy.

Tension between the Haldeman-Ehrlichman grouping in the White House, who resented Kissinger's "superstar" publicity, and Kissinger reached a peak between Kissinger's Oct. 26, 1972, announcement that "peace is at hand" in Vietnam, and the actual cease-fire accord in January, 1973. Kissinger told several close friends in that interval that he was seriously considering resigning as the President's national security adviser.

The conflict inside the White House, never officially disclosed, included disagreement about whether to push ahead with Kissinger's admittedly ambiguous cease-fire draft accord with Hanoi over the bitter opposition of South Vietnamese President Nguyen Van Thieu. President Nixon's inner circle of staff aides was strongly opposed, on grounds that this would dishonor the administration with its right-wing supporters. Instead, the President ordered the massive December bombings of North Vietnam, despite furious outcries on the political left.

Throughout his administration President Nixon, in addition to negotiating with China, with the Soviet Union, North Vietnam and other adversaries, was constantly engaged in maneuvering around political forces on the American scene.

These internal political maneuverings constitute the least-told portion of the history of the Nixon administration's foreign policy.

Every President engages in negotiating with, or circumventing, domestic forces in pursuit of his objectives.

In President Nixon's case, however, the domestic strategy was extraordinary. He and Kissinger both were determined to shut out from their secrets the federal bureaucracy, which they distrusted. Moreover, the President was intent on a profound shift of American policy toward the Soviet Union and China. This meant that the President was embarked on overturning basic ideology of Republican rightists, the original core of his political support. The challenge for the President was how to set the stage for the policy shift without arousing a furious political outcry that could block it.

As perceived from the White House, therefore, almost everyone outside it was a potential blocking force: the federal bureaucracy inherited from previous Democratic administrations; the liberal "Eastern Establishment" which would agree with his Sino-Soviet policy but would oppose continuation of the Vietnamese war; allies who would "leak" to protect their own interests, and political rightists in the Republican and Democratic parties and in the American military establishment who would raise outcries over his turnabout with China and the Soviet Union.

Before he became President, Mr. Nixon had moved considerably ahead of the right wing of his party in examining the power realities of the nuclear age, although relatively few Americans were aware of that.

Although he was an early disciple of John Foster Dulles, by 1967 Mr. Nixon had made a major departure from Dulles' anti-Communist dogma.

Writing in Foreign Affairs, the organ of the "Eastern Establishment," Mr. Nixon added up the military, economic, social, political and intellectual damage inflicted on the United States by the Vietnamese war, and concluded:

"Other nations must recognize that the role of the United States as world policeman is likely to be limited in the future."

Looking beyond Vietnam, Mr. Nixon was most troubled by the realization that "the Soviets may reach nuclear parity with the United States" in the coming decade, and that China, "within three to five years, will have a significant nuclear capability . . ."

This realignment of world military power, Mr. Nixon said, requires that "every step possible must be taken to avert direct confrontations between the nuclear powers. To achieve this, it is essential to minimize the number of occasions on which the great powers have to decide whether or not to commit their forces."

The dual themes, retrenchment of American military involvement abroad and the diminution of East-West confrontation, were the genesis of what came to be called the Nixon Doctrine. The parallel views of Kissinger, read by the President, brought Kissinger into the White House.

Disposing of the Vietnamese war was the obstacle impeding the larger world strategy.

Initially, by propounding the concept of "linkage"—that all East-West problems were linked, including Vietnam, nuclear arms control, the continuing crisis in the Middle East resulting from the 1967 Arab-Israeli war—the Nixon-Kissinger policy attempted to induce the Soviet Union to bring enough pressure on North Vietnam to end the war in South Vietnam.

That effort failed. North Vietnam was carefully positioned between China and the Soviet Union, arch rivals for Marxist-Leninist paramountcy. The Kremlin could not put adequate pressure on Hanoi to make it shift course in the war, even if it wished to do so, without exposing the Soviet Union to charges of betraying

Communist interests. In addition, if either China or the Soviet Union balked at supplying arms and other war supplies, North Vietnam could sustain the war with supplies from either one of them. Only if the United States engaged the self-interest of both China and the Soviet Union could it obtain any leverage against North Vietnam.

The Nixon administration therefore devised a weblike scenario of intertwined secret diplomatic strategies, with Hanoi, with Moscow, with Peking. Simultaneously, while threading a path through this diplomatic maze by subterranean channels, the Nixon administration had to fend off escalating domestic demands for fulfillment of its priority commitment to end the war.

Time was the imperative to allow the Nixon administration's strategic threads to be drawn together. "Buying time" from the American public became the driving dilemma inside the administration.

Phased American troop withdrawals from South Vietnam were the prime device chosen to buy time. Beginning with an initial withdrawal increment of 25,000 men, dramatically announced by President Nixon and South Vietnamese President Nguyen Van Thieu at Midway Island on June 8, 1969, the administration spaced out troop pullbacks over a four-year period, with careful calibration of American public and congressional pressures.

The technique was comparable to turning a valve to permit steam to escape from a boiler to avoid an explosion. As the pressure mounted, more steam—troops —were let out. Each batch of withdrawals was proclaimed new evidence of the success of "Vietnamization," turning the war over to the South Vietnamese.

While this process stretched out, the administration periodically circulated hints that secret diplomacy was on the verge of producing the hoped-for peace accord. Critics were repeatedly disarmed by administration charges that their demands for more flexible conditions for ending the war, or setting deadlines for unilateral U.S. withdrawal, jeopardized administration strategy when diplomatic success was within tantalizing range.

142

Once the national boiler almost did explode, when President Nixon sent American troops, joined by South Vietnamese forces, into a new theater for U.S. military action, across the Cambodian border in April, 1970. Violent dissent spilled out across many college campuses, and the United States had political war casualties on its home front.

Essentially, however, the administration's strategy of containment succeeded—but at a price. The price was rising disaffection among the public and in Congress, a feeling of being out-manipulated with a mounting curve of attempts to limit the President's warmaking powers.

The strategists in the White House had a much different perspective. The multiple, hidden diplomacy which preoccupied them, they were convinced, ultimately would produce enough spectacular dividends to thrust the Vietnam turmoil into the shadows.

It was in the midst of the Nixon administration's completely hidden secret three-tiered diplomacy with Peking, with Moscow, with Hanoi, that the storm of alarm over security leaks broke on June 13, 1971, with the first published installment of the Pentagon Papers on the Vietnam war.

"There was every reason to believe," President Nixon said afterward in defense of the extraordinary countermeasures he instituted, that "this was a security leak of unprecedented proportions."

At first glance, Kissinger told friends afterward, he assumed that the leaker was Laird, happy to see blame poured on the Kennedy and Johnson administrations for leading the United States into the morass of Vietnam. On second thought, Kissinger, as well as the President, was stunned by the thought that a leak hemorrhage across the government could spill into public print all the tightly guarded secrets on their China-Soviet-Vietnam diplomacy. They dared not tell even the nation's highest courts the specifics of these fears because the secrecy in large part was to conceal their plans from the federal bureaucracy.

Not until a month later, on July 15, 1971 did the White House disclose that for 2½ years, starting "within two weeks" of the President's inauguration, the Nixon administration was engaged in secret explorations with the People's Republic of China.

Only marginal, public-conditioning steps were disclosed during that time, salami slices of relaxations on trade and travel between the United States and China. These were to reinforce U.S. intentions in the secret diplomacy with China, and progressively to prepare American public opinion for the reversal of American policy.

The dramatic "ping-pong diplomacy," the first official visit of an American group to Communist China, a table tennis team with accompanying newsmen, in April, 1971, became part of the mutual public scene-setting.

Leakage of the Pentagon Papers in fact did nothing to impair, or diminish, the surprise of the disclosure on July 15, 1971, that Kissinger had secretly traveled to Peking the previous week, conferred with Premier Chou En-lai, and arranged for a spectacular visit to China by President Nixon, which took place the following February after a subsequent Kissinger preparatory visit.

The shock was great to the absolutist anti-Communist political allies of President Nixon; but attrition and the conditioning of public opinion had reduced their ranks and their impact. By the time the President traveled to Peking his mission was hailed by most Americans, and the world, as enlightened statesmanship, although in Japan the initial disclosure of Kissinger's secret diplomacy was labeled the first of the "Nixon shocks."

A reverse use of the disclosure of secret diplomacy was made by the Nixon administration on Jan. 25, 1972, to out-maneuver critics, predominantly on the political left, who challenged the administration's claims that it was exhausting all diplomatic possibilities for ending the war in Vietnam.

For 30 months, President Nixon dramatically revealed on national television that Kissinger and North

Vietnamese Politburo member Le Duc Tho periodically met secretly in Paris, behind the back of the formal negotiations conducted by publicly assigned diplomats. This was unknown as well to almost all senior officials of the State Department, including those who thought they were supervising all the diplomacy on Vietnam.

"There was never a leak," President Nixon said proudly.

The President actually was disclosing failure of 12 rounds of Kissinger-Tho diplomacy; nevertheless, that publicly strengthened the administration's hand.

Similarly, super-secret "back channel" negotiations were conducted between the United States and the Soviet Union, over the heads of American-Soviet negotiators in the nuclear SALT negotiations, and in the planning of President Nixon's first summit trip to Moscow.

On October, 1971, announcement of the President's plan to visit the Soviet Union for summit talks, eight months before the event, was a prime example of how the Nixon administration used its secret and its public strategy for mutually reinforcing purposes.

By announcing the Moscow visit before he made the Peking trip, but with the actual Soviet trip set for the following May, the President served notice to both Communist nations that he was pursuing a triangular strategy, which left the United States free to tilt in either direction. Also, by displaying this surge of interwoven high-stakes diplomacy, the Nixon administration gained time, and advantage, over its Vietnam critics, who had accused it of pursuing only sterile diplomacy.

These "closely inter-related" and "highly sensitive foreign policy initiatives" were inseparable, and "leaks of secret information about any one could endanger all," President Nixon insisted in 1973 when the Watergate tide was cresting around the White House. Alarm that the Pentagon Papers disclosure represented "a security leak of unprecedented proportions," he said, precipitated the creation of the White House anti-leak "plumbers" unit, and the launching of other extraordinary precautions, including the wiretapping of members of Kissinger's National Security Council staff with Kissinger's endorsement.

Not until early 1974 did the outside world learn that the "plumbers" discovered, in late 1971, that Navy personnel inside the White House were spying on Kissinger's operations and passing information to the Joint Chiefs of Staff. The bureaucracy, too, was trying to pierce the secrecy wall.

The secrecy web, however, remained essentially intact and effective.

President Nixon, in February, 1972, achieved his dramatic meeting with China's Mao Tse-tung and Premier Chou En-lai after "almost three years of the most painstaking, meticulous and necessarily discreet preparation." A generation ' of hostile confrontation was over.

The following May, in Moscow, President Nixon completed his double-summit triumph. After signing the world's first nuclear arms limitation accord and an array of other agreements, President Nixon and Soviet Communist Party chief Leonid I. Brezhnev, cocktails in hand and with Brezhnev's left hand around the President's shoulder, celebrated "peaceful coexistence" before 1,500 guests in the Kremlin.

Among the onlooking Politburo members was dour Mihail Suslov, chief ideologist of the Communist Party and for a generation the archetypal champion of struggle with the West. Suslov managed a slight smile as he shook hands with the President.

President Nixon had boldly gambled and won. Despite a gross affront he delivered to Soviet prestige earlier in May, by ordering the mining of North Vietnam's harbors to cut off Soviet seaborne arms deliveries, the Soviet Union's self-interests in East-West detente had induced it, after a brief period of soul-searching, to proceed with the summit meeting.

The Nixon administration had diplomatically encircled North Vietnam by forging new ties with its two major allies, China and the Soviet Union. It required nearly a year more of diplomatic bargaining between Kissinger and Le Duc Tho, however, with active intervention by the Soviet Union, plus the punishing B-52 bombing of North Vietnam in December, 1972, to produce the Vietnam cease-fire accord of January, 1973. Most of what followed in the diplomatic history of the Nixon administration lacked equivalent drama, except for the outbreak of the Middle East war in October, 1973, with its threat of a confrontation despite detente.

Soviet leader Brezhnev's return summit trip to the United States in June, 1973, was anti-climactic compared with the first summit. Its most novel result was an agreement on the prevention of nuclear war, which caused disquiet among some allies, notably France, about U.S.-Soviet "hegemony."

The realities of bargaining out specific measures for development of East-West detente were compounded by a morning-after reaction in Congress to the inflated expectations aroused by the hyperbole of detente rhetoric.

In 1973 and 1974, the Nixon administration was confronted by powerful demands in Congress for freer Soviet emigration treatment of Jews and other minorities as the bargaining price for easing restrictions on Soviet trade, and hardened demands for greater protection of American security interests in the continuing nuclear strategic arms negotiations with the Kremlin. Weakened by the Watergate furor, the President's ability to deliver on his detente commitments was impaired.

Detente, as the nation's policy, was widely hailed, nevertheless, here and abroad as the Nixon administration's most striking accomplishment, even though some of the strongest original advocates grumbled that it was paying the East more dividends than the West.

In the final accounting, President Nixon was not toppled from office over international ends, but domestic means. The extreme practices that his administration employed on the domestic scene in the name of protecting the secrecy of his foreign policy proved his undoing. The excesses of security control, paradoxically, might have been regarded as less unbearable in the era of confrontation than in the era of negotiation he fostered. His 1968 projection was wrong; the country cannot run itself domestically without a President keenly attuned to American values.

CHAPTER THIRTEEN

THE MORAL LEGACY: "MY ADVICE WOULD BE TO STAY AWAY"

By Laurence Stern

A national correspondent for The Washington Post, Laurence Stern formerly was in charge of national news coverage for The Post and the editor of the Style *section.*

> "Thy death bed is no lesser than thy
> land
> Wherein thou liest in reputation
> sick . . ."
> —John of Gaunt to Richard II,
> Shakespeare

> "We have a cancer within, close to
> the presidency
> that is growing. It is growing
> daily . . ."
> —John Dean to Richard Nixon

John W. Dean III may have been the agent and the prophet of the undoing. But among the sad young men of the Watergate scandal, it was Gordon Strachan who gave the sharpest utterance to the moral legacy of the Nixon presidency.

Strachan was asked at the Senate Watergate committee hearings what advice he would give to young people about government service in view of his own plunge into "the Watergate pit."

"My advice," Strachan replied, "would be to stay away."

This was Watergate's leitmotif, sounded in vary-

149

ing tones by the contrite juniors and the weathered professionals—by the ruined and by the repentant.

Richard M. Helms, the former boss of the Central Intelligence Agency and a lifelong specialist in the uses of governmental craft, found himself making a strange admission during another Senate hearing that touched on Watergate.

"Giving assistance to the presidency," he observed to the Senate Foreign Relations Committee, "has not been a crime until relatively recently."

Then came the transcripts, with their pornographic starkness, which revealed not the quest for truth as advertised by the President but a savage and frantic effort to keep the prosecutors off the trail leading toward the Oval Office.

The transcripts introduced into the lexicon of American politics a new vocabulary that seemed to be drawn from the language of back-street combat rather than sober presidential deliberation—such words as "stonewalling" and "hanging tough."

While he was solemnly pledging to the American people a full investigation of Watergate, he was also, the transcripts revealed, rehearsing self-exculpatory scenarios with Dean, John Ehrlichman and H. R. (Bob) Haldeman in the privacy of the Oval Office as the tape recorder quietly revolved.

"President: I didn't tell him [Dean] to go get the money did I? Haldeman: No. President: You didn't either, did you? Haldeman: Absolutely not! I said you got to talk to Mitchell . . . President: We've got a pretty good record on that one, John, at least."

A half century earlier, when Richard Nixon was 10, he was lying in front of the family fireplace with newspapers full of the new revelations of the Teapot Dome scandal spread over the floor, according to a reminiscence of his mother, Hannah Nixon.

Suddenly, Mrs. Nixon recounted to biographer Bela Kornitzer, young Nixon looked up and said: "Mother, I would like to become a lawyer—an honest lawyer who can't be bought by crooks."

When he launched his second campaign for the presidency in the nomination hall at Miami Beach in 1968, President Nixon promised to heed the "real voice of America"—that of "the forgotten Americans—the non-shouters, the non-demonstrators."

He promised a rule of law and order. "Government can pass laws," he said. "But respect for law can come only from people who take the law into their hearts and minds—and not into their hands."

Five years later, when advised by Ehrlichman that a high-ranking Justice Department official, Robert Mardian, was coaching Watergate witnesses to lie, the President had this tape-recorded reaction:

"Oh."

The newspapers that are now spread out in front of other fireplaces have made a hollow thing of President Nixon's summons back to the old-fashioned virtues of work and thrift and civic orderliness.

The moral legacy he pledged has been mocked by the billowing revelations of Watergate. His personal real estate deals, his tax windfalls and loan transactions with private financiers all seemed to give the lie to the "cloth coat" morality he once professed to follow.

It has added up to the greatest political scandal in American history, dwarfing Teapot Dome.

On the public opinion fever charts the moral atmosphere of the Nixon years was becoming inseparable from what John Dean called the "cancer" of Watergate.

Public distrust of government entered into a steepening decline during 1973, although the trend had been gradually downward since 1958, according to the latest survey on the subject by the University of Michigan's Institute for Social Research. This growing disenchantment with government was found in all socio-economic sectors of American society—most keenly among the college-educated.

"The legacy is clearly one of sustained distrust of virtually all political institutions, especially the electoral process," said Warren Miller, director of the institute's Center for Political Studies.

Faith in the electoral process, Miller and his fellow

researchers found, was the one confidence index that held steady through the years. Until 1973.

"Now all of a sudden it seems that the consequences of Watergate has been to bring into question not only the President and presidential government in Washington but the entire efficacy of elections in getting a response from government," Miller said.

The Michigan sample shows that the percentage of those throughout the U.S. population who felt that elections force the government to heed popular views declined from 56 to 33 per cent.

During the Year of Watergate those who believe government is run in behalf of a "few interests" rose from 59 to 72 per cent of the population; those who felt they could trust their government only "some of the time" went from 46 to 66 per cent; those who felt "quite a few of those who run the government are crooked" went up from 38 to 53 per cent.

In Miller's view the tentative foreign policy triumphs of rapprochement with the Soviet Union and China are transitory in their impact. The enduring theme, as he sees it, is the increasing cynicism of Americans toward governmental processes—a trend that began in the 1960s with a growing polarization of national opinion on such issues as race, welfare policy, public schools and law and order.

Finally, less than two weeks after the release of the Watergate transcripts, the Harris Survey concluded that 49 per cent of the American people wanted President Nixon impeached and removed from office, while 14 per cent did not and 10 per cent were undecided.

Many more, 64 per cent, believed that the President knew about the White House cover-up of Watergate, and 59 per cent believed that Mr. Nixon knowingly falsified his income tax returns.

The wave of public antipathy toward the President seemed to spring from the latent puritanism that still seems to reside in the American conscience and to which he so often appealed.

Richard M. Nixon coveted the presidency and lived within its shadow of influence longer than most men. It was his tragic lot to have brought the office to its lowest level of public esteem since the Harding administration.

Each of our Presidents has left some characteristic imprint—a style, a sense of program, a quality of leadership—that marked his place in the national memory.

Harry S Truman was the embodiment of plain-spoken feistiness. Franklin D. Roosevelt was the consummate political craftsman. John F. Kennedy is remembered for charm and dry, Brahmin wit. Dwight D. Eisenhower symbolized soldierly rectitude, and Lyndon B. Johnson a sense of coarse, hard-driving ambition.

Until the Watergate transcripts Mr. Nixon had been remote, almost to the point of personal invisibility. In the White House he alternated between deep seclusion in the Oval Office and carefully programmed public appearances.

He sought to project himself onto the pages of his autobiography, "Six Crises." But what emerges is a sort of Kama Sutra of his emotional reactions to threatening events in physical terms, much as the ancient Hindu manual dealt with the act of love.

"In such periods of intense preparation for battle," he wrote of the Hiss case, "most individuals experience all the physical symptoms of tension—they become edgy and short-tempered, some can't eat, others can't sleep . . . I had a similar experience during the Hiss case. But what I had learned was that feeling this way before a battle was not something to worry about—on the contrary, failing to feel this way would mean that I was not adequately keyed up, mentally and emotionally, for the conflict ahead."

Political process was a series of challenge and crisis which one met, surmounted with an inevitable letdown afterward. But the book fails to project a sense of the underlying beliefs and values which carried President Nixon along his 30-year political career.

And so the question still haunts us at the door of the

now-vacated Oval Office in which Richard M. Nixon immersed himself alone for the countless hours of his presidency.

Who was there?

CHAPTER FOURTEEN

THE SEVEN CRISES OF RICHARD M. NIXON

THE HISS CASE

... On that evening of August 5, as I reviewed Hiss' testimony, I realized that this case presented a crisis infinitely greater and more complex than anything I had faced running for Congress in 1946.—Aug. 5, 1948

THE FUND

As I waited for them, I knew that if the reports with regard to the Herald Tribune were accurate, I had been hit by a real blockbuster. I had firmly believed up to this time that since the attack was strictly partisan and would not stand up on its merits, our strategy of continuing to play it down would not pay off and it would be forgotten within a few days. I still believe this would have been the case had the attack continued to come from only Democrats and from newspapers which were opposed to Eisenhower as well as to me. But when Republicans as well as Democrats began to demand my scalp, the roof caved in.—September, 1952

THE HEART ATTACK

"Dick," said a familiar voice, "this is Jim Hagerty—the President has had a coronary."

... This was far different from any other crisis I had faced in my life and had to be handled differently. I had always believed in meeting a crisis head on. The difficult period is reaching a decision, but once that has been done, the carrying-out of the decision is easier than the making of it. In meeting any crisis in life, one must either fight or run away. But one must do something. Not knowing how to act or not being able to act is what tears your insides out.—Sept. 24, 1955

CARACAS

It was past 2 a.m. when I finally turned out the light and tried to get some sleep. I had only eight hours in which to decide whether or not to keep the appointment at San Marcos. Whether, in effect, to fight or run away from this crisis which had implications far beyond my personal safety. I slept very little that night. I could feel the tension building up. Outside the hotel, I could hear the chants of the mob swirling around the hotel, "Fuera Nixon, Fuera Nixon, Fuera Nixon."

As I tossed in bed, I knew from previous experience that this necessary period of indecision was far more wearing than tomorrow's activities would be, no matter which way I decided. This was part of the crisis syndrome as I knew it.—May, 1958

DEBATING KHRUSHCHEV

Now we were going at it toe-to-toe. To some, it may have looked as though we had both lost our tempers. But exactly the opposite was true. I had full and complete control of my temper and was aware of it. I knew the value of keeping cool in a crisis, and what I said and how I said it was done with as much calm and deliberation as I could muster in a running, impromptu debate with an expert.—July, 1959

1960 CAMPAIGN

It was now almost midnight. In fifteen minutes I would have to go downstairs alone to the Ambassador ballroom and speak . . . I thought back over other crises which had confronted me as I prepared for speeches or key press conferences: the fund speech in 1952; my White House press conference after the President's stroke in 1957; trying to hold my temper as I met the press in Lima and Caracas after the riots there in 1958;

those tense moments when Khrushchev had verbally as-saulted me at the American Exhibition in Moscow and I had a split second to decide whether to remain silent, to retreat, or to fight back.

But this was the greatest test of all. How could I be gracious, and yet not concede outright?—Nov. 1960

WATERGATE

Nixon: How much money do you need?

Dean: I would say these people are going to cost a million dollars over the next two years.

Nixon: We could get that. On the money, if you need the money you could get that. You could get a million dollars. You could get it in cash. I know where it could be gotten. It is not easy, but it could be done. But the question is who the hell would handle it? Any ideas on that?—March 21, 1973

CHAPTER FIFTEEN

ALL THE PRESIDENT'S MEN

H. R. (Bob) HALDEMAN—47, an advertising executive with J. Walter Thompson Co., was President Nixon's former chief of staff and had worked for Richard Nixon since 1956. Haldeman has been indicted for conspiracy, obstruction of justice and perjury in the Watergate cover-up. He pleaded not guilty on March 9, 1974.

JOHN D. EHRLICHMAN—49, formerly a Senate lawyer, was assistant to the President for domestic affairs until his resignation April 30, 1973. Ehrlichman was indicted Sept. 4, 1973, by a Los Angeles County grand jury on charges of burglary, conspiracy and perjury in connection with the "plumbers" break-in at the office of Dr. Lewis Fielding. He pleaded not guilty Sept. 7, 1973, was indicted March 1, 1974, by the original Watergate grand jury for the conspiracy to impede the Watergate investigation, obstruction of justice and lying to FBI agents and the grand jury and pleaded not guilty. He was indicted March 7, 1974, by the second Watergate grand jury on charges of conspiracy and lying to FBI agents and the grand jury about the Los Angeles break-in and pleaded not guilty. The California charges of burglary and conspiracy were dropped March 13, 1974. But on July 12, 1974, he was found guilty of perjury and conspiracy in the Fielding break-in and on July 31, 1974, sentenced to a minimum of 20 months in prison.

JOHN W. DEAN III—35, a former House Judiciary Committee and Justice Department lawyer, was counsel to the President from 1970 until he was fired on April 30, 1973. Dean pleaded guilty on Oct. 19, 1973 to an information charging conspiracy to obstruct justice and defraud the U.S. government. Sentencing was deferred. Dean agreed to testify for the prosecution in future trials of White House officials allegedly involved in the Watergate scandal in exchange for immunity from federal prosecution for any other Watergate-related crimes. On August 2, 1974, he was sentenced by Federal Judge John J. Sirica to serve from a minimum of one year to a maximum of four years in prison for conspiracy to obstruct justice in the Watergate case.

JOHN N. MITCHELL—60, former Attorney General, was campaign director of the Committee for the re-election of the President until July 1, 1972, when he returned to the New York law firm of Mudge Rose Guthrie & Alexander. He was acquitted in a New York trial in April, 1974, on charges of perjury and conspiracy in connection with a secret campaign contribution from Robert L. Vesco. Mitchell still faces formal charges of conspiracy, obstruction of justice, making false statements to a grand jury or a court, perjury and making false statements to the FBI in the Watergate cover-up.

ALFRED C. BALDWIN III—37, a former FBI agent and security guard for Martha Mitchell, admits he transcribed the wiretapped conversations of Democratic officials in the Watergate bugging, but was granted immunity in exchange for his testimony before a federal grand jury in which he gave a full account of the Watergate raid.

BERNARD L. BARKER—56, of Cuba, worked for the CIA at the time of the Bay of Pigs invasion. Barker formed a real estate firm, Barker Associates, in Miami. He was arrested inside the Democratic National

Committee headquarters and pleaded guilty. He was sentenced to a prison term of 18 months to six years, but was freed on Jan. 4, 1974, pending outcome of his appeal.

ALEXANDER P. BUTTERFIELD—48, former classmate of H. R. Haldeman and 20-year Air Force veteran, was hired in December, 1968, to work at the Executive Mansion. Butterfield left the White House March 14, 1973, to become administrator of the Federal Aviation Administration. It was through his testimony that the Senate Watergate committee learned that tape recorders had secretly monitored President Nixon's conversations since 1971.

J. FRED BUZHARDT JR.—49, former Air Force officer and lawyer, was general counsel of the Defense Department. He joined the White House in May, 1973, and is now counsel to the President. While Defense Department general counsel, Buzhardt denied a request from E. Howard Hunt Jr. to see classified defense documents on the Pentagon Papers. Buzhardt headed Mr. Nixon's special Watergate legal team.

DWIGHT L. CHAPIN—33, who worked under H. R. (Bob) Haldeman at the J. Walter Thompson advertising agency in Los Angeles, was appointments secretary to the President. He was convicted in April, 1974, of perjury in connection with his relationship to political saboteur Donald H. Segretti. On May 15, 1974, Chapin was sentenced to a prison term of 10 to 30 months. He is free pending appeal.

KENNETH W. CLAWSON—37, joined the White House staff in 1972 after leaving the reportorial staff of The Washington Post. Clawson became director of communications. He was a member of the "attack group" which met daily to map propaganda strategy during the 1972 re-election campaign, and was named as author of a spurious letter which damaged Sen. Edmund S. Muskie's New Hampshire primary effort by an insulting reference to "Canucks." He has denied writing the "Canuck" letter.

CHARLES W. COLSON—42, was special counsel to the President until his resignation in February, 1973, to return to private law practice. Colson was indicted March 1, 1974, by the original Watergate grand jury on charges of conspiracy to impede the Watergate investigation and obstruction of justice. He pleaded not guilty March 9, 1974, was indicted March 7, 1974, by the second Watergate grand jury on a charge of conspiracy to violate the constitutional rights of Dr. Lewis Fielding and pleaded not guilty on March 9, 1974. On June 21, 1974, he received a one-to-three year sentence and a $5000 fine for obstruction of justice in the prosecution of Daniel Ellsberg.

G. BRADFORD COOK—37, practiced corporate and securities law in Chicago for 10 years before joining the Securities and Exchange Commission. Cook resigned as SEC chairman in the wake of allegations that he had deleted references to a secret $200,000 contribution to the Committee for the Re-election of the President from a commission complaint against Robert L. Vesco.

LEONARD GARMENT—50, a law partner of Mr. Nixon's New York firm. Garment joined the White House in May, 1969. He was President Nixon's White House counsel and a Watergate troubleshooter. In January, 1974, Garment returned to his former position as assistant to the President.

VIRGILIO R. GONZALEZ—46, a native of Cuba, previously employed in Miami as a locksmith, was arrested inside the Democratic National Committee offices. He pleaded guilty and was sentenced to a prison term of one to four years. He was released on parole March 7, 1974.

L. PATRICK GRAY III—57, was acting head of the FBI during the first Watergate investigation and resigned April 27, 1973, when it was revealed that he had destroyed material given him by John W. Dean III and John D. Ehrlichman. He is practicing law in New London, Conn.

ALEXANDER M. HAIG JR.—49, entered the White House in January, 1969, as a colonel and senior military adviser to Henry A. Kissinger, assistant to the President for national security affairs. While at the White House, Haig became a full general, served as deputy assistant to the President for national security affairs and became Mr. Nixon's chief of staff, replacing H. R. (Bob) Haldeman.

RICHARD M. HELMS—61, an officer of the Central Intelligence Agency from its formation, served as its director from 1966 until his appointment as U.S. ambassador to Iran. Helms was approached by White House aides to assist in the cover-up by persuading the FBI to call off its investigation of the Mexican "laundering" of Watergate funds. This he refused to do. Helms has been called back to the U.S. several times to testify in Watergate-related matters.

E. HOWARD HUNT JR.—55, who pleaded guilty in the first Watergate trial in 1973, was a 21-year veteran of the CIA who retired in 1970. He was brought to the White House by his friend Charles W. Colson and engaged in political spying, including the Ellsberg psychiatrist's office break-in and gathering information on Sen. Edward M. Kennedy. Hunt had been sentenced to a prison term of 30 months to eight years and ordered to pay a $10,000 fine, but was released Jan. 2, 1974, pending outcome of his appeal.

HERBERT W. KALMBACH—52, President Nixon's personal attorney, raised secret funds to help support the Watergate defendants and pay their legal fees. He has pleaded guilty to peddling an ambassadorship and for illegal fund raising in 1970. In exchange for his offer of cooperation, Special Prosecutor Leon Jaworski promised not to bring further charges. Sentencing has been deferred.

RICHARD G. KLEINDIENST—50, an Arizona lawyer prominent in Sen. Barry Goldwater's 1964 presidential campaign, was deputy attorney general from 1969 until February, 1972, when he succeeded John N. Mitchell as Attorney General. He resigned April 30, 1973, because of his close personal ties to persons implicated in the Watergate case. On May 16, 1974, Kleindienst pleaded guilty to a misdemeanor charge involving his testimony at his Senate confirmation hearings and received a suspended sentence.

EGIL KROGH JR.—34, worked briefly for John D. Ehrlichman in his Seattle law firm and became his deputy at the White House. Krogh resigned May 9, 1973 from his job as under secretary of transportation after taking full responsibility for the burglary of Daniel Ellsberg's psychiatrist's office by two Watergate conspirators. Krogh was given a six-month sentence in prison for conspiracy to violate the rights of a citizen in approving the burglary.

FREDERICK C. LaRUE—45, a wealthy Mississippi oil man, was an aide and close friend of John N. Mitchell when Mitchell directed the 1972 Nixon compaign. LaRue has pleaded guilty to charges of conspiracy to obstruct justice in the Watergate cover-up; sentencing has been deferred.

G. GORDON LIDDY—43, a former FBI agent, prosecutor and unsuccessful candidate for Congress, worked with the White House "plumbers" on the Ellsberg psychiatrist's office break-in. As an aide at the Nixon re-election committee, he directed the Watergate break-in. Aside from a criminal sentence, he has been found in contempt of Congress and contempt of court as he has refused to cooperate in any investigation.

JEB STUART MAGRUDER—39, who had California advertising and management experience, served successively as special assistant to the President, campaign chief of staff and deputy director of the Committee for the Re-election of the President. Magruder resigned from his Commerce Department job in April, 1973, and has pleaded guilty to obstruction of justice and defrauding the United States in the cover-up. On May 21, 1974 he was sentenced to a 10-month to 4-year term in federal prison.

ROBERT C. MARDIAN—50, former assistant attorney general in charge of the Justice Department's Internal Security Division was political coordinator for the Nixon re-election committee. Mardian has been indicted for conspiracy in connection with the Watergate cover-up.

EUGENIO R. MARTINEZ—50, native of Cuba, was a salesman in the real estate office of Bernard L. Barker. He was arrested inside the Democratic National Committee offices and pleaded guilty. Martinez was sentenced to a prison term of one to four years, and released on parole March 7, 1974.

JAMES W. McCORD JR.—50, a retired CIA official, joined the Nixon re-election committee in 1972 as security coordinator and was among the five men caught in Democratic National Committee headquarters. A letter he sent to Judge John J. Sirica in March 1973 is credited with having been a major factor in the collapse of the Watergate cover-up. McCord was sentenced to a prison term of one to five years but is free pending outcome of his appeal.

KENNETH W. PARKINSON—46, a Washington lawyer who was retained by the Committee for the Re-election of the President following the Watergate break-in to represent the committee in several suits brought by Democratic Party officials and others. Parkinson allegedly acted as a middleman between the original Watergate defendants and the committee officials involved in the cover-up. He was indicted March 1, 1974, for conspiracy and obstruction of justice.

HERBERT L. PORTER—36, formerly a successful computer salesman, was scheduling director of the Committee for the Re-election of the President. He pleaded guilty to lying to the FBI about the disposition of funds of the committee and was released from prison May 17, 1974, after serving 27 days of a 30-day sentence. He is on one year probation.

C. G. (BEBE) REBOZO—60, a Florida millionaire, has been a long-time Nixon friend. Rebozo has been involved in Mr. Nixon's real estate transactions and accepted the $100,000 Hughes cash contribution which was investigated by the Senate Watergate committee.

DONALD H. SEGRETTI—32, a California attorney, was released on March 25, 1974, after serving six months at the Federal Correctional Institution at Lompoc for his efforts to sabotage the primary election campaigns of Democratic presidential candidates.

HUGH W. SLOAN JR.—33, who had worked for the Republican Congressional Campaign Committee and on the White House staff, resigned from his position as treasurer of the re-election finance committee. Sloan disbursed funds to the Watergate conspirators.

JAMES D. ST. CLAIR—53, was a top-ranking Boston trial lawyer before he came to the White House. St. Clair became special counsel to the President Jan. 5, 1974, and served as his chief Watergate attorney.

MAURICE H. STANS—65, formerly a New York investment banker, was Secretary of Commerce in the first Nixon Cabinet and chairman of the Finance Committee to Re-elect the President. Stans was acquitted in April, 1974, in a New York trial on charges of perjury and conspiracy in the case of a $200,000 campaign contribution from Robert L. Vesco and alleged influence peddling before the Securities and Exchange Commission.

GORDON C. STRACHAN—30, an attorney who worked for H. R. (Bob) Haldeman in the White House, was liaison for Haldeman with the re-election committee in the 1972 campaign. He has been indicted on charges of conspiracy, obstruction of justice, and making false statements to a grand jury or a court in the Watergate cover-up. He pleaded not guilty on March 9, 1974, and is awaiting trial.

FRANK STURGIS—38, resided in Miami where he was active in anti-Castro affairs. He was arrested inside the Democratic National Committee headquarters and pleaded guilty to the break-in, illegal wiretapping and eavesdropping. Sturgis was sentenced to a prison term of one to four years, scheduled to be released on parole March 7, 1974, but released by court order on Jan. 18, 1974, pending outcome of his appeal.

ROBERT L. VESCO—37, a New Jersey financier, was being investigated by the Securities and Exchange Commission when he made a secret $200,000 cash contribution to the Nixon re-election committee in April, 1972. Vesco was indicted by a New York grand jury for attempting to obstruct the SEC investigation and is currently a fugitive in Costa Rica.

ROSE MARY WOODS—55, has been with Mr. Nixon since 1951, as his personal secretary. Miss Woods testified that she might have accidentally caused a 4½-minute hum in the June 20 taped conversation between Mr. Nixon and H. R. (Bob) Haldeman but sees no way that she could have been responsible for an 18-minute blank in the recording.

DAVID YOUNG—37, a lawyer, joined the White House in 1970 as an assistant on Henry A. Kissinger's National Security Council staff and was detailed in 1971 to John D. Ehrlichman's Domestic Council. Young, who had worked with Egil Krogh in supervising the "plumbers" involved in the burglary of Daniel Ellsberg's psychiatrist's office, was granted limited immunity from prosecution in July, 1973, in exchange for cooperating with the Senate Watergate committee.

RONALD L. ZIEGLER—35, was brought to the White House as press secretary for President Nixon after having worked in advertising with H. R. (Bob) Haldeman. As many of the original Nixon team left the White House under a Watergate cloud. Ziegler remained to become one of the President's closest associates and advisors. His title is assistant to the President.

CHAPTER SIXTEEN

THE NIXON YEARS: A CHRONOLOGY

By Kenneth Bredemeier

1969

Jan. 20—Richard M. Nixon is inaugurated the nation's 37th President as 100,000 people jam Washington's streets to celebrate, or in the case of Vietnam war protesters, pitch objects and shout obscenities at the new Chief Executive.

Jan. 21—The nation's new Attorney General, John N. Mitchell, assures Americans of "vigorous" law enforcement.

March—The United States begins 14 months of secret bombings of Cambodia, officially recognized as a neutral country.

March 28—General of the Army Dwight D. Eisenhower, the 34th President of the United States dies after a long illness.

April 3—The Vietnam war death toll reaches 33,641 —a dozen more than the Korean War—making Vietnam the third costliest foreign war in U.S. history.

April 7—The Supreme Court rules unanimously that laws prohibiting reading or looking at obscene material in one's home are unconstitutional.

April 17—Sirhan Sirhan is convicted of first-degree murder in the killing of Sen. Robert F. Kennedy.

May 1—The Senate and House push investigations into campus disturbances, while Attorney General Mitchell urges educators to arrest and prosecute campus demonstrators to "end minority tyranny" and Assistant Attorney General William H. Rehnquist attacks "the new barbarians" on campuses.

May 5—Life magazine reveals that Supreme Court

Justice Abe Fortas for 11 months held a $20,000 fee from the family foundation of Louis E. Wolfson, but returned the money after Wolfson was indicted (and later jailed) for selling unregistered securities.

May 15—Supreme Court Justice Fortas resigns.

May 21—Warren Earl Burger, a judge on the U.S. Circuit Court of Appeals for the District of Columbia is nominated by President Nixon to succeed Earl Warren as chief justice of the United States.

June 3—As antiwar protests multiply, President Nixon sharply criticizes student demonstrators.

June 8—President Nixon and President Nguyen Van Thieu of South Vietnam meet at Midway in the Pacific to discuss the war. President Nixon then announces that 25,000 American troops will be withdrawn from the war by the end of August, the first U.S. reduction in combat forces.

June 9—Interest on prime-rate bank loans, the rate banks charge their most credit-worthy customers, increases to a new record high 8½ per cent.

June 13—The Department of Justice reveals in federal court in Chicago that it has wiretapped antiwar activists without court approval and the government claims it has a legal right to eavesdrop on any domestic group "which seeks to attack and subvert the government by unlawful means."

July 15—Secretary of Defense Melvin R. Laird says the United States has "turned the corner" toward peace in Vietnam.

July 16—Apollo 11 blasts off from Cape Kennedy with astronauts Neil A. Armstrong, Edwin E. Aldrin Jr. and Michael Collins aboard.

July 18—Mary Jo Kopechne, a 28-year-old Washington secretary, is killed when a car in which she is riding, driven by Sen. Edward M. Kennedy (D-Mass.), plunges off a bridge into a pond on Chappaquiddick Island, off Martha's Vineyard, Mass. Kennedy does not report the accident till the next morning.

July 20—As millions watch on television around the world, Neil Armstrong takes man's first step on the moon, proclaiming: "That's one small step for man, one giant leap for mankind."

July 21—The Nixon administration lifts various travel and trade restrictions to ease relations with the People's Republic of China.

July 25—Kennedy appears on national television and terms "indefensible" his failure to report immediately the accident in which Miss Kopechne was killed. Saying he is considering resigning his Senate seat, he asks for "the advice and opinion" of Massachusetts residents. He pleads guilty to a state charge that he left the scene of the accident and receives a two-month suspended sentence.

July 25—In Guam, President Nixon enunciates the Nixon Doctrine: Asian security must be borne by Asians.

July 30—Kennedy says he will retain his Senate seat after receiving a tremendous vote of confidence from the people of Massachusetts.

Aug. 2—Several hundred thousand flag-waving Romanians give President Nixon an enthusiastic welcome in Bucharest. He is the first American President to visit a Communist country in 24 years.

Aug. 8—President Nixon calls for a sweeping revision of the nation's welfare system—the family assistance plan—that would more than double the number of people eligible for government assistance.

Aug. 9—Five persons, including movie actress Sharon Tate, are discovered brutally murdered in a posh section of Los Angeles.

Aug. 10—Rep. Wright Patman (D-Tex.), chairman of the House Banking and Currency Committee, charges that C. G. (Bebe) Rebozo, a friend of President Nixon's was handed several "special favors" by the Small Business Administration, including an $80,000 loan approved despite the objections of the agency's staff.

Aug. 16—About 300,000 people, most of them college-aged sons and daughters of middle America, flock to the four-day Woodstock Music Festival, which comes to symbolize the youthful counterculture. Massive traffic jams are created and there are shortages of food, water and medical supplies.

Aug. 18—President Nixon nominates Clement F. Haynsworth Jr., the conservative chief judge of the Fourth U.S. Circuit Court of Appeals, to replace Fortas.

Sept. 23—Secretary of Labor George P. Shultz announces institution of the so-called Philadelphia Plan, a program setting minority hiring quotas for six skilled construction crafts working on federal projects in the city.

Oct. 15—Millions of Americans demonstrate against the war on Vietnam Moratorium Day. Speeches, prayer vigils, candlelight parades and some violence mark the day.

Oct. 19—Vice President Spiro T. Agnew, in a sharp attack on antiwar demonstrators, says the Vietnam Moratorium Day was "encouraged by an effete corps of impudent snobs who characterize themselves as intellectuals."

Oct. 20—President Nixon defends his choice of Judge Haynsworth for a seat on the Supreme Court, accusing the judge's critics of being "vicious" character assassins.

Oct. 29—In a unanimous decision, the Supreme Court rebuffs the Nixon administration and orders elimination of school segregation "at once."

Nov. 13—In a Des Moines speech, Vice President Agnew sharply criticizes alleged bias on network news shows.

Nov. 14, 15—About 250,000 Americans gather in Washington for the second Vietnam Moratorium. The demonstration includes a single-file "March Against Death" past the White House. Small bands of radical youths throw rocks and bottles at the Justice Department and hoist the Vietcong flag.

Nov. 16—The first reports of what comes to be called the Mylai massacre are published. American infantrymen, early on March 16, 1968, ordered South Vietnamese villagers out of their homes, according to news reports then dynamited or burned the villagers' homes

171

and shot the people to death. The death toll may have exceeded 500.

Nov. 20—Vice President Agnew questions the news judgment of the press and points to The Washington Post and The New York Times as two newspapers that need more competition.

Nov. 21—On a roll-call vote, the Senate rejects, 55 to 45, Judge Haynsworth for a seat on the Supreme Court.

Nov. 24—Army 1st Lt. William L. Calley Jr. is charged with the murder of 109 men, women and children in the Mylai incident, and he will face a general court-martial, the Army announces.

Dec. 1—The Selective Service System stages its first draft lottery since 1942.

Dec. 15—President Nixon announces another 50,000-man U.S. troop cut in Vietnam, saying that "if Hanoi is willing to talk seriously, they will find us flexible and forthcoming."

1970

Jan. 1—President Nixon signs a bill creating the Council on Environmental Quality and promises to fight pollution so that "the decade of the '70s will be known as the time when this country regained a productive harmony between man and nature."

Jan. 5—Joseph A. (Jock) Yablonski, defeated as a reform candidate for the presidency of the United Mine Workers in December, and his wife and daughter are found dead in their Clarksville, Pa., home. Police say they were murdered several days before.

Jan. 19—Inflation in 1969 was 6.1 per cent, the highest since 1951.

Jan. 19—His nomination of Clement Haynsworth rejected, President Nixon nominates Judge G. Harrold Carswell of Florida, a member of the Fifth U.S. Circuit Court of Appeals, to fill the Supreme Court vacancy left by the resignation of Justice Fortas.

Feb. 2—President Nixon proposes the nation's first $200 billion budget.

Feb. 6—Unemployment, the Labor Department reports, is 3.9 per cent.

Feb. 8—George C. Wallace, the former governor of Alabama and 1968 presidential candidate, urges Southern defiance of federal court desegregation orders, and says he will run for President again in 1972 "if Nixon doesn't do something about the mess our schools are in."

March 5—Presidential adviser Daniel Patrick Moynihan espouses a policy of "benign neglect" toward Negroes and a group of civil rights leaders claims it is "a calculated, aggressive and systematic" administration effort to "wipe out" civil rights advances.

March 5—President Nixon and Soviet Premier Aleksei N. Kosygin hail the start of the nuclear-weapons-ban treaty.

March 6—Explosions and fire demolish a Greenwich Village town house in New York City, killing three, whom police say are young revolutionaries who manufactured bombs. One dead woman is said to be a member of the radical Weathermen faction of the Students for a Democratic Society.

March 10—An explosion in a car near the Bel Air, Md., courthouse where black militant H. Rap Brown is to be tried on arson and incitement to riot charges kills two men. Maryland state police say the two men were carrying an explosive device in the car.

March 16—The State Department says Americans can travel to the People's Republic of China for "any legitimate purpose."

April 8—The Senate rejects Judge Carswell, 51 to 45, for a seat on the Supreme Court, the second defeat of a Nixon high court nominee.

April 20—President Nixon tells the nation in a televised speech that 150,000 more troops will be brought home over the next year.

April 21—Millions of Americans observe Earth Day, focusing new attention on the planet's pollution problems.

April 30—In another televised address on the war, President Nixon announces he has sent American troops into a section of Cambodia in hopes of destroying North Vietnamese "headquarters" and "sanctuaries."

May 4—National Guard gunfire kills four students at Kent State University in Ohio after campus protest over the Cambodian invasion.

May 5—Campus demonstrations escalate sharply as students protest the killings at Kent State.

May 6—Interior Secretary Walter J. Hickel sends a letter to President Nixon claiming the administration is rejecting American youth, thus contributing to the student revolt.

May 8—President Nixon says U.S. combat forces will start pulling out of Cambodia the following week and all will be out by mid-June.

May 9—President Nixon visits anti-war protesters at the Lincoln Memorial before dawn and spends an hour chatting with them. Later, as many as 100,000 people protest the war peaceably near the White House, although some disrupt traffic and hurl objects.

May 12—Judge Harry A. Blackmun is unanimously approved by the Senate for the Supreme Court seat resigned by Associate Justice Fortas.

May 14—Two blacks are killed by police gunfire aimed at a student dormitory at Jackson State College in Mississippi.

May 26—New York City union officials present the President a hard hat at the White House and voice support for his war policies.

June 3—President Nixon declares the Cambodian invasion a success.

June 5—The Senate Foreign Relations Committee reports that American military experts believed Communist troops were moving away from the South Vietnamese border before U.S. combat forces invaded Cambodia.

June 5—At a secret White House meeting, President Nixon orders an interagency committee to make plans for stepped-up domestic intelligence.

June 22—President Nixon signs legislation lowering the voting age to 18.

June 25—The interagency committee on domestic

intelligence secretly recommends a plan drawn up by White House aide Tom Charles Huston which entails surreptitious entry and other activities it says are "clearly illegal."

July 23—President Nixon approves the interagency committee's plans for "clearly illegal" covert activities.

July 28—FBI Director J. Edgar Hoover protests the July 23 Nixon decision and the President rescinds his approval of the committee's plans.

Aug. 7—Israeli-Arab fighting halts as American-sanctioned 90-day cease-fire takes effect, but Arab guerrilla representatives say they will try to wreck it.

Aug. 12—The President signs postal reform legislation that creates the independent U.S. Postal Service.

Aug. 26—American women celebrate the 50th anniversary of women's suffrage, part of a new focus on emerging women's liberation from traditional family-oriented roles.

Sept. 6—Four jetliners are hijacked by Arab commandos and three of them are flown to Arab nations in the Middle East. The fourth plane lands in London after security agents kill one hijacker and wound another.

Oct. 12—President Nixon vetoes legislation that would have limited radio and television spending by political candidates in 1972.

October—President Nixon and Vice President Agnew campaign extensively for various House and Senate candidates. Agnew is the Republicans' cutting edge and he denounces the "radical liberal" members of the Senate up for re-election, especially Republican Charles E. Goodell of New York. Agnew and other Republicans, with tacit White House backing, support the eventual New York winner, James L. Buckley, the Conservative Party nominee. The President tells voters it is "time to draw the line" against youthful terrorists, campus violence and crime. "It is time for the great silent majority of Americans to stand up and be counted," he says.

"If a candidate has condoned violence, lawlessness, then you know what to do," he says. Toward the end of the campaign dissidents in San Jose, Calif., hurl eggs and stones at the President, narrowly missing him. The Democrats say the Nixon-Agnew campaign tactics are divisive and attempt to exploit the fears of Americans.

Nov. 3—The election results are mixed. The GOP gains two Senate seats, but loses nine in the House and 11 governorships. The President claims an "ideological" majority in the Senate, although the Democrats still maintain a numerical majority.

Nov. 9—Former French President Charles deGaulle dies at age 79, the last survivor of World War II Allied leaders.

Nov. 23—Defense Secretary Laird reveals unsuccessful raid on POW camp near Hanoi—an attempt to free U.S. prisoners but the raiders found the camp deserted.

Nov. 21—Hanoi reports "wave after wave" of American bombers have attacked North Vietnam.

Nov. 25—President Nixon asks and gets the resignation of Interior Secretary Hickel, a frequent critic of the administration.

Nov. 27—FBI chief Hoover charges two Roman Catholic war protesters, the Revs. Daniel J. and Philip F. Berrigan, with plotting to kidnap a government official as a hostage to gain the release of political prisoners and an end to the Indochina bombing.

Dec. 4—The November unemployment rate is 5.8 per cent, the Labor Department says, the highest in 7½ years.

Dec. 14—President Nixon names former Texas Gov. John B. Connally, a Democrat, Treasury Secretary.

1971

Jan. 18—Sen. George McGovern (D-S.D.) announces his candidacy for the Democratic nomination for President. He vows to end U.S. involvement in Southeast Asia.

Jan. 22—In his State of the Union address, President Nixon proposes revenue sharing—at least $16 billion in unattached federal funds annually to state and local governments—as a means of revising the accumulation of power in Washington.

Early February—Technicians install tape recording equipment in the Oval Office of the White House, the President's Executive Office Building office, the Cabinet Room and the Lincoln Sitting Room to record conversations for posterity. The recording system is not revealed.

Feb. 19—The Democratic National Committee approves wide-ranging reforms for the selection of delegates to its 1972 convention. They allow much greater participation for blacks, women and youths.

March 1—A bomb explodes in the U.S. Capitol. No one is injured in the early morning blast, but there is extensive property damage. An anonymous caller said the bomb was a protest against American military involvement in Laos.

March 23—President Nixon raises milk price supports, reportedly after key dairy industry officials restate their promise to raise $2 million for his 1972 re-election campaign.

March 29—An Army court-martial finds Lt. Calley guilty of the premeditated murder of at least 22 South Vietnamese civilians at Mylai. Two days later he is sentenced to life imprisonment.

April 7—President Nixon announces that another 100,000 American combat troops will be removed from South Vietnam by Dec. 1, which would leave 184,000 there.

April 9—A U.S. Ping-Pong team enters the People's Republic of China for a series of exhibition matches. It is the first official group of Americans to visit Mainland China in nearly two decades.

April 14—President Nixon removes the 20-year ban on American trade with the People's Republic of China.

April 20—The Supreme Court unanimously rules that busing can be used to achieve racial desegregation in public schools in the dual black-white school systems of the South. But de facto segregation in the North is excluded from the decision.

May 3—Antiwar protesters disrupt traffic and engage in widespread civil disobedience. District of Columbia police arrest 7,000 in one day and 5,000 more the next two days.

May 9—West Germany, Switzerland, the Netherlands and Austria announce the upward revaluation, or "float," of their currencies against the fixed value of the dollar. The move is seen as promoting more flexible exchange rates in the world's monetary system.

June 1—President Nixon defends the mass arrests of war protesters in Washington and rejects claims that police abused constitutional rights of the demonstrators.

June 11—Attorney General Mitchell defends wiretapping of "dangerous" radicals without court approval, claiming that domestic revolutionaries are as serious as "any threat from abroad."

June 13—The New York Times starts publication of the highly classified Pentagon papers, a government history of American involvement in Vietnam. Within the week, President Nixon authorizes establishment of a "special investigations unit," later known as the "plumbers," to "stop security leaks and to investigate other sensitive security matters." John D. Ehrlichman, the President's chief domestic adviser, is appointed to supervise the operation, with Egil Krogh, an Ehrlichman deputy, in direct charge. David Young, E. Howard Hunt Jr. and G. Gordon Liddy are also members of the unit. H. R. (Bob) Haldeman, the White House chief of staff, and presidential counsel John W. Dean III are among a select few who know about formation of the "Plumbers."

June 28—Daniel Ellsberg, a Defense Department official in the Johnson years, admits he leaked the Pentagon papers to the press. A federal grand jury indicts him on a charge of stealing the documents.

June 30—After a month of drama in lower courts, the Supreme Court rules, 6 to 3, that The New York Times and The Washington Post are free to publish articles based on the Pentagon papers because the government has not proved national security was endangered.

June 30—The 26th Amendment to the U.S. Constitution, giving persons between 18 and 21 the right to vote in all elections, takes effect.

July 15—In a surprise announcement, President Nixon says he will visit China in early 1972 at the invitation of Premier Chou En-lai. The visit, the President reveals, was arranged during a secret trip to Peking by presidential foreign affairs adviser Henry A. Kissinger.

Aug. 11—Ehrlichman approves a memo written by Krogh and Young that proposes "a covert operation" to get Ellsberg's psychiatric records "if done under your assurance that it is not traceable."

Aug. 15—After rejecting imposition of wage-price controls for months, President Nixon announces a 90-day freeze on wages and prices and a 10 per cent import surcharge.

Sept. 3—Hunt, Liddy, Bernard Barker, Eugenio Martinez and Felipe DeDiego burglarize the Los Angeles office of Ellsberg's psychiatrist. The CIA had given Hunt a special camera, a wig, and a "speech-altering device" for the mission.

Sept. 13—Thirty-one prisoners and nine hostages are killed when 1,500 New York state troopers, sheriff's deputies and guards retake control of the Attica State Prison in Attica, N.Y., after 1,200 inmates controlled it for four days.

Sept. 16—At Colson's suggestion, Hunt begins to compose fake diplomatic cables to implicate the Kennedy administration in the 1963 assassination of South Vietnamese President Ngo Dinh Diem.

Sept. 17—Supreme Court Justice Hugo Black retires for health reasons after 34 years-on the high court. He dies a week later.

Sept. 23—Supreme Court Justice John M. Harlan retires after 16 years, thus giving President Nixon the chance to appoint two new justices at the same time.

Oct. 7—President Nixon unveils details of his Phase II anti-inflation program. He establishes a Price Commission, and a Pay Board to regulate prices and wages.

Oct. 12—The President says he will visit Moscow in May, 1972, three months after his trip to Peking.

Oct. 21—President Nixon nominates two judicial conservatives to the Supreme Court—Richmond, Va., attorney Lewis F. Powell Jr. and Assistant U.S. Attorney General William F. Rehnquist.

Oct. 25—The U.N. General Assembly seats the People's Republic of China and expels nationalist China over the protests of the United States.

Dec. 3—India and Pakistan wage war, largely in East Pakistan. India recognizes the rebel Bangladesh government and after 15 days of fighting East Pakistani forces surrender. The United States charges that India was largely responsible for the war.

Dec. 6—Lewis F. Powell Jr. is confirmed by the Senate as an associate Supreme Court justice.

Dec. 10—William F. Rehnquist is confirmed by the Senate for a seat on the Supreme Court.

Dec. 18—President Nixon announces that the Group of 10 major industrial nations has agreed on an 8.57 per cent devaluation of the dollar against gold.

Dec. 20—President Nixon terminates the 10 per cent import surcharge.

Dec. 26-30—U.S. fighter planes bomb North Vietnam in the heaviest air raids since the November, 1968, bombing halt by President Johnson.

1972

Jan. 1—Formal repatriation of Bengali natives begins and an estimated 1 million refugees return from India to Bangladesh following the Pakistani surrender.

Jan. 4—Sen Edmund S. Muskie of Maine announces his candidacy for the 1972 Democratic presidential nomination and he is presumed by political writers to be the front-runner.

Jan. 7—Richard M. Nixon formally says he will run for a second term as President.

Jan. 20—The McGraw-Hill Book Co. and Life magazine say they are suspending publication of the purported Clifford Irving biography of Howard Hughes pending a probe of a Swiss bank account into which their money for the industrialist was deposited.

Jan. 27—Secretary of Commerce Maurice H. Stans resigns and becomes the chief fund-raiser for the President's re-election campaign.

Jan. 27—At a meeting in Mitchell's office attended by Mitchell, Dean and Jeb Stuart Magruder, Liddy describes a $1 million plan, which Mitchell later says included "mugging squads, kidnaping teams, prostitutes to compromise the opposition and electronic surveillance." Liddy is instructed to devise a more "realistic" plan.

Jan. 31—The Federal Aviation Administration orders airports to start using a baggage and passenger screening system to prevent hijackings.

Feb. 4—Mitchell, Dean, Magruder and Liddy meet again to discuss Liddy's revised $500,000 campaign plan, which includes wiretapping and photography. Mitchell makes no final decision, although later Magruder says Mitchell selected the Democratic National Committee at the Watergate for surveillance.

Feb. 15—Attorney General Mitchell resigns and 15 days later becomes chief to the Nixon re-election campaign.

Feb. 20-27—President Nixon arrives in Peking for his historic visit as millions of Americans watch on television via satellite. At an elaborate banquet in Peking, Mr. Nixon proposes that China and the United States begin a "long march" toward peace. Throughout the week, the President has long and seemingly friendly discussions with the Chinese leaders, including Chairman Mao Tse-tung.

Feb. 29—Newspaper columnist Jack Anderson releases a "confidential" memorandum said to have been written by Dita Beard (Washington lobbyist for International Telephone and Telegraph Corp.) which connects an ITT commitment to help fund the Republican National Convention with a Justice Department antitrust suit settlement favoring ITT.

March 7—Muskie wins the year's first presidential primary in New Hampshire, but McGovern does better than expected.

March 14—Alabama Gov. George C. Wallace wins

a big victory in the Florida primary, besting Minnesota Sen. Hubert H. Humphrey, Washington Sen. Henry M. Jackson, Muskie, New York Mayor John V. Lindsay and McGovern.

March 22-23—Four of the labor representatives on the President's new Pay Board quit and charge that the administration is guilty of "flagrant favoritism to big business and the banks."

March 30—At a Key Biscayne, Fla., meeting, Mitchell, Magruder and Frederick C. LaRue, a Mitchell campaign aide, listen to Liddy's third campaign proposal. Magruder later says Mitchell approved spending $250,000 for it, but Mitchell says he did not.

April 4—Four bank drafts totaling $89,000 are issued by a Mexico City bank. The money came from Texas contributors to the Nixon campaign, and the donation was moved through Mexico to avoid disclosure.

April 6—A Harrisburg, Pa., federal court jury convicts the Rev. Philip Berrigan of attempting to smuggle a letter out of prison, but the jury is deadlocked on other charges of conspiracy in connection with an alleged plot to kidnap presidential adviser Kissinger.

April 7—The new federal campaign contribution reporting law takes effect, but millions of dollars in secret donations to the President's re-election campaign have been collected before this date.

April 10—International financier Robert L. Vesco, who is under investigation by a New York grand jury in connection with Securities and Exchange Commission fraud, gives chief Nixon fund-raiser Stans a $200,000 cash campaign donation.

April 16—American war planes raid Haiphong and Hanoi, two cities the United States has not attacked since 1968.

April 19—A $25,000 check and the $89,000 in Mexican bank drafts are deposited in the Miami bank account of Bernard L. Barker's firm. He later withdraws the money in $100 bills and it is used in the Watergate operation.

April 27—Muskie, defeated in presidential primary

elections in Pennsylvania and Massachusetts during the week, withdraws as an active presidential candidate.

May 2—J. Edgar Hoover, for 48 years the FBI's director, dies.

May 3—President Nixon designates L. Patrick Gray III, an assistant attorney general, as the acting FBI director.

May 9—President Nixon announces that the United States has mined the North Vietnam harbors of Haiphong and six other ports. Hundreds of U.S. bombers continue their massive raids over North Vietnam.

May 15—Gov. Wallace, campaigning for the Democratic presidential nomination in Laurel, Md., is shot and paralyzed from the waist down, and three others are injured. A Milwaukee man Arthur H. Bremer, is charged with the assault.

May 22-29—President Nixon arrives in Moscow, becoming the first U.S. President to visit the Soviet Union. During his week-long visit, the President confers at length with Communist Party chief Leonid I. Brezhnev and other Soviet officials. The two countries sign several agreements, pledging co-operation in the fields of health, the environment, science and space. More importantly, the two superpowers agree to a historic pact to limit for the first time the growth of strategic missiles and missile launchers.

May 28—The Democratic National Committee's headquarters in the Watergate office complex are successfully entered, and eavesdropping devices implanted, by the Hunt-Liddy team.

June 17—James McCord, Frank Sturgis and three Cubans, Barker, Martinez and Virgilio Gonzalez, are caught by Washington police inside the Democrats' Watergate headquarters and police confiscate their cameras, sophisticated eavesdropping equipment and $2,300 in cash, mostly in $100 bills with serial numbers in sequence.

June 19—The Supreme Court rules that electronic surveillance by the federal government without court approval is unconstitutional.

June 19—White House press secertary Ronald L.

Ziegler says he won't comment on the Watergate break-in, calling it "a third-rate burglary attempt."

June 22—Hurricane Agnes lashes the East Coast, causing more than $3 billion in property damage and killing 120 people. Especially hard hit is Pennsylvania.

June 29—The Supreme Court, in a 5-4 decision, rules that the death penalty is unconstitutional because it is "cruel and unusual punishment."

June 29—Stans gives Herbert W. Kalmbach, the President's personal attorney, $75,000 after the lawyer says, "I am here on a special mission on a White House project and I need all the cash I can get." It is the first of about $500,000 paid to buy the silence of the Watergate conspirators.

July 1—Mitchell quits as the President's campaign manager, citing personal reasons.

July 6—Sloan, after agreeing to lie about the amount of money disbursed to Liddy, says he will not commit perjury.

July 6—Gray talks with the President and tells him that "people on your staff are trying to wound you by using the CIA and FBI and by confusing the question of CIA interest in, or not in, people the FBI wishes to investigate." Gray says Mr. Nixon tells him, "Pat, you just continue to conduct your aggressive and thorough investigation."

July 12—McGovern wins the Democratic presidential nomination.

July 13—McGovern picks Sen. Thomas F. Eagleton of Missouri as his vice presidential running mate.

July 25—Eagleton reveals that from 1960 to 1966 he underwent psychiatric treatment including electric shock treatment for "depression." McGovern declares he will keep Eagleton as his running mate.

July 31—Eagleton quits as the Democratic vice presidential nominee at McGovern's request.

Aug. 5—McGovern picks a new vice presidential running mate, former Peace Corps director R. Sargent Shriver.

Aug. 15—The Soviet Union, according to Jewish sources, has started charging exit fees of $5,000 to

$25,000 for educated Jews who wish to emigrate to Israel.

Aug. 22—President Nixon is renominated by the Republican National Convention.

Aug. 26—The 20th Olympic Summer Games open in Munich.

Aug. 26—The General Accounting Office, Congress' fiscal watchdog, reports "apparent violations" of the Federal Election Campaign Act by the Nixon re-election committee.

Aug. 29—President Nixon says Dean has conducted a thorough investigation of the Watergate break-in and "I can state categorically that his investigation indicates that no one in the White House staff, no one in this administration, presently employed was involved in this very bizarre incident. What really hurts is if you try to cover it up." Dean later testifies that he had not heard of his investigation until the President's statement.

Sept. 5—Eight Arab commandos raid the dormitory of the Isareli team at the Olympic Games and capture 11 hostages. As the world watches on television, tense negotiations proceed throughout the day. Finally, the commandos arrange to be transported with their hostages to an airport outside Munich where they are promised an airplane to fly out of the country. In an ensuing airport gun battle with West German police, all of the hostages, five of the eight commandos and one policeman are killed.

Sept. 8—Israeli jets stage a massive attack on 10 guerrilla bases deep inside Syria and Lebanon in retaliation for the Munich assault.

Sept. 15—Liddy, Hunt and the five men caught inside the Watergate on June 17 are indicted by a federal grand jury.

Sept. 16—Attorney General Kleindienst says the Watergate probe by the FBI and the U.S. Attorney's office in Washington was "one of the most intensive, objective and thorough" in many years.

Oct. 3—The House Banking and Currency Committee votes not to hold hearings on Nixon campaign finances that would have touched on the funding of the Watergate operation.

Oct. 10—The Washington Post reveals that the Watergate break-in was part of a massive campaign of political spying and sabotage conducted on behalf of the President's re-election and directed by White House and re-election committee officials.

Oct. 25—Haldeman is revealed by The Post as among those authorized to approve payments from a secret espionage and sabotage fund. Ziegler denies the story as "the shoddiest type of journalism . . . that I do not think has been witnessed in the political process for some time."

Oct. 26—"Peace is at hand," Kissinger tells a Washington news conference. He says final peace terms could be worked out in one more negotiating session with the North Vietnamese. Under the proposed terms, U.S. troops would be withdrawn from South Vietnam within 60 days and POWs would be released.

Nov. 7—Richard M. Nixon and Spiro T. Agnew are re-elected in a landslide with 61 per cent of the popular vote. They win in every state except Massachusetts.

Nov. 14—For the first time in history the Dow-Jones industrial index of 30 blue-chip stocks closes over 1,000.

Dec. 16—Kissinger says Hanoi has stopped bargaining in "good faith and good will."

Dec. 18—President Nixon orders large-scale bombing of the Hanoi-Haiphong area and the attacks level wide areas of the two cities.

Late December—Gray, he later says, burns the Hunt documents along with the Christmas trash.

Dec. 28—Harry Truman, the 33rd President of the United States, dies at 88.

Dec. 29—Life magazine ceases publication.

Dec. 30—The President ends the massive bombing of North Vietnam with the announcement that peace talks will resume on Jan. 8. U.S. losses during the bombing have been heavy, both in aircraft and in men.

1973

Jan. 3—Hunt reiterates his demands for more money and executive clemency, Dean later testifies.

Jan. 11—President Nixon ends all mandatory wage and price controls.

Jan. 11—Sen. Sam J. Ervin Jr. (D-N.C.) agrees to lead a Senate investigation of Watergate.

Jan. 11—Hunt pleads guilty to six charges against him in the Watergate case. Four other defendants—Barker, Martinez, Gonzalez and Frank Sturgis—follow suit four days later. And on Jan. 30, Liddy and McCord are convicted.

Jan. 12—John J. Caulfield, a White House aide and security operative, meets McCord on the George Washington Parkway in Virginia and offers him executive clemency "from the highest level of the White House." McCord refuses.

Jan. 16—"Are you being paid by anybody for anything?" Judge John J. Sirica asks the Watergate defendants. "No," they reply in unison.

Jan. 14—Caulfield and McCord meet again and McCord later says Caulfield tells him: "The President's ability to govern is at stake. Another Teapot Dome scandal is possible and the government may fall."

Jan. 20—President Nixon is inaugurated for a second term and he says "we stand on the threshold of a new era of peace."

Jan. 22—The Supreme Court overrules state abortion restrictions during the first three months of pregnancy and says during the next six months the state may "regulate the abortion procedure in ways that are reasonably related to maternal health."

Jan. 23—Lyndon B. Johnson, the nation's 36th President, dies at 64.

Jan. 23—President Nixon announces that the Vietnam war, the nation's longest and most divisive, is to end on Jan. 28. The peace agreement, hammered out in further Paris negotiations between Kissinger and North Vietnam's Le Duc Tho, calls for withdrawal of the last 23,700 American troops in Vietnam and return of U.S. prisoners of war within 60 days.

Jan. 26-28—A Gallup Poll puts the President's popularity at a high of 68 per cent.

Jan. 27—Defense Secretary Laird announces the end of the military draft.

Feb. 2—Judge Sirica says that he is "not satisfied" that the whole Watergate story has been revealed.

Feb. 7—The Senate votes, 70 to 0, to establish a committee with four Democrats and three Republicans to investigate Watergate and other 1972 campaign abuses.

Feb. 12—Operation Homecoming begins: The first 142 American POWs are released and they and other POWs come home to joyous reunions with their families.

Feb. 12—The United States, for the second time in 14 months, devalues the dollar against most major world currencies, this time by 10 per cent.

Feb. 27—Members of the militant American Indian Movement seize the trading post and church at historic Wounded Knee on the Oglala Sioux reservation in South Dakota.

March 7—At his confirmation hearings to be FBI director, Gray discloses he has given Dean 82 FBI reports.

March 9—Ehrlichman says the President will veto appropriations bills and if Congress overrides the vetoes, Mr. Nixon will impound the funds.

March 19—McCord writes Judge Sirica a letter charging that perjury was committed at the Watergate trial, that defendants were pressured to plead guilty and keep quiet, that higher-ups were involved, and that "several members of my family have expressed fear for my life if I disclose knowledge of the facts of this matter."

March 21—President Nixon, he says later, learns of "serious charges which came to my attention," and he begins "intensive new inquiries into this whole matter."

March 21—Within hours of the White House meeting, arrangements are made to pay Hunt $75,000.

March 23—Judge Sirica makes McCord's letter public and gives four of the Watergate defendants provisional sentences in an effort to encourage them to talk to the grand jury.

March 30—The White House offers to let administration staff testify in closed session before the Senate Watergate committee. Ervin later calls such an offer "executive poppycock" and says Nixon staff members are not "nobility and royalty."

April 5—Gray's nomination as FBI director is withdrawn.

April 5—In San Clemente, Ehrlichman discusses the directorship of the FBI with the federal judge in the current Ellsberg case, W. Matt Byrne Jr.

April 7—Judge Byrne rejects the FBI directorship.

April 12—Magruder confesses his perjury to the prosecutors.

April 17—President Nixon says that a new "intensive" investigation has produced "major developments" and "real progress . . . in finding the truth" about Watergate.

April 17—Presidential press secretary Ziegler says all previous statements about Watergate are "inoperative."

April 27—Judge Byrne discloses a Justice Department memorandum on the break-in at Ellsberg's psychiatrist's office.

April 30—President Nixon accepts the resignations of Haldeman, Ehrlichman and Kleindienst and fires Dean. Mr. Nixon accepts responsibility for Watergate.

May 7—The new Attorney General, Elliot L. Richardson, promises to appoint a special prosecutor in the growing Watergate scandal and give him "all the independence, authority and staff support" he needs.

May 10—Mitchell and Stans are indicted by a federal grand jury in New York on perjury and conspiracy charges in connection with the $200,000 campaign contribution of financier Robert L. Vesco.

May 11—Judge Byrne dismisses all charges in the Pentagon papers case against Daniel Ellsberg. The judge cites government misconduct as the reason.

May 11—West Germany and East Germany establish formal relations.

May 17—The televised Senate Watergate hearings begin.

May 18—Archibald Cox, former solicitor general of the United States, is named by Richardson as the Watergate special prosecutor.

June 21—The Supreme Court, in a series of 5-to-4 votes on obscenity cases, says states can ban books, magazines, movies and plays which are offensive to local standards even if they are acceptable in other parts of the country.

July 12—President Nixon is hospitalized with viral pneumonia.

July 16—White House aide Alexander Butterfield reveals the White House tape-recording system.

July 17—The Senate approves the controversial Alaska oil pipeline after Vice President Agnew votes in favor of blocking further court challenges to the project by environmentalists and thus breaks a 48-48 deadlock.

July 25—The President says he will not release White House tapes to Cox because it would jeopardize the "independence of the three branches of government."

July 31—Rep. Robert F. Drinan (D-Mass.) is the first member of Congress to introduce an impeachment resolution against President Nixon.

Aug. 22—President Nixon names Henry A. Kissinger, for 4½ years his top national security adviser and foreign affairs specialist, to be Secretary of State, replacing William P. Rogers, who resigns.

Aug. 22—President Nixon, in his first press conference in five months, declares Watergate "water under the bridge." He says he accepts all the blame for the White House climate which led to the break-in and cover-up.

Sept. 4—Ehrlichman, Krogh, David Young and G. Gordon Liddy are indicted by a California grand jury in Los Angeles in connection with the break-in at Ellsberg's psychiatrist's office.

Sept. 6—Former United Mine Workers president Boyle is arrested and charged with the 1969 murder of his one-time opponent for the union presidency, Joseph A. (Jock) Yablonski.

Sept. 11—A four-man military junta overthrows Marxist Chilean President Salvadore Allende in a violent coup. Santiago police say Allende committed suicide rather than surrender to the new regime.

Oct. 6—A major Mideast war erupts with the Israelis fighting Arabs on two fronts—the Egyptians along the Suez Canal and the Syrians on the Golan Heights. In 16 days of fighting, both the Israelis and Arabs suffer major losses of weapons, planes and troops.

Oct. 10—In a dramatic appearance in federal court in Baltimore, Vice President Spiro T. Agnew pleads no contest to a charge of income tax evasion, climaxing a lengthy investigation into kickbacks he allegedly accepted from contractors while he was Baltimore County executive, governor of Maryland and Vice President. He is fined $10,000 and placed on three years' probation.

Oct. 12—President Nixon, in a White House ceremony, nominates House Minority Leader Gerald R. Ford of Michigan to be Vice President.

Oct. 17—The oil-producing Arab nations impose an embargo on further shipment of oil to the United States in an effort to get the United States to change its pro-Israeli foreign policy.

Oct. 20—Cox, in a televised press conference, defends his decision not to compromise with the President on the tapes issue and emphasizes that he will not resign. A few hours later, Nixon press secretary Ziegler announces the firing of Cox and abolition of the special prosecutor's office, the resignation of Richardson and the firing of Deputy Attorney General William D. Ruckelshaus for their refusal to fire Cox. The episode comes to be known as the "Saturday Night Massacre."

Oct. 23—The White House says it will release the tapes Cox sought.

Oct. 30—The House Judiciary Committee starts consideration of possible impeachment procedures.

Oct. 31—The White House says that two of the nine

tape recordings scheduled for submission to Judge Sirica do not exist.

Nov. 1—Sen. William B. Saxbe (R-Ohio) becomes President Nixon's fourth Attorney General, and Houston lawyer Leon Jaworski is appointed as the new special prosecutor.

Nov. 3—The Gallup Poll records President Nixon's lowest approval rating to date—27 per cent.

Nov. 7—In a wide-ranging talk on the energy crisis, President Nixon calls for a return to daylight savings time on a year-round basis, reduced fuel oil allocations, widespread establishment of car pools and 50-mile-per-hour speed limits. He also asks Congress to relax environmental standards when necessary to meet the shortage of oil caused by the Arabs' oil embargo.

Nov. 14—White House attorneys learn there is an 18½-minute gap in the June 20, 1972, tape of a Haldeman-Nixon meeting and it is revealed publicly a week later.

Nov. 17-20—President Nixon, in a series of appearances in the South, seeks public support for his embattled presidency. At one point, he says: "People have got to know whether or not their President is a crook. Well, I'm not a crook."

Nov. 26—President Nixon's secretary, Rose Mary Woods, says she may have accidentally erased the 18½ minutes of the 18½ minutes.

Nov. 27—Gerald R. Ford is confirmed by the Senate as Vice President.

Dec. 8—President Nixon reveals his personal finances. He has become a millionaire during his term in office and paid less than $1,000 in taxes in both 1970 and 1971.

1974

Jan. 15—A panel of technical experts determines that the 18½-minute gap in the June 20 tape is the result of five separate manual erasures.

Feb. 4—President Nixon proposes the nation's first

$300 billion budget—$304.4 billion for fiscal year 1975.

Feb. 5—Patricia Hearst, of Hearst newspaper family, is kidnaped by the Symbionese Liberation Army in Berkeley.

Feb. 6—The House votes 410 to 4 to proceed with the impeachment probe and to give the House Judiciary Committee broad subpoena powers.

February—Lines at gasoline stations through much of the nation grow rapidly. Some motorists wait hours to buy a few gallons of gas.

March 1—Seven key former Nixon administration and campaign officials—Mitchell, Haldeman, Ehrlichman, Strachan, Robert Mardian, Kenneth Parkinson and Colson—are indicted by a grand jury for allegedly conspiring to cover up the Watergate burglary.

March 7—Ehrlichman, Colson and five others are indicted by a federal grand jury in the break-in at Ellsberg's psychiatrist's office.

April 3—The Internal Revenue Service says Mr. Nixon owes $432,787 in back taxes and interest penalties totaling another $33,000. The assessment is made largely because the IRS finds that the President's deduction for donation of his vice presidential papers was made after the date such contributions were prohibited. Mr. Nixon says he will pay the entire sum.

April 28—Mitchell and Stans are acquitted of all charges against them in the Vesco case.

April 30—The White House releases 1,239 pages of edited transcripts and they reveal brutally frank White House discussions on Watergate and administration and political personalities.

May 2—The Maryland Court of Appeals bars former Vice President Agnew from the practice of law, calling him "morally obtuse."

May 7—The President's chief defense lawyer, James D. St. Clair, says no more White House Watergate conversations will be turned over to either the special prosecutor or the House Judiciary Committee.

May 9—The House Judiciary Committee begins

formal hearings on the possible impeachment of President Nixon.

May 16—Richard G. Kleindienst becomes the first of the nation's 68 attorneys general to plead guilty to a criminal offense, that he refused to testify accurately during his Senate confirmation hearing. He later was sentenced to a month in jail and fined $100, but both were suspended.

May 21—Jeb Stuart Magruder, once the deputy director of President Nixon's re-election campaign, is sentenced to a prison term of 10 months to four years for his part in the Watergate cover-up.

May 24—Special Watergate prosecutor Jaworski appeals directly to the Supreme Court to decide whether the President can withhold evidence in the criminal cases of his former aides. The Supreme Court a week later agrees to hear the case, bypassing the U.S. Court of Appeals.

June 3—Former presidential aide Charles W. Colson pleads guilty to obstructing justice for devising a White House scheme to influence the outcome of Daniel Ellsberg's Pentagon Papers trial by defaming Ellsberg and destroying his public image.

June 14—President Nixon, on a trip to the Mideast, gives Egypt nuclear energy for peaceful purposes and later does the same for Israel.

June 21—Former White House aide Charles W. Colson is sentenced to one to three years imprisonment and fined $5,000 for obstructing justice in the prosecution of Pentagon Papers defendant Daniel Ellsberg.

June 28—President Nixon and Soviet leader Leonid Brezhnev, at a summit meeting in Moscow, agree to a further limitation of defensive anti-ballistic missiles in their two countries.

July 9—Earl Warren, the retired chief justice of the Supreme Court, dies at 83.

July 12—John D. Ehrlichman, once the No. 2 man on President Nixon's White House staff, is convicted of perjury and violating the civil rights of Ellsberg's psychiatrist in connection with the break-in at the doctor's office.

194

July 24—The Supreme Court, ruling unanimously that President Nixon has no right to withhold evidence in criminal proceedings, orders him to turn over 64 White House tapes of Watergate discussions, 63 of them between the President and key aides. The President agrees to turn over the tapes.

July 24—After 10 weeks of evidence gathering, the House Judiciary Committee begins debate on articles of impeachment against Richard Nixon.

July 27—The Judiciary committee, on a 27-to-11 vote, recommends that President Nixon be impeached because his actions formed a "course of conduct or plan" to obstruct the investigation of the Watergate break-in and to cover up other unlawful activities.

July 29—The committee votes 28 to 10 for a second article of impeachment, alleging the President's repeated misuse of his power to violate the constitutional rights of American citizens.

July 29—Former Treasury Secretary John B. Connally is indicted by a federal grand jury on charges of taking illegal payoffs, conspiracy to obstruct justice and perjury. The grand jury charged that Connally received $10,000 for recommending an increase in milk price supports, conspired to concoct a false story to thwart investigators probing the alleged bribe and then lied to the grand jury which was investigating the alleged gifts.

July 30—The Judiciary committee adopts 21 to 17 a third article of impeachment against President Nixon for defying its subpoenas. The committee concluded its historic inquiry after rejecting two additional articles —one involving the secret bombing of Cambodia (26 to 12), and the other, tax fraud and unconstitutional receipt of emoluments from the federal government for his private homes (26 to 12).

July 31—John D. Ehrlichman is sentenced by U.S. District Court Judge Gerhard A. Gesell to serve a minimum of 20 months to a maximum of five years in prison. The former White House domestic affairs adviser was convicted July 12, 1974, on charges of conspiracy and perjury growing out of the burglary of the office of Daniel Ellsberg's psychiatrist.

Aug. 2—Judge John J. Sirica sentences former White House counsel John Dean to a minimum of one year to a maximum of four years in prison for conspiracy to obstruct justice in the Watergate case.

Aug. 5—Three new transcripts, recounting conversations on June 23, 1972, between Richard Nixon and H. R. Haldeman, are released by the White House. The tapes reveal that President Nixon personally ordered a cover-up of the facts of Watergate within six days after the illegal entry into the Democrats' national headquarters. The transcripts completely undermine the President's previous insistence that he was uninvolved in the cover-up, and show that he directed efforts to hide the involvement of his aides in the Watergate break-in through a series of orders to conceal details about the break-in known to himself but not to the FBI. With the transcripts' release, the President released a statement about his position and noted, "Although I recognized that these presented potential problems, I did not inform my staff or counsel of it, or those arguing my case, nor did I amend my submission to the Judiciary Committee in order to include and reflect it."

Aug. 6—With resignation demands coming from some of his staunchest supporters in Congress, President Nixon tells his Cabinet that he does not intend to resign and believes that the constitutional process should be allowed to run its course.

Aug. 6—House Minority Leader John J. Rhodes (R-Ariz.) tells a news conference that he will vote for Article I of impeachment, charging President Nixon with obstruction of justice, after reading the June 23, 1972, transcripts Mr. Nixon released August 5.

Aug. 6—All 10 Republicans on the House Judiciary Committee who had voted against impeachment turn around and announce they would vote in favor of at least the obstruction of justice article.

Aug. 6—The Senate Foreign Relations Committee reaffirms its decision that Henry A. Kissinger's role in the wiretapping of subordinates and newsmen did not constitute grounds to bar his confirmation as Secretary of State. The committee had undertaken its inquiry at Kissinger's request, following the publication of FBI reports which said the secretary, then the President's national security adviser, was the person who requested the wiretaps that were intended to stop leaks of national security information. Kissinger threatened to resign unless his name was cleared.

Aug. 7—President Nixon meets for a half hour with Senate Minority Leader Hugh Scott, House Minority Leader John Rhodes, and Senator Barry Goldwater. He was told that he had about 15 votes against conviction in the Senate and perhaps only 10 votes against impeachment in the House.

Aug. 7—The President is reported to be nearing a decision to resign, but there is no official White House confirmation.

Aug. 7—With expectations of an imminent resignation and hopes by investors for a new and more stable administration to deal with the nation's economic problems, the Dow Jones average of 30 industrials closes up 23.78 points to 797.56 for the third biggest gain of the year.

Aug. 8—In his 37th address to the nation, the 37th President of the United States, Richard Milhous Nixon, announces on television that he would resign his office, effective at noon, Aug. 9. At that time, Gerald Rudolph Ford, whom Mr. Nixon nominated for Vice President on Oct. 12, 1973, would be sworn in as the 38th President, to serve out the 895 remaining days of Mr. Nixon's second term.

I. IMPEACHMENT

Article I of the Resolution of Impeachment

Following is Article I, with amended language in italics, as adopted by the House Judiciary Committee, July 27, 1974, in a 27-to-11 vote.

In his conduct of the office of President of the United States, Richard M. Nixon, in violation of his constitutional oath faithfully to execute the office of President of the United States and, to the best of his ability, preserve, protect, and defend the Constitution of the United States, and in violation of his constitutional duty to take care that the laws be faithfully executed, has prevented, obstructed, and impeded the administration of justice, in that:

On June 17,1972, and prior thereto, agents of the Committee for the Re-election of the President committed *unlawful* entry of the headquarters of the Democratic National Committee, in Washington, District of Columbia, for the purpose of securing political intelligence. Subsequent thereto, Richard M. Nixon, using the powers of his high office, *engaged personally and through his subordinates and agents in a course of conduct or plan designed* to delay, impede, and obstruct the investigation of such illegal entry; to cover up, conceal and protect those responsible; and to conceal the existence and scope of other unlawful covert activities.

The means used to implement this *course of conduct or plan* have included one or more of the following:

(1) Making false or misleading statements to lawfully authorized investigative officers and employees of the United States:

(2) Withholding relevant and material evidence or information from lawfully authorized investigative officers and employees of the United States;

(3) Approving, condoning, acquiescing in, and counseling witnesses with respect to the giving of false or misleading statements to lawfully authorized investigative officers

and employees of the United States and false or misleading testimony in duly instituted judicial and congressional proceedings;

(4) Interfering or endeavoring to interfere with the conduct of investigations by the Department of Justice of the United States, the Federal Bureau of Investigation, the Office of Watergate Special Prosecution Force *and congressional committees;*

(5) Approving, condoning, and acquiescing in, the surreptitious payment of substantial sums of money for the purpose of obtaining the silence or influencing the testimony of witnesses, potential witnesses or individuals who participated in such *unlawful* entry and other illegal activities;

(6) Endeavoring to misuse the Central Intelligence Agency, an agency of the United States;

(7) Disseminating information received from officers of the Department of Justice of the United States to subjects of investigations conducted by lawfully authorized investigative officers and employees of the United States for the purpose of aiding and assisting such subjects in their attempts to avoid criminal liability;

(8) Making *or causing to be made* false or misleading statements for the purpose of deceiving the people of the United States into believing that a thorough and complete investigation had been conducted with respect to allegations of misconduct on the part of personnel of the executive branch of the United States and personnel of the Committee for the Re-election of the President, and that there was no involvement of such personnel in such misconduct; or

(9) Endeavoring to cause prospective defendants, and individuals duly tried and convicted, to expect favored treatment and consideration in return for their silence or false testimony, or rewarding individuals for their silence or false testimony.

In all of this, Richard M. Nixon has acted in a manner contrary to his trust as President and subversive of constitutional government, to the great prejudice of the cause of law and justice and to the manifest injury of the people of the United States.

Wherefore Richard M. Nixon, by such conduct, warrants impeachment and trial, and removal from office.

Article II of the Resolution of Impeachment

Article II of the Resolution of Impeachment, with amended language in italics, as adopted by the House Judiciary Committee July 29, 1974, in a 28-to-10 vote.

Using the powers of the office of President of the United States, Richard M. Nixon, in violation of his constitutional oath faithfully to execute the office of President of the United States and, to the best of his ability, preserve, protect, and defend the Constitution of the United States, and in disregard of his constitutional duty to take care that the laws be faithfully executed, has repeatedly engaged in conduct violating the constitutional rights of citizens, impairing the due and proper administration of justice and the conduct of lawful inquiries, or contravening the laws governing agencies of the executive branch and the purposes of these agencies.

This conduct has included one or more of the following:

(1) He has, acting personally and through his subordinates and agents, endeavored to obtain from the Internal Revenue Service, in violation of the constitutional rights of citizens, confidential information contained in income tax returns for purposes not authorized by law, and to cause, in violation of the constitutional rights of citizens, income tax audits or other income tax investigations to be initiated or conducted in a discriminatory manner.

(2) He misused the Federal Bureau of Investigation, the Secret Service, and other executive personnel, in violation or disregard of the constitutional rights of citizens, by directing or authorizing such agencies or personnel to conduct or continue electronic surveillance or other investigations for purposes unrelated to national security, the enforcement of laws, or any other lawful function of his office; he did direct, authorize, or permit the use of information obtained thereby for purposes unrelated to national security, the enforcement of laws, or any other lawful function of his office; and he did direct the concealment of certain records made by the Federal Bureau of Investigation of electronic surveillance.

(3) He has, acting personally and through his subordinates and agents, in violation or disregard of the consti-

tutional rights of citizens, authorized and permitted to be maintained a secret investigative unit within the office of the President, financed in part with money derived from campaign contributions which, unlawfully utilized the resources of the Central Intelligence Agency, engaged in covert and unlawful activities, and attempted to prejudice the constitutional right of an accused to a fair trial.

(4) He has failed to take care that the laws were faithfully executed by failing to act when he knew or had reason to know that his close subordinates endeavored to impede and frustrate lawful inquiries by duly constituted executive, judicial, and legislative entities concerning the unlawful entry into the headquarters of the Democratic National Committee, and *the cover-up thereof, and concerning other unlawful activities including those relating to the confirmation of Richard Kleindienst as Attorney General of the United States, the electronic surveillance of private citizens, the break-in into the offices of Dr. Lewis Fielding, and the campaign financing practices of the Committee to Re-elect the President.*

(5) In disregard of the rule of law, he knowingly misused the executive power by interfering with agencies of the executive branch, including the Federal Bureau of Investigation, the Criminal Division, and the Office of Watergate Special Prosecution Force, of the Department of Justice, and the Central Intelligence Agency, in violation of his duty to take care that the laws be faithfully executed.

In all of this, Richard M. Nixon has acted in a manner contrary to his trust as President and subversive of constitutional government, to the great prejudice of the cause of law and justice and to the manifest injury of the people of the United States.

Wherefore Richard M. Nixon, by such conduct, warrants impeachment and trial, and removal from office.

Article III of the Resolution of Impeachment

Article III of the Resolution of Impeachment, with amended language in italics, as adopted by the House Judiciary Committee July 30, 1974, in a vote of 21 to 17.

In his conduct of the office of President of the United States, Richard M. Nixon, contrary to his oath faithfully to execute the office of President of the United States and, to the best of his ability, preserve, protect, and defend the Constitution of the United States, and in violation of his constitutional duty to take care that the laws be faithfully executed, has failed without lawful cause or excuse to produce papers and things as directed by duly authorized subpoenas issued by the Committee on the Judiciary of the House of Representatives on April 11, 1974, May 15, 1974, May 30, 1974, and June 24, 1974, and willfully disobeyed such subpoenas. The subpoenaed papers and things were deemed necessary by the Committee *in order to resolve by direct evidence fundamental, factual questions relating to Presidential direction, knowledge or approval of actions demonstrated by other evidence to be substantial grounds for impeachment of the President.* In refusing to produce these papers and things *Richard M. Nixon, substituting his judgment as to what materials were necessary for the inquiry, interposed the powers of the presidency against the lawful subpoenas of the House of Representatives, thereby assuming to himself functions and judgments necessary to the exercise of the sole power of impeachment vested by the Constitution in the House of Representatives.*

In all of this, Richard M. Nixon has acted in a manner contrary to his trust as President and subversive of constitutional government, to the great prejudice of the cause of law and justice and to the manifest injury of the people of the United States.

Wherefore, Richard M. Nixon by such conduct, warrants impeachment and trial, and removal from office.

II. THE NEW TAPES

Nixon's Response to the Supreme Court Decision

On July 24, 1974, the Supreme Court ruled unanimously, and definitely, in an 8-to-0 ruling that President Nixon must turn over tape recordings of White House conversations needed by Watergate Special Prosecutor Leon Jaworski for the trial of the President's highest aides.
Ordering compliance with a trial subpoena "forthwith," the court rejected Mr. Nixon's broad claims of unreviewable executive privilege and said they "must yield to the demonstrated, specific need for evidence in a pending criminal trial."
Chief Justice Warren E. Burger delivered the historic judgment in a packed and hushed courtroom. His 31-page opinion drew heavily on both the great cases of the court's past, as well as the pro-prosecution edicts of a court dominated by Nixon appointees.
One justice, William H. Rehnquist, disqualified himself because of his previous association with former Attorney General John N. Mitchell in the Justice Department.

Following is the July 24, 1974, White House statement on the Supreme Court decision read by the President's special counsel, James D. St. Clair:

I have reviewed the decision of the Supreme Court with the President. He's given me this statement, which he's asked me to read to you. And this is the President's statement as he gave it to me:

"My challenge in the courts to the subpoena of the special prosecutor was based on the belief that it was unconstitutionally issued, and on my strong desire to protect the principle of presidential confidentiality in a system of separation of powers.

"While I am, of course, disappointed in the result, I respect and accept the court's decision, and I have instructed Mr. St. Clair to take whatever measures are necessary to comply with that decision in all respects. For the future it will be essential that the special circumstances of this case not be permitted to cloud the right of Presidents to maintain the basic confidentiality without which this office cannot function. I was gratified, therefore, to note that the court reaffirmed both the validity and the importance of the principle of executive privilege, the principle I had sought to maintain. By complying fully with the court's ruling in this case, I hope and trust that I will contribute to strengthening rather than weakening this principle for the future, so that this will prove to be not the precedent that destroyed the principle but the action that preserved it."

That concludes the President's statement. As we all know, the President has always been a firm believer in the rule of law, and he intends his decision to comply fully with the court's ruling as an action in furtherance of that belief. Therefore, in accordance with his instructions, the time-consuming process of reviewing the tapes subject to the subpoena, and the preparation of the index and analysis required by Judge Sirica's order, will begin forthwith.

Thank you all very much.

The Nixon Statement Upon Releasing the New Tapes

Following is the statement by President Nixon, Aug. 5, 1974.

I have today instructed my attorneys to make available to the House Judiciary Committee, and I am making public, the transcripts of three conversations with H. R. Haldeman on June 23, 1972. I have also turned over the tapes of these conversations to Judge Sirica, as part of the process of my compliance with the Supreme Court ruling.

On April 29, in announcing my decision to make public the original set of White House transcripts, I stated that "as far as what the President personally knew and did with regard to Watergate and the cover-up is concerned, these materials—together with those already made available—will tell it all."

Shortly after that, in May, I made a preliminary review of some of the 64 taped conversations subpoenaed by the special prosecutor.

Among the conversations I listened to at that time were two of those of June 23. Although I recognized that these presented potential problems, I did not inform my staff or my counsel of it, or those arguing my case, nor did I amend my submission to the Judiciary Committee in order to include and reflect it. At the time, I did not realize the extent of the implications which these conversations might now appear to have. As a result, those arguing my case, as well as those passing judgment on the case, did so with information that was incomplete and in some respects erroneous. This was a serious act of omission for which I take full responsibility and which I deeply regret.

Since the Supreme Court's decision 12 days ago, I have ordered my counsel to analyze the 64 tapes, and I have listened to a number of them myself. This process has made it clear that portions of the tapes of these June 23 conversations are at variance with certain of my previous statements. Therefore, I have ordered the transcripts made available immediately to the Judiciary Committee so that they can be reflected in the committee's report, and included in the record to be considered by the House and Senate.

In a formal written statement on May 22 of last year, I said that shortly after the Watergate break-in I became concerned about the possibility that the FBI investigation might lead to the exposure either of unrelated covert activities of the CIA, or of sensitive national security matters that the so-called "plumbers" unit at the White House had been working on, because of the CIA and plumbers connections of some of those involved. I said that I therefore gave instructions that the FBI should be alerted to coordinate with the CIA, and to ensure that the investigation not expose these sensitive national security matters.

That statement was based on my recollection at the time—some 11 months later—plus documentary materials and relevant public testimony of those involved.

The June 23 tapes clearly show, however, that at the time I gave those instructions I also discussed the political aspects of the situation, and that I was aware of the advantages this course of action would have with respect to limiting possible public exposure of involvement by persons connected with the re-election committee.

My review of the additional tapes has, so far, shown no other major inconsistencies with what I have previously submitted. While I have no way at this stage of being certain that there will not be others, I have no reason to believe that there will be. In any case, the tapes in their entirety are now in the process of being furnished to Judge Sirica. He has begun what may be a rather lengthy process of reviewing the tapes, passing on specific claims of executive privilege on portions of them, and forwarding to the special prosecutor those tapes or those portions that are relevant to the Watergate investigation.

It is highly unlikely that this review will be completed in time for the House debate. It appears at this stage, however, that a House vote on impeachment is, as a practical matter, virtually a foregone conclusion, and that the issue will therefore go to trial in the Senate. In order to ensure that no other significant relevant materials are withheld, I shall voluntarily furnish to the Senate everything from these tapes that Judge Sirica rules should go to the special prosecutor.

I recognize that this additional material I am now furnishing may further damage my case, especially because attention will be drawn separately to it rather than to the evidence in its entirety. In considering its implications, therefore, I urge that two points be borne in mind.

The first of these points is to remember what actually happened as a result of the instructions I gave on June 23. Acting Director Gray of the FBI did coordinate with Director Helms and Deputy Director Walters of the CIA. The CIA did undertake an extensive check to see whether any of its covert activities would be compromised by a full FBI investigation of Watergate. Deputy Director Walters then reported back to Mr. Gray that they would not be compromised. On July 6, when I called Mr. Gray, and when he expressed concern about improper attempts to limit his investigation, as the record shows, I told him to press ahead vigorously with his investigation—which he did.

The second point I would urge is that the evidence be looked at in its entirety, and the events be looked at in perspective. Whatever mistakes I made in the handling of Watergate, the basic truth remains that when all the facts were brought to my attention, I insisted on a full investigation and prosecution of those guilty. I am firmly convinced that the record, in its entirety, does not justify the extreme step of impeachment and removal of a President. I trust that as the constitutional process goes forward, this perspective will prevail.

The Complete Transcript of the New Tapes

President Nixon personally ordered a cover-up of the facts of Watergate within six days after the illegal entry into the Democrats' national headquarters on June 17, 1972, according to the following transcripts of Mr. Nixon's conversations with H. R. Haldeman on June 23, 1972. The transcripts were released by the White House Aug. 5. 1974.

10:04 to 11:39 a.m.

(Unintelligible)

P (Unintelligible) . . . they've got a magnificent place—

H No, they don't. See, that was all hand-held camera without lighting—lousy place. It's good in content, it's terrible in film quality.

P (Unintelligible) Rose, she ought to be in here.

H No, well let her in if you want to, sure—

P. That's right. Got so goddamned much (scratching noises).

H Goddamned.

P I understand, I just thought (unintelligible). If I do, I just buzz.

H Yeah. Ah—

P Good, that's a very good paper at least (unintelligible). The one thing they haven't got in there is the thing we mentioned with regard to the armed services.

H I covered that with Ehrlichman who says that can be done and he's moving. Not only armed services, but the whole government.

P GSA? All government?

H All government procurement, yeah. And, I talked to John about that and he thought that was a good idea. So, Henry gets back at 3:45.

P I told Haig today that I'd see Rogers at 4:30.

H Oh, good, O.K.

P Well, if he gets back at 3:45, he won't be here until 4:00 or 4:30.

H It'll be a little after 4:00 (unintelligible) 5:00.

P Well, I have to, I'm supposed to go to Camp David. Rogers doesn't need a lot of time, does he?

H No sir.

P Just a picture?

H That's all. He called me about it yesterday afternoon and said I don't want to be in the meeting with Henry, I understand that but there may be a couple of points Henry wants me to be aware of.

P Sure.

P (Unintelligible) call him and tell him we'll call him as soon as Henry gets here, between 4:30 and 5:00 (unintelligible). Good.

H O.K., that's fine.

H Now, on the investigation, you know the Democratic break-in thing, we're back in the problem area because the FBI is not under control, because Gray doesn't exactly know how to control it and they have—their investigation is now leading into some productive areas—because they've been able to trace the money—not through the money itself —but through the bank sources—the banker. And, and it goes in some directions we don't want it to go. Ah, also there have been some things—like an informant came in off the street to the FBI in Miami who was a photographer or has a friend who is a photographer who developed some films through this guy Barker and the films had pictures of Democratic National Committee letterhead documents and things. So it's things like that that are filtering in. Mitchell came up with yesterday, and John Dean analyzed very carefully last night and concludes, concurs now with Mitchell's recommendation that the only way to solve this, and we're set up beautifully to do it, ah, in that and that—the only network that paid any attention to it last night was NBC—they did a massive story on the Cuban thing.

P That's right.

H That the way to handle this now is for us to have Walters call Pat Gray and just say, "Stay to hell out of this—this is ah, business here we don't want you to go any further on it." That's not an unusual development, and ah, that would take care of it.

P What about Pat Gray—you mean Pat Gray doesn't want to?

H Pat does want to. He doesn't know how to, and he doesn't have, he doesn't have any basis for doing it. Given this, he will then have the basis. He'll call Mark Felt in, and the two of them—and Mark Felt wants to cooperate because he's ambitious—

P Yeah.

H He'll call him in and say, "We've got the signal from across the river to put the hold on this." And that will fit rather well because the FBI agents who are working the case, at this point, feel that's what it is.

P This is CIA? They've traced the money? Who'd they trace it to?

H Well they've traced it to a name but they haven't gotten to the guy yet.

P Would it be somebody here?

H Ken Dahlberg.

P Who the hell is Ken Dahlberg?

H He gave $25,000 in Minnesota and, ah, the check went directly to this guy Barker.

P It isn't from the committee though, from Stans?

H Yeah. It is. It's directly traceable and there's some more through some Texas people that went to the Mexican bank which can also be traced to the Mexican bank—they'll get their names today.

H —And (pause)

P Well, I mean, there's no way—I'm just thinking if they don't cooperate, what do they say? That they were approached by the Cubans. That's what Dahlberg has to say, the Texans too, that they—

H Well, if they will. But then we're relying on more and more people all the time. That's the problem and they'll stop if we could take this other route.

P All right.

H And you seem to think the thing to do is get them to stop?

P Right, fine.

H They say the only way to do that is from White House instructions. And it's got to be to Helms and to—ah, what's his name . . . . . .? Walters.

P Walters.

H And the proposal would be that Ehrlichman and I call them in, and say, ah—

P All right, fine. How do you call him in—I mean you just—well, we protected Helms from one hell of a lot of things.

H That's what Ehrlichman says.

P Of course, this Hunt, that will uncover a lot of things. You open that scab there's a hell of a lot of things and we just feel that it would be very detrimental to have this thing go any further. This involves these Cubans, Hunt, and a lot of hanky-panky that we have nothing to do with ourselves. Well what the hell, did Mitchell know about this?

H I think so. I don't think he knew the details, but I think he knew.

P He didn't know how it was going to be handled though —with Dahlberg and the Texans and so forth? Well who was the asshole that did? Is it Liddy? Is that the fellow? He must be a little nuts!

H He is.

P I mean he just isn't well screwed on is he? Is that the problem?

H No, but he was under pressure, apparently, to get more information, and as he got more pressure, he pushed the people harder to move harder—

P Pressure from Mitchell?

H Apparently.

P Oh, Mitchell. Mitchell was at the point (unintelligible).

H Yeah.

P All right, fine, I understand it all. We won't second-guess Mitchell and the rest. Thank God it wasn't Colson.

H The FBI interviewed Colson yesterday. They determined that would be a good thing to do. To have him take an interrogation, which he did, and that—the FBI guys working the case concluded that there were one or two possibilities—one, that this was a White House—they don't think that there is anything at the election committee—they think it was either a White House operation and they had some obscure reasons for it—non-political, or it was a—Cuban and the CIA. And after their interrogation of Colson yesterday, they concluded it was not the White House, but are now convinced it is a CIA thing, so the CIA turnoff would—

P Well, not sure of their analysis, I'm not going to get that involved. I'm (unintelligible).

H No, sir, we don't want you to.

P You call them in.

H Good deal.

P Play it tough. That's the way they play it and that's the way we are going to play it.

H O.K.

P When I saw that news summary, I questioned whether it's a bunch of crap, but I thought, er, well it's good to have them off us a while, because when they start bugging us, which they have, our little boys will not know how to handle it. I hope they will though.

H You never know.

P Good.

H Mosbacher has resigned.

P Oh, yeah?

H As we expected he would.

P Yeah.

H He's going back to private life (unintelligible). Do you want to sign this or should I sent it to Rose?

P (scratching noise)

H Do you want to release it?

P O.K. Great. Good job, Bob.

H Kissinger?

P Huh? That's a joke.

H Is it?

P Whenever Mosbacher came for dinners, you see he'd have to be out escorting the person in and when they came through the receiving line, Henry was always with Mrs. Mosbacher and she'd turn and they would say this is Mrs. Kissinger. He made a little joke.

H I see. Very good. O.K.

P Well, good.

H (unintelligible) Congressional guidance to get into the Mills thing at all. It was reported that somebody— Church met with Mills.

P Big deal. (unintelligible)

H Well, what happened there is—that's true—Church went Um?

P Is it pay as you go or not?

H Well, Church says it is, our people don't believe it is. Church told Mills that he had Long's support on adding Social Security and Wilbur equivocated on the question, when Johnny Burns talked to him about whether he would support the Long/Church amendment, but Long and Church telling him that it is fully funded—and our people are afraid Mills is going to go along if they put the heat on him as a partisan Democrat to say that this would be damned helpful just before our convention to stick this to the White House. Ah, Johnny Burns, he talked to Wilbur about it afterwards and this has been changed, so don't be concerned about it—you should call Mansfield and you should tell Mansfield that Burns is going to fight this in conference and that he will demand that it go to rules and he will demand a three-day lay-over, which means he will

carry the conference over until July 7, which would be
—and then before they even start the action, so it will
mean they have to stay in—they can't—

P All right.

H (Unintelligible).

P Go ahead.

H Clark made the point that he should handle this not
you, and is doing this through Scott to Byrd, who is
acting (unintelligible) still in the hospital. And he, Clark's
effort is going to be to kill the Church/Long amendment.
They got another tactic which is playing a dangerous game,
but they are thinking about, which is, if they put Social
Security on (unintelligible) that they will put revenue
sharing and H.R. 1 in it and really screw it up.

P I would. Not dangerous at all. Buck up.

H They're playing with it—they understand. Clark is
going off with the mission to kill it.

P Revenue sharing won't kill it, but H.R. 1 would.

H So, that's what he is off to.

P But, boy if the debt ceiling isn't passed start firing
(expletive deleted) government workers, I really mean it
—cut them off. They can't do this—they've got to give us
that debt ceiling. Mills has said that he didn't (unintelligible) on the debt ceiling earlier. Well, it's O.K—it's O.K.

H Well, Burns says that he is justifying it on the basis
that they have told him that it's finance. Ehrlichman met
with them—the Republicans on Senate Finance yesterday
and explained the whole thing to them. They hadn't understood the first six-months' financing and they are with
it now and already to go and hanging on that defense. He
feels, and they very much want, a meeting with you before
the recess, finance Republicans.

P All right. Certainly.

H So we'll do that next week. Did you get the report
that the British floated the pound?

P No. I don't think so.

H They did.

P That's devaluation?

H Yeah. Flanigan's got a report on it here.

P I don't care about it. Nothing we can do about it.

H You want a run-down?

P No, I don't.

H He argues it shows the wisdom of our refusal to
consider convertibility until we get a new monetary system.

212

P Good. I think he's right, It's too complicated for me to get into. (unintelligible) I understand.

H Burns is concerned about speculation about the lira. the dollar.

P Yeah. O.K. Fine.

H Burns is concerned about speculation about the liraa.

P Well, I don't give a (expletive deleted) about the lira. (Unintelligible)

H That's the substance of that.

P How are the House guys (unintelligible) Boggs (unintelligible).

H All our people are, they think it's a great—a great ah—

P There ain't a vote in it. Only George Shultz and people like that think it's great (unintelligible). There's no votes in it, Bob.

P Or do you think there is?

H No, (unintelligible) I think it's—it looks like a Nixon victory (shuffling) major piece of legislation (unintelligible).

P (unintelligible)

H Not til July, I mean, our guys' analysis is that it will—not going to get screw up. The Senate will tack a little bit of amendment on it, but not enough to matter and it can be easily resolved in conference.

P Well, what the hell, why not accomplish one thing while we're here.

H Maybe we will.

P Yep. Not bad.

H In spite of ourselves.

P O.K. What else have you got that's amusing today?

H That's it.

P How's your (unintelligible) (Voices fade) coverage?

H Good newspaper play—lousy television—and they covered all the items, but didn't (unintelligible) you gotta (unintelligible) but maximum few minutes (unintelligible). ible).

P (unintelligible)

H Sure. One thing, if you decide to do more in-office ones—

P Remember, I, I—when I came in I asked Alex, but apparently we don't have people in charge. I said I understood, that you had told me that the scheme was to let them come in and take a picture—an Ollie picture—but (expletive deleted), what good does an Ollie picture do?

213

H Doesn't do any good.

P Don't know what it was but apparently he didn't get the word.

H Well, I think we ought to try that next time. If you want to see if it does us any good, and it might, let them.

P Well, why wasn't it done this time?

H I don't know.

P It wasn't raised?

H I don't know. You said it—

P Because I know you said—and Ollie sat back there and (unintelligible) and I said (unintelligible). But (expletive deleted) Ollie's pictures hang there and nobody sees them except us.

H Now what you've got to—it's really not the stills that do us any good on that. We've got to let them come in with the lights.

P Well in the future, will you make a note. Alex, Ron or whoever it is—no Steve. I have no objection to them coming in, and taking a picture with stills, I mean with the camera. I couldn't agree more. I don't give a (expletive deleted) about the newspapers.

H You're going to get newspaper coverage anyway.

P What (unintelligible) good objective play—

H Oh, yeah.

P In terms of the way it was—

H Or in the news.

P Needless to say, they sunk the bussing thing, but there was very, very little on that (unintelligible) Detroit (unintelligible).

H Two networks covered it.

P We'll see what Detroit does. We hope to Christ the question (unintelligible) SOB, if necessary. Hit it again. Somebody (unintelligible) bussing thing back up again.

H What's happened on the bussing thing. We going to get one or not? Well, no we're out of time. No. After.

P I guess it is sort of impossible to get the word to the research people that when you say 100 words, you mean 100 words.

H Well, I'm surprised because this is Buchanan, and I didn't say time on this one. I said 100 words and Pat usually takes that seriously but that one—I have a feeling maybe what happened is that he may have started short and he may have gotten into the editing—you know the people—the clearance process—who say you have to say such and such, although I know what's happened.

P I don't know—maybe it isn't worth going out and (unintelligible). Maybe it is.

H Well, it's a close call. Ah, Ehrlichman thought you probably—

P What?

H Well, he said you probably didn't need it. He didn't think you should, not at all. He said he felt fine doing it.

P He did? The question, the point, is does he think everybody is going to understand the bussing?

H That's right.

P And, ah, well (unintelligible) says no.

H Well, the fact is somewhere in between, I think, because I think that (unintelligible) is missing some—

P Well, if the fact is somewhere in between, we better do it.

H Yeah, I think Mitchell says, "Hell yes. Anything we can hit on at anytime we get the chance—and we've got a reason for doing it—do it."

P When you get in—when you get in (unintelligible) people, say, "Look the problem is that this will open the whole, the whole Bay of Pigs thing, and the President just feels that ah, without going into details—don't, don't lie to them to the extent to say there is no involvement, but just say this is a comedy of errors, without getting into it, the President believes that it is going to open the whole Bay of Pigs thing up again. And, ah, because these people are plugging for (unintelligible) and they should call the FBI in and (unintelligible) don't go any further into this case period! (inaudible) our cause—

H Get more done for our cause by the opposition than by us.

P Well, can you get it done?

H I think so.

P (unintelligible) moves (unintelligible) election (unintelligible).

H They're all—that's the whole thing. The Washington Post said it in its lead editorial today. Another "McGovern's got to change his position." That that would be a good thing, that's constructive. Ah, the white wash for change.

P (unintelligible) urging him to do so—say that is perfectly all right?

H Cause then they are saying—on the other hand—that he was not so smart. We have to admire the progress he's made on the basis of the position he's taken and maybe he's right and we're wrong.

215

P (Inaudible) I just, ha ha.

H Sitting in Miami (unintelligible) our and a little bit. They eliminated their law prohibiting male (unintelligible) from wearing female clothes—now the boys can all put on their dresses—so the gay lib is going to turn out 6,000 (unintelligible).

P (unintelligible).

H I think.

P They sure test the effect of the writing press. I think, I think it was still good to have it in the papers, but, but, let's—perfectly—from another standpoint, let's just say look, "Because (unintelligible) people trying and any other damned reason, I just don't want to go out there (unintelligible) what better way to spend my time than to take off two afternoons or whatever it was to prepare for an in-office press conference." Don't you agree?

H That's, that's—

P (unintelligible) I spend an hour—whatever it was— 45 minutes or so with television executives (unintelligible) all in and outs (unintelligible). "Look, we have no right to ask the President anything (unintelligible) biased." (unintelligible) says I'm going to raise hell with the networks. And look, you've just not got to let Klein ever set up a meeting again. He just doesn't have his head screwed on. You know what I mean. He just opens it up and sits there with eggs on his face. He's just not our guy at all is he?

H No.

P Absolutely, totally, unorganized.

H He's a very nice guy.

P People love him, but damn is he unorganized.

H That's right, he's not.

P But don't you agree that (unintelligible) worth doing and that it's kind of satisfying.

H Sure. And as you point out there's some fringe benefits with—going through the things is a good exercise for you—

P That's right.

H In the sense of getting caught up on certain items—

P Right.

H It's a good exercise for the troops in having to figure out what the problems are and what the answers are to them.

P Three or four things. Ah—Pat raised the point last night that probably she and he and the girls ought to stay

216

in a hotel on Miami Beach. First she says the moment they get the helicopter and get off and so forth, it destroys their hair and so forth. And of course, that is true—even though you turn them off and turn them on so on. The second point is—

H Could drive over—

P Well, the point is, I want to check with Dean to be sure what the driving time is. If the driving time with traffic is going to be up to an hour—

H Oh no.

P With the traffic—

H But they have an escort.

P How long would it take?

H Half an hour. Less than half an hour. You can make it easy in a half hour without an escort and they would—they should have an escort. They should arrive with—and they may not like it—it may bother them a little, but that's what people expect—and you know at the conventions—every county—

P She has another point though which I think will please everybody concerned. She says, "Now, look. You go there—she says so far as she was concerned she would be delighted—the girls would be delighted to every reception—everything that they have there." They want to be busy. They want to do things and they want to be useful. Of course, as you know, our primary aim is to see that they are on television (unintelligible) coming into the hall (unintelligible) shooting the hall (unintelligible) plan on television. My point is, I think it would be really great if they did the delegations of the big states. Just to stop in you know. Each girl and so forth can do—

H Sure.

P The second thing is—just go by and say hello, and they'll do the handshakers (unintelligible) you know (unintelligible).

H Well, the big point is, there's, there's several major functions that they may want to tie that into.

P Yeah. Yeah.

H There's—a strong view on the part of some of our strategists that we should be damned careful not to over use them and cheapen them. That they should—there is a celebrity value you can lose by rubbing on them too much—

P I couldn't agree more.

217

H and so we have to—their eagerness to participate should not go—

P California delegation (unintelligible) think I'm here. I mean we're going to have (unintelligible).

P You understand—they're willing. Have them do things—do the important things, and so forth, and so on.

H There's the question. Like Sunday night they have the (unintelligible) whether they should go to that—now at least the girls should go. I think I ought to go too!

P Yep.

H You know, whether Pat—one thought that was raised was that the girls and their husbands go down on Sunday and Pat wait and come down with you on Tuesday. I think Pat should go down and should be there cause they'll have the salute—

P (Inaudible)

H She should arrive separately. I think she should arrive with the girls. Another thought was to have the girls arrive Sunday, Pat arrive Monday and you arrive Tuesday. I think you're overdoing your arrivals.

P No, no, no. She arrives with the girls and they—they should go. I agree.

H But, I don't think you have to be there until Tuesday.

P I don't want to go near the damned place until Tuesday. I don't want to be near it. I've got the arrival planned (unintelligible) my arrival of, ah—

H Now we're going to do, unless you have some objection, we should do your arrival at Miami International not at Homestead.

P Yes, I agree.

H Ah, we can crank up a hell of an arrival thing.

P All right.

P (unintelligible) is for you, ah, and perhaps Colson probably (inaudible).

P I was thumbing through the, ah, last chapters of (unintelligible) last night and I also read the (unintelligible) chapters (unintelligible). Warm up to it, and it makes, ah, fascinating reading. Also reminds you of a hell of a lot of things that happened in the campaign—press you know, election coverage, the (unintelligible) etc., etc.

H Yeah.

P. So on and so on. I want you to reread it, and I want Colson to read it, and anybody else.

H O.K.

P And anybody else in the campaign. Get copies of the

book and give it to each of them. Say I want them to read it and have it in mind. Give it to whoever you can, O.K.?

H Sure will.

P Actually, the book reads awfully well—have to look at history I want to talk to you more about that later in terms of what it tells us about how our campaign should be run, O.K.?

H O.K. In other words, (unintelligible) the media and so forth—

P to a great extent, is responsible to what happened to Humphrey both in '68. If that's true, it did not apply in 1960. The media was just as bad (unintelligible) two weeks. In 1960 we ran—

H It was a dead heat.

P All the way through the campaign and it never changed, clearly. It may be—it may be that our—as you read this on how (unintelligible) our campaign was—how much television, you know. We didn't have (unintelligible) at all. It may be that our '60 campaign (unintelligible) was extremely much more effective and it may be too, that we misjudged the (unintelligible). You read it through and (unintelligible) see what I mean. I mean, it's it's—even realize that '68 was much better organized. It may be we did a better job in '60. It just may be. It may tell us something. Anyway would you check it over?

H Yep.

P (unintelligible) check another thing—gets back? Convention?

H He was, I'm not sure if he still is.

P Could find out from him what chapters of the book he worked on. Ah, I don't want coverage of the heartattack thing. I did most of the dictating on the last two but I've been curious (unintelligible). But could you find out which chapters he worked on. Also find out where Moscow is— what's become of him—what's he doing ten years. Say hello to him (unintelligible) might find it useful (unintelligible) future, despite the (unintelligible). You'll find this extremely interesting, read (unintelligible).

H Read that a number of times (unintelligible) different context—

P Ah, I would say another thing—Bud Brown (unintelligible) did you read it? (Unintelligible) candidates. I don't know who all you discussed that with. Maybe it's not been handled at a high enough level. Who did you discuss that with? (Unintelligible)

219

H MacGregor and Mitchell. MacGregor and Mitchell, that's all.

P Yep. (Unintelligible) I don't mind the time—the problem that I have with it is that I do not want to have pictures with candidates that are running with Democrats —or against Democrats that may either be (unintelligible) or might be for us. On the other hand, all sophisticated Democratic candidates you understand—the damned candidates (unintelligible) they gotta get a picture with the President. The way to have the pictures with the candidate —this would be a very clever thing, is to call both Democrats—the good Southern Democrats and those few like (unintelligible), who did have a picture with me, see, and then call them up and say look (unintelligible) came on and they took a picture and maybe (unintelligible) President. Wants you to know that if you would like a picture, if you would like to come down to the office, you know, you can have a picture taken that you are welcome to use. How does that sound to you as a (unintelligible)? Let me say this. I'm not—I'm not—I think that getting to the candidates out there that are very busy and so forth may help us a bit. If the candidates run too far behind you, it drags you too much.

H Yeah. That's right.

P On the, on the other side, I don't think it's going to hurt you particularly if you always (unintelligible) there's some quality—

H O yeah, but they aren't going to (inaudible).

P (Unintelligible) quite candid with you—I think when I ran in '46, remember, I would have gotten on my hands and knees for a picture with Harold Stassen and (unintelligible) whole story. We (unintelligible) to do what we can (unintelligible) in the House and the Senate—as well as we can.

H (Unintelligible) have our loyalists feel that we're—

P That's right. (Unintelligible) and I'll be glad to do it next week, and I think on that basis we can handle the Democrats. Say, "Look they had a picture," and then call each one. I mean they'll have to check this list. Check each one (unintelligible) and say, look (unintelligible) if you'd like a picture with him—not on a basis of support—See?

H Yeah.

P (Unintelligible) not going to make any statement— not going to make any statement. (Unintelligible) have a picture, he'd be glad to have a picture (unintelligible).

H Picture of the—

P That's right. Be glad to if you like, but it's up to you and so forth.

H You did the Democrats in here. Would you do a, would you do the Republicans? Do a different picture (unintelligible) full shot.

P Yeah. Another point I was going to mention to you, Bob, is the situation with regard to the girls. I was talking to Pat last night. Tricia and I were talking, and she mentioned—Tricia said that apparently when she was in Allentown there were 20 or 30 thugs—labor thugs out booing.

H Hmmm.

P And when she went to Boston to present some art—her Chinese things to the art gallery there—two the (unintelligible) from the press were pretty vicious. What I mean is they came through the line and one refused to shake. One was not with the press. Refused to shake hands, so forth and so on. Tricia (unintelligible) very personal point, (unintelligible) good brain in the head. She said first she couldn't believe that the event that they do locally (unintelligible) understand. You know she does the Boys' Club, the Art Gallery (unintelligible). She says the important thing is to find this type of (unintelligible) to go into the damn town (unintelligible) do television which of course, they do. (Unintelligible) she says why (unintelligible) control the place. She says in other words, go in and do the Republican group. Now, sure isn't (unintelligible) to say you did the Republican group, as it is the Allentown Bullies Club? But, that's the paper story. The point is, I think Parker has to get a little more thinking in depth, or is it Codus now who will do this?

H They are both working on it.

P What's your off-hand reaction on that, Bob? I do not want them, though, to go in and get the hell kicked (unintelligible).

H There's no question, and we've really got to work at that.

P Yep (unintelligible).

H Ya, but I think—I'm not sure—if you can't get the controlled non-political event, then I think it is better to do a political event (unintelligible).

P For example—now the worst thing (unintelligible) is to go to anything that has to do with the arts.

H Ya, see that—it was (unintelligible) Julie giving that time to the Museum in Jacksonville.

221

P The arts you know—they're Jews, they're left wing—in other words, stay away.

P Make a point.

H Sure.

P Middle America—put that word out—Middle America-type of people (unintelligible), auxiliary, (unintelligible). Why the hell doesn't Parker get that kind of thing going? Most of his things are elite groups except, I mean, do the cancer thing—maybe nice for Tricia to go up—ride a bus for 2 hours—do some of that park in Oklahoma—but my view is, Bob, relate it to Middle America and not the elitist (unintelligible). Do you agree?

H Yep. Sure do.

P I'm not complaining. I think they are doing a hell of a job. The kids are willing—

H They really are, but she can improve.

P There again, Tricia had a very good thought on this, but let's do Middle America.

H Yep.

P (Unintelligible).

P I don't know whether Alex told you or not, but I want a Secret Service reception some time next week. I just gotta know who these guys are (Unintelligible). Don't you think so? I really feel that they're there—that ah, I see new guys around—and Jesus Christ they look so young.

H Well, they change them—that's one (unintelligible) any reception now would be totally different (unintelligible).

P Get 100 then—so it's 200 and I shake their hands and thank them and you look (unintelligible) to (unintelligible). They have a hell of a lot of fellas, let's face it, (unintelligible) friends (unintelligible), but I just think it's a nice—

H They all—you have such—that's why it's a good thing to do, cause they are friends—and they have such overriding respect for you and your family that a

P I wouldn't want the whole group—something like (unintelligible). Third point—I would like a good telephone call list for California, but not a huge book, and the kind—This would be a good time where (unintelligible) and just give thanks to people for their support. For example, Colson had me call (unintelligible) the other day—(unintelligible) thing to do, but, here you could take the key guys that work—I wouldn't mind calling a very few key contributors—maybe, but we're talking about magnitude of ten—very key ten.

H Ten—you mean ten people?

P Ya

H Oh, I thought you meant $10,000.

P No, ten. Ten. I was thinking of very key (unintelligible), people like—that work their ass off collecting money, just to say that—people that—the people that are doing the work—very key political (unintelligible) just to pat them on the back. I mean that means a helluva lot—very key political VIPs, you know, by political VIPs—ah (unintelligible) just get the South get a better (unintelligible). Our problem is that there are only two men in this place that really give us names—that's Rose—the other is Colson, and we just aren't getting them. But I mean ah, and then editors—by editors and television people—like a (unintelligible) call, but a few key editors who are just busting their ass for us where there's something to do. But give me a good telephone list, and Rose should give me a few personal things—like I do a lot of things, but I called (unintelligible) here today some (unintelligible) and things of that sort. But I think this would be a very good use of my time while I'm in California.

P I never mind doing it you know when I've got an hour to put my feet up and make a few calls—don't you agree?

H Yep.

P I think of campaign—that's going to be a hell of a (unintelligible). I think sometimes when we're here in Washington, you know, supposedly doing the business of the government, that I can call people around the country—people that will come out for us—and so forth—like (unintelligible) for example, Democrats come out for us. They're (unintelligible) right across the board—Democrat or labor union. (unintelligible)

H Ya.

P Religious leaders (unintelligible) say something. You gotta be careful some ass over in (unintelligible) checked on (unintelligible) that's why you can't have Klein (unintelligible). He just doesn't really have his head screwed on Bob. I could see it in that meeting yesterday. He does not.

H That's right.

P He just doesn't know. He just sort of blubbers around. I don't know how he does TV so well.

223

H Well, he's a sensation on that—that goes to the (unintelligible) meaning of the thin, you know. What's his drawback, is really an asset.

P Ya. If you would do this. Pat, and tell Codus, (unintelligible), but I will go to Camp David (unintelligible) half hour. Key Biscayne—she might want to stay there if she can go in less than a half hour with an escort. Do you think you can? Frankly, Miami Beach (unintelligible) but we can arrange it either way? Leave it to her choice.

H It wouldn't take as long.

P Leave it to her choice—she'd—it's.—

H She'd—it's so miserable. If she's at Miami Beach she'll be a prisoner in that hotel.

P Yeah. Tell her, tell her that's fine. But it's up to her.

H Fair enough!

P I'll be anxious to (unintelligible). I suppose most of our staff (unintelligible) but that Six Crises is a damned good book, and the (unintelligible) story reads like a novel —the Hiss case—Caracas was fascinating. The campaign of course for anybody in politics should be a must because it had a lot in there of how politicians are like. (unintelligible) elections, and how you do things. (unintelligible) as of that time. I think part of the problem as an example, for example, I'm just thinking—research people something they really missed (unintelligible) Burns. Pat and I, she said (unintelligible) no, she had remembered. She remembered (unintelligible) that was pretty far back (unintelligible). (unintelligible) and Jimmy Burns said well (unintelligible) hard for me to come, but I just want you to know (unintelligible) but because (unintelligible) want you to know you are still my friend (unintelligible). Wonderful item to put in.

H Is that in the book?

P It's in the book! Hell yes. It's in the book.

H Is it?

P (Unintelligible) Why don't you reread it?

Enter Z (Ronald L. Ziegler) We're delaying our briefing until noon for the higher education (unintelligible) and so forth. But I thought, if you agree, that I would not for press purposes, but pust sit on the side for this economic thing.

Z Well there's the entire cabinet of economic advisers, I mean Council of Economic Advisers, plus Shultz—fairly big group.

P Shultz.

Z Well.

H (Unintelligible)

P See what I mean?

H Sure.

P It's the kind of thing that I get in toasts and that sort of thing, but, but you see, I don't think our guys do that kind of—that should be must reading—that book is crammed full—crammed full—see. It would be helpful for those to get it. O.K. Oh, can we can take another second? I mean, on that thing on the All Time Baseball Greats—I would like to do that and, if you could, if you could get it.

Unidentified Voice There's already a story at random—

P I saw it.

UV Indicating that you were going to

P If you would get that—if you would get the three or four. I don't want the—I'm only speaking of the All Time Greats.

UV Right.

P And then, and then get me a couple of other people (unintelligible) very badly (unintelligible) and I'll go down through the—quietly (unintelligible).

UV So do you want names from me or just a list of others you have picked?

H No, just the names that have been picked (unintelligible) various people.

UV Right.

P (Unintelligible)

UV Right, I got it.

P. O.K.

UV Yes Sir. (Unintelligible)

H You did, huh.

Z Yeah. Incidentally, in the news summary (unintelligible) preferred television. Did you see that? (unintelligible) I talked to

H We may (unintelligible) we may not.

Z No, the point I'm making—

P I know Ron, but let me say—but I think—apparently, the Today show this morning (unintelligible) two minutes of television.

Z I thought he got good play. Particularly in the light of the fact that ah, helluva a lot of other (unintelligible) would take place in the nation.

P Right.

H We have an overriding—

P What, weren't, how about the guys that were there?

They were pleased with the—

Z (unintelligible) and then (unintelligible)

P Huh?

P Cause I didn't think they would—

Z But they always are—

P Helluva a lot of news and—

H Well that snaps all our own machinery into motion too.

Z (Unintelligible) damn. Feel it?

P (Unintelligible) that's good, warm—

Z Right. They came to me and then said (unintelligible).

P (Unintelligible) should have some more.

Z And, they liked the color. They made the point about —you know. How relaxed you were, and at the end, sitting down and talking about the baseball thing after the whole thing—after it was over. You know, you just chipped those things off with such ease and so forth. It was so good.

1:04 to 1:13 p.m.

P O.K., just postpone (scratching noises) (unintelligible) Just say (unintelligible) very bad to have this fellow Hunt, ah, he knows too damned much, if he was involved—you happen to know that? If it gets out that this is all involved, the Cuba thing it would be a fiasco. It would make the CIA look bad, it's going to make Hunt look bad, and it is likely to blow the whole Bay of Pigs thing which we think would be very unfortunate—both for CIA, and for the country, at this time, and for American foreign policy. Just tell him to lay off. Don't you?

H Yep. That's the basis to do it on. Just leave it at that.

P I don't know if he'll get any ideas for doing it because our concern political (unintelligible). Helms is not one to (unintelligible)—I would just say, look it, because of the Hunt involvement, whole cover basically this

H Yep. Good move.

P Well, they've got some pretty good ideas on this Meany thing. Shultz did a good paper. I read it all (voices fade).

2:20 to 2:45 p.m.

H No problem.

P (Unintelligible)

H Well, it was kind of interest. Walters made the point

and I didn't mention Hunt, I just said that the thing was leading into directions that were going to create potential problems because they were exploring leads that led back into areas that would be harmful to the CIA and harmful to the government (unintelligible) didn't have anything to do (unintelligible).

(Telephone)

P Chuck? I wonder if you would give John Connally a call he's on his trip—I don't want him to read it in the paper before Monday about this quota thing and say— look, we're going to do this, but that I checked, I asked you about the situation (unintelligible) had an understanding it was only temporary and ah (unintelligible) O.K.? I just don't want him to read it in the papers. Good. Fine.

H (unintelligible) I think Helms did to (unintelligible) said, I've had no—

P God (unintelligible).

H Gray called and said, yesterday, and said that he thought—

P Who did? Gray?

H Gray called Helms and said I think we've run right into the middle of a CIA covert operation.

P Gray said that?

H Yeah. And (unintelligible) said nothing we've done at this point and ah (unintelligible) says well it sure looks to me like it is (unintelligible) and ah, that was the end of that conversation (unintelligible) the problem is it tracks back to the Bay of Pigs and it tracks back to some other the leads run out to people who had no involvement in this, except by contracts and connection, but it gets to areas that are liable to be raised? The whole problem (unintelligible) Hunt. So at that point he kind of got the picture. He said, he said we'll be very happy to be helpful (unintelligible) handle anything you want. I would like to know the reason for being helpful, and I made it clear to him he wasn't going to get explicit (unintelligible) generality, and he said fine. And Walters (unintelligible). Walters is going to make a call to Gray. That's the way we put it and that's the way it was left.

P How does that work though, how they've got to (unintelligible) somebody from the Miami bank.

H (unintelligible). The point John makes—the Bureau is going on this because they don't know what they are uncovering (unintelligible) continue to pursue it. They don't need to because they already have their case as far as the charges against these men (unintelligible) and ah, as they pursue (unintelligible) exactly, but we didn't in any way say we (unintelligible). One thing Helms did raise. He said, Gray—he asked Gray why they thought they had run into a CIA thing and Gray said because of the characters involved and the amount of money involved, a lot of dough (unintelligible) and ah, (unintelligible)

P (Unintelligible).

H Well, I think they will.

P If it runs (unintelligible) what the hell who knows (unintelligible) contributed CIA.

H Ya, it's money CIA gets money (unintelligible) I mean their money moves in a lot of different ways, too.

H (Unintelligible).

P Well you remember what the SOB did on my book? When I brought out the fact, you know—

H Ya.

P That he knew all about Dulles? (Expletive deleted) Dulles knew. Dulles told me. I know, I mean (unintelligible) had he telephone call. Remember, I had a call put in— Dulles just blandly said and knew why.

H Ya.

P Now, what the hell! Who told him to do it? The President? (Unintelligible).

H Dulles was no more Kennedy's man than (unintelligible) was your man (unintelligible).

P (unintelligible) covert operation—do anything else (unintelligible)

H The Democratic nominee, we're going to have to brief him.

P Yes sir. Brief him (unintelligible). We don't (unintelligible).

H Oh no. Tell him what we want him to know. I don't think you ought to brief him.

P Me? Oh, hell no!

H (unintelligible) you would have been if Johnson called you in—

P Johnson was out of office.

H That's the point—he was.

P Eisenhower, Eisenhower did not brief Kennedy.

H And wouldn't be proper anyway (unintelligible) because you're too (unintelligible)

P (unintelligible) Same thing that Eisenhower did. Course Eisenhower (unintelligible)

Phone rings

P Ya. Ah, I'll call him tomorrow.

H (Unintelligible) sure, that you want to

P No. I just simply think that we provide for (unintelligible) from the appropriate authorities (unintelligible) of course not, and I don't think we ought to let Kissinger brief—I'd just have Helms (unintelligible)

(unidentifiable)

P What did you say that poll, Gallup (unintelligible) wonder why he got it out so quickly. Usually lead time is two weeks.

H Well, actually, this is where lead time usually was and until the last few months (unintelligible). This time he's putting it out fast.

P (Unintelligible) want to get it out before the Convention.

H Well, because he's got a trial heat, and he wants to put this out before—set the stage for the trial heats.

P (Unintelligible) before the Convention. (Unintelligible) God damn (unintelligible) well what do you.

H Sure.

P You know we sat here and talked about (unintelligible) year and a half ago. But we had no idea—we thought they do it on the Today show (unintelligible) and all that (expletive deleted). And at that time (unintelligible) took events didn't we?

H (Unintelligible) always known was the case, but—

P China, May 8, and Russia. That's all.

H If you don't have the events you gotta make (unintelligible) everything (unintelligible) better off putting three months or three year's effort against one event than you are putting the same amount, tenth of that effort, non-event type thing.

P I'm really impressed with Shultz and all those guys—

H I told him.

P Fine.

H I talked to Shultz about calling Connally and I said that you had mentioned how impressed you were with the paper he had done (unintelligible).

P Eisenhower—(unintelligible) sure elections (inaudible) and then in November, before the election, he dropped a 57 (unintelligible). The reason for that was nothing he did, Congressional election (unintelligible).

H Ya.

P I'm saying to you, McGovern candidate (unintelligible)

problem got to take on (unintelligible). In 1958 (unintelligible) March, (unintelligible) 52

H Eisenhower?

P Eisenhower.

H (Unintelligible)

P Yes sir (unintelligible) May 54-31, June 53-32, July 52-32, August (unintelligible) September (unintelligible) October (unintelligible) 26, November election 52—(unintelligible) January. For example, here's early July 1961, July 57. August 61. September—September 58, October 58, November 58. That's when we were running. We were running lower (unintelligible). A little lower (unintelligible) Kennedy, you really can't tell about that. At the eve, his lowest was 62 (unintelligible) elections. But in 63 at the end he was 57. Johnson then, of course, he was up in the 80s. We've never been very high.

H That's incredible. I don't think you ever will get up in the 80s.

P No. Well Johnson, of course—66, 46, 56 September, October 44, November 44, December 48, that's all. Except his negatives were higher 42, 44, 41 our negatives have never been that high. He run around 49 (unintelligible).

H Ya.

P Then it goes on 46, 48, 45, 41, 39, 39, 38, 51, 46, 58, 48, 39, 40, 41 (unintelligible) then back up to 49, 46, 42. The point that I'm trying to make (unintelligible) cause you're under attack.

H Sure.

P (Unintelligible).

H Before the public eye—the focus of attention is on the negatives of the Administration. It's an interesting point. Buchanan, in response to the response to his attack—

P Ya.

H Argues quite strongly that the point that the attacks should always turn to the positive side. He argues that this is wrong, and the attacks, should stay on the negative side. Do not try to weave in also positive points. That there should be an attack program that is purely attack.

P Except on foreign policy.

H That's what he is talking about primarily. You hammer your strong point.

P I just think you've got to hit that over and over again. We gotta win—

H You don't argue against our hammering our strong point. His argument is when you are attacking—we should do some of our advertising—should be an attack on Mc-Govern advertising—and that attack should not (unintelligible) Nixon strongpoints. It should only (unintelligible) McGovern negative points.

P Ya.

H Argument being that it is impossible in this election for you to get less than 40% of the vote, equally impossible for you to get more than 60. (unintelligible) that up over there. We should go over early if we could get this (unintelligible) on the networks. Wait until 3:00—we got a problem because of what it is. (Unintelligible) because they are shooting with one camera (siren) (unintelligible) we're better off.

P Clear over there on the other side? You get the word to them.

Z Yes sir. But I don't want to take your time to do it.

P I'll go across—I just wanted to (unintelligible)

Z Yes sir. Absolutely.

P And, based from the thing this morning, do you feel it worthwhile to (unintelligible) till Monday?

Z Yes, sir.

H Well, let's do it earlier in the day, because we are (unintelligible) jeopardizing

Z At 2:00.

P Are you set up? You want me to come right this minute?

Z Well, I don't—anytime you feel comfortable.

P (Unintelligible),

Z As soon as possible.

H His argument is to start with, you got 40% of the people who will vote for you no matter what happens.

P I agree.

H And you got 40% of the people that will vote against you no matter what happens, so you got 20% of the vote left in the middle who may vote for you or may not—and that 20% is what you gotta work on. His argument is that you're so well known, your pluses are as clear as your minuses; that getting one of those 20, who is an undecided type, to vote for you on the basis of your positive points is much less likely than getting him to vote against McGovern by scaring him to death about McGovern; and that that's the area that we ought to be playing.

P Well.

H (Unintelligible).

P Well, I am not going to do it. I really want you to

231

bring in Flanigan and all these others (unintelligible) and lay it to them (unintelligible).

H Yep.

P Don't you think he'll agree? Oh, you don't?

H No, I think they will. They'll agree for awhile (unintelligible) agree—they will say well why not do it anyway.

P No, No, Nope, No—Never! I can't take it for granted. Listen, he could think I'm setting him up (unintelligible) reasonable man. God damn it, (unintelligible) I have him be against Muskie. We don't give a (expletive deleted). Or, Nixon! Muskie—screw him otherwise—fine. I don't know if our people would be scared (unintelligible) about Muskie.

H (Unintelligible) they are. They aren't, but I think you got to build that up. His point is that so little is known, better chance of (voices fade)